CONSIDER THE LILIES

A History of St Mary's Calne

CONSIDER THE LILIES

A History of St Mary's Calne

Elizabeth Christie

THIRD MILLENNIUM
PUBLISHING, LONDON

Consider the Lilies: A History of St Mary's Calne

2013 © St Mary's Calne and
Third Millennium Publishing Limited

First published in 2013 by Third Millennium Publishing Limited,
a subsidiary of Third Millennium Information Limited.

2–5 Benjamin Street
London
United Kingdom
EC1M 5QL
www.tmiltd.com

ISBN: 978 1 908990 18 1

British Library Cataloguing in Publication Data

A CIP catalogue record for this book is availablefrom the British Library.

Editor	Pamela Hartshorne
Design	Susan Pugsley
Production	Bonnie Murray
Reprographics	Studio Fasoli, Verona, Italy
Printing	Printer Trento, Italy

Contents

Foreword from the Headmistress

Consider the Lilies is a tribute to St Mary's Calne. Reaching our 140-year anniversary is a landmark by any measure. This is a beautiful and compelling history book that not only looks back on our tremendous heritage, but one that helps us look forward to an exciting future.

It took courage and vision to found a girls' school at a time when women were denied the right to vote and university entrance for them was a radical idea. For 140 years St Mary's Calne has provided opportunities for girls to shine, to take their place in the world as leaders. These pages bear witness to this remarkable achievement. It is an inspiring story and, we think, a fascinating read for all generations of pupils and alumnae.

Written by Calne Old Girl Elizabeth Christie, the school's first archivist, this book explores St Mary's from 1873 to 2013. The many facts and dates serve as markers for key moments in our history, but we have also taken great care to celebrate our community's character and characters. The indefinable, yet palpable, St Mary's Calne spirit is as much a part of our history as any event, staff member or building. Nowhere is that spirit more evident than in the resiliency, authenticity and warmth of our pupils and alumnae. There is something different about a St Mary's Calne girl – I believe this in my heart.

Dr Felicia Kirk

Opposite: *The Millennium Sundial*

CHAPTER ONE

The Early Years 1873–1915

The parish church of St Mary the Virgin has stood part-way up a small hill in the Wiltshire town of Calne since Norman times. Nestled under the western edge of the Marlborough downs, Calne lies at the meeting point of Abberd Brook and the River Marden, the waters of which were for many hundreds of years vital to the town's thriving woollen industry. When the Industrial Revolution led to the decline of the West Country wool trade, the local economy became dependent on the expanding bacon-curing business set up by the Harris family. By the middle of the 19th century, Harris' was a major employer and, helped by the arrival of the railway, Calne continued its gradual expansion into the tenanted strips and open fields around the town. When the Revd John Duncan took up the position of Vicar in 1865, Calne was a busy market town with many local shops and small businesses but was suffering from the problems of poor public health associated with its main industry and with the limited services.

Opposite: *An 1850 etching of the Church of St Mary the Virgin, Calne*

Intelligent, straightforward and with high integrity, it was not long before he became a well-respected member of the community. He dedicated much of his time to pastoral duties and had a particular interest in local education.

In the mid 19th century there were several schools in Calne serving different sections of the population. John Duncan soon became aware that there were no good schools based on an Anglican doctrine for the daughters of the tradespeople of the town and of the farmers in surrounding villages. He described how he urged others in the parish to recognise the need for such a school.

This was a time of national concern about girls' schooling, and the pioneering work of Miss Buss and Miss Beale showed that girls could benefit from an ambitious education. John Duncan was an admirer of Nathaniel Woodard, who was founding schools that aimed to provide a sound education grounded in the Anglican tradition, and so it was against this background that Canon Duncan sought the help of the local church community. By 1872 he had enough people interested in giving support that he could move forward his dream of providing a school based on Woodard's principles.

Prominent among these people was Miss Ellinor Gabriel, who lived in Horsebrook House on The Green above the church in Calne. Described by Miss Richardson,

Above: *The Parish Church in Calne*

Left: *Canon John Duncan*

A Scotsman by birth and the son of a ship-owner of Aberdeen, John Duncan described how as a child he was devoted to sports, his pony, fishing and exploring the countryside around his home. At 14 he began to work in earnest with such good results that a couple of years later he took the highest honours at Aberdeen University. He then studied in London and Berlin before travelling for some months on the continent.

An early dissatisfaction with his religious upbringing led to John Duncan joining the Church of England in 1854. He began his career as a Classics Master at a local school in Calne, and through Archdeacon Drury, the incumbent at Bremhill, he met Bishop Hamilton of Salisbury. The Bishop's influence led to John Duncan's ordination and a curacy in Sherborne. He had been Perpetual Curate of Lyneham for six years when called by the Bishop of Salisbury to the important benefice of Calne.

This was not an easy calling, as Calne had a strongly influential nonconformist population at the time, however John Duncan had the qualities to embrace the task.

the first headmistress, as having 'invariable kindness', she agreed to become the superintendent of the new school and to bear the financial responsibilities of the enterprise.

Ellinor Gabriel was a woman of wide interests and with a great dedication to the causes dear to her heart. St Mary's has a scrap book of cuttings which she gathered from the 1850s to the 1880s. These give a wonderful insight into local and national issues that concerned, informed or amused her.

A suitable house was found on the lower side of The Green, which Miss Gabriel bought, and with help from other donors she equipped it to meet the requirements of a school. Built in the early 19th century of stone, it is a well-proportioned attractive house of two storeys, with attic bedrooms. A parapet runs along the roofline and a pediment covers a central porch. Standing between other houses, like them it is now a listed building. Miss Gabriel's office was on the left of the entrance and was described as being 'very sparsely furnished with a desk and two stools'. There was an area outside at the back which provided a limited space for recreation.

Miss Ellinor Gabriel

Some of the items in the scrap book of Ellinor Gabriel

- *Births, marriages and deaths*
- *Book reviews*
- *Many poems, often on the subjects of religion and death*
- *A foreign correspondent's report on 'The New Queen of Madagascar'*
- *A letter to a newspaper signed 'your obedient servants, Mappin and Webb', on the occasion of a swarm of bees landing on a man in Regent Street*
- *An article on the dangers of travelling abroad and the risk of disease, entitled 'Climate and Consumption'*
- *A report on a lecture at the Royal Institution by Professor Huxley on 'Dogs and the problems connected with them'*
- *A report on 'meeting a Filey fishing lass collecting bait'*
- *A letter from Smyrna describing a train accident involving the Bishop of Gibraltar in which 12 carriages on a train pulling 21 were disconnected unnoticed by the driver, who carried on to his destination*
- *The opening of an orphans' home in Calne*
- *An obituary of the Prince Consort*
- *A gypsy recipe for cooking hedgehogs*
- *Pictures of 'British Life Contrivances for saving ship-wrecked and drowning persons', including a motor life-line and Price Albert's life-ladder*
- *Sign language instructions*
- *A description of an emigration journey from Calne to Adelaide in Australia*
- *A report on the anniversary of the Battle of the Nile*
- *An article on the Great Clock at Strasbourg*
- *Post Office information on letter rates*

The Opening of St Mary's School

So it was that in January 1873 St Mary's School was opened for six day girls and three boarders whose families had connections to the church. The first applicant on the school list, Elizabeth Colson, described how on that day Miss Richardson was introduced to each of her pupils by Canon Duncan, who then told those present that they were leaders in a new venture which he hoped would carry on for many years to follow. They then sang, 'Oh happy band of pilgrims'. Alice Frayling, one of the early pupils, later said, 'It was a venture of faith, a grain of mustard seed. It ascended as children of many prayers do succeed.'

Alice arrived at the school in 1879 in the footsteps of Laura, her older sister who started in 1876 and continued later as a staff member and matron. Along with Elizabeth Colson in the first group of girls, was Amy Heath, who is recorded in the school's minute book as having gained a third-class honours in the Junior Cambridge Local Examination in 1876.

Top far left: *The first school house on The Green in Calne as it is today*

Top left: *The opening page of St Mary's School minute book 1873*

Left: *Extracts from the minute book 1875 and 1876*

12

Right: *Mrs Penelope Murray*

Below right: *Pupil list from 1887 with a red cross by the names of those who died*

first deputy head, Miss Amy Williams. Mrs Murray and her daughter Alice Duncan helped with French, literature and music. Alice had married John Duncan in 1871. An accomplished artist, she also taught drawing, painting, geometry and perspective, and gave dancing lessons in the winter. The church organist, Mr Bellamy, instructed the girls in music, with some of them progressing to take public examinations. His successor as organist, Mr Pullein, taught at St Mary's for 57 years, retiring in 1943. Alice Frayling described in a letter years later that Canon Duncan gave a weekly scripture lesson, and Mrs Murray took a litany class once a week followed by a homily which frequently delayed tea. One early pupil described these as 'happy days'.

Alice also tells how the children in the school were divided into three classes, with the oldest children in the schoolroom, and the little ones in the classroom. There were few books and these were exclusively school property, with pupils being charged 2s 6d per term for their use.

Fees received from the pupils in 1873 amounted to £186 3s 10d, with an expenditure that year of £296 0s 2d. A similar shortfall was seen year by year, being covered at first by Miss Gabriel and later by Mrs Murray.

Canon Duncan had been convinced of the importance of regular examination of the girls to keep standards high. Initially he carried this out himself, but later an external assessor came into the school. These included a Miss Pearce from St Andrew's University and E.J. Aston from

Among others present at the opening day of the school was Canon Duncan's mother-in-law, Mrs Penelope Murray. Mrs Murray, the widow of the Revd George Murray who was the eldest son of the Bishop of Rochester, had come to live in Calne in 1868. Married in 1848, by 1854 she was left on her own to bring up five children. Mrs Murray was described in a school magazine of 1910 at the time of her death as 'a woman of strong character and highly intellectual, of charming manners united to a gentle dignity. To know her was to love her. To watch the beautiful consistency of her life was an inspiration'. Penelope Murray had been a staunch supporter of the Vicar and was to play a pivotal role in the early success of St Mary's School.

School Life

As life settled down in St Mary's, the pupils were taught a range of subjects by Miss Richardson, remembered as a disciplinarian with a strong sense of humour, and the

*'I send you the result of the examination of
St Mary's School which is most creditable
both to the scholars and to their teachers.
They have made considerable advance in the
last year and if I had known how much they
had improved I should have given them less
easy questions. There is no doubt of Mable
Heath and Alice Frayling being best in their
respective divisions, but there were some very
good papers done by the others. Lilian Heath
failed in arithmetic but she must be consoled
by the excellence of her dictation and pay
more attention to her sums for the time to
come. The maps of India were very neatly
done even those where cities were wrongly
placed were worthy of credit for
the mountains and rivers.'*

– Report on examination results, Christmas 1883
by Mr W.P. Bingham

Jesus College, Oxford. The reports of these visits give an
interesting insight into school life through that time.

Prizegiving took place annually, at first at Christmas
time, when the formal part of the day was followed by a
Shakespeare production by the older girls and then 'dancing
until after mid-night'. In later years prizegiving was held in
the summer term in Mrs Murray's garden with an outside
speaker, who on one occasion was Earl Nelson. Prizes were
presented for academic achievement, and in areas such as
general improvement, drawing, drill and needlework. In later
years, scholarships were awarded and the notable musical
achievements of the pupils were recognised.

Pupil numbers grew to 14 by the end of the first year
and over the next few years they increased to around
20–25, including some junior girls and boys.

A Change of Leader

Mrs Murray's greater involvement in the school was soon
required as in 1879, after six and a half years of managing
St Mary's and meeting the deficit in the budget, Ellinor
Gabriel decided she could no longer continue.

John Duncan describes how at this point he feared for
the future of the school and felt it was essential to found
St Mary's on a permanent basis with its own freehold
premises. With generous donations from several people

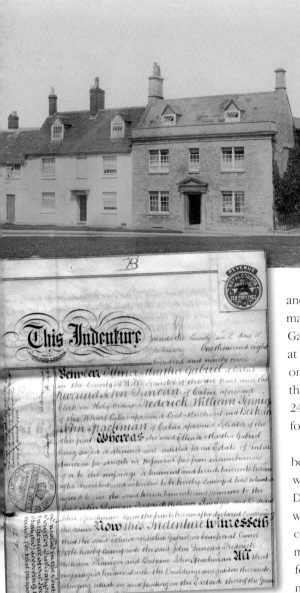

Top: *An archive picture of the four St Mary's houses (left)and recent photo of the old school houses (right)*

Above: *Conveyance document between Ellinor Martha Gabriel and Revd J. Duncan and others*

and a £500 gift of his own, he managed to raise £1,313 15s 6d. Miss Gabriel sold him the school house at half its value and Mrs Murray took on the task of superintendent. With the conveyance of the property on 24 April 1880, St Mary's School was founded as a permanent institution.

Mrs Murray's willingness to become superintendent of St Mary's was something for which Canon Duncan was forever grateful. He was generous in his praise of her contribution in both time and money. She remained at St Mary's for 17 years, during which time she managed the running of the school, kept the accounts and covered the annual financial deficit. Retirement came in 1896, when Mrs Murray moved to Bath, but she continued to give financial support to the school and attended St Mary's for prizegiving until her death in 1910. She had made arrangements that any deficit in the two terms after her death should be paid from her estate.

Although Ellinor Gabriel had stepped back from the running of the school she remained a generous supporter until her death in 1900. In 1887 she gave £1,000 to be invested in order to provide three scholarships in memory of her sister Frances, and in 1890 she bought and gave to St Mary's two houses adjoining the schoolhouse to provide extra accommodation. The same year Mrs Murray also bought and gave to the school a house on the other side of the original school house. These four houses can be seen on The Green in Calne today and remained in use by St Mary's until the school moved to its present site in 1908. At Prize Day in 1896 Canon Duncan recognised the great debt St Mary's owed to Miss Gabriel and Mrs Murray, saying 'To the money they have given must be added the thought, the care, the anxiety, the watchfulness, the love, the work they have lavished on it. They are of immeasurable value.'

While Canon Duncan, a man described as having 'a remarkable aptitude for business', was the prime mover in managing the financial affairs of St Mary's, he did have support from other members of the community. Conveyance documents show that transfers were made to Canon John Duncan, Clerk in Holy Orders; Frederick Pinniger, Coal Merchant; and Bertram Spackman, Solicitor. Others who gave financial support included Albert Buckeridge, P. Hewett and Robert Heath: local people, some of whom we know to have had children in the school. We know also that all of these people, other than P. Hewett, showed further commitment to St Mary's by acting as trustees. It was truly a community undertaking.

'It was a narrow passage room between the study and the corridor, very simply fitted with prie-dieu, gilt cross, candlesticks and candelabra. There was a coloured glass window in one corner, with a bench underneath where hymn books were kept. Coconut matting covered the floor and kneelers were provided for the children. The opening service was a great occasion. Mrs Murray, Miss Gabriel and the whole school were present, while Canon Duncan, vested in cassock and surplice, performed the Act of Dedication.'

– A DESCRIPTION OF THE FIRST SCHOOL CHAPEL, KNOWN AS THE ORATORY

'The walls were matchboard to a depth of three feet, above which was a broad band of chocolate, the remaining wall space being primrose and the ceiling pale blue. Red and white striped blinds completed the colour scheme'. Round the cornice were quotations such as 'Help thyself and God will help thee.'

– A DESCRIPTION OF THE ENLARGED SCHOOLROOM FROM MISS LEESON'S TIME

The Early Headmistresses

From the opening of St Mary's in 1873 to the arrival of Miss Dyas in 1888, four headmistresses oversaw the education of the pupils. They each brought their own influence to school life. After Miss Richardson, who kept in contact with the school and attended the 1934 reunion, came Miss Jones. She was remembered for her enthusiasm for producing Shakespeare plays in which she also acted. Alice Frayling described how Miss Jones ruled with a rod of iron, while her deputy, Miss Culpin, ruled by love: 'A smile of approbation from Miss Jones was highly prized.'

Miss Pells, who followed, was described as 'a very clever and efficient teacher'. Miss Edwards, a colleague, said that Miss Pells was 'a truly clever teacher, very self-reliant, tall, spare of build and with very, very, dark eyes'. While the girls sat at needlework she read and explained the works of Dickens, Tennyson and Longfellow and read Shakespeare plays. She would take the pupils for long Sunday walks with her dog. Her tenure at St Mary's was short, as she went on to Newnham to study a course in Higher Education. However, it was during her time that the first Oratory was furnished and dedicated in a narrow, passage-like room. St Mary's was intensely proud of its Oratory and morning and afternoon prayers were held here.

Miss Pells was succeeded by Miss Leeson, who was responsible for a change in the organisation of the school into forms and a considerable expansion to the fabric of the school, including enlarging the schoolroom. The playground at the back of the building was extended and surfaced and the first bazaar was held, raising £10. This allowed a library to be supplied with books, and tennis racquets, balls and a net to be bought for the new court on a field provided by a parent, Dr Coleman.

Above: *The school accounts for 1881*

Left: *A plaque given by the leaving girls of 1927*

Right: *Miss Dyas with her pupils*

Top right: *Miss Florence Dyas*

September 18th – I did not finish my German and so got reproved, oh that German 'tis so silly.

September 28th – I have been horrid all day and of all the most unlucky girls, I got an order mark. If I could but leave other people and their business alone instead of speaking to them. We have been having a chatteration giving our different opinions of heaven and hell and Judas Iscariot. Oh! That dreadful composition. I don't know what to say a bit. I wish I was home for bed tonight. My school mattress looks awfully hard, and I am as cold as ice.

October 29th – It is Miss Dyas's birthday today, we boarders gave her a glorified cross for her prayer desk. She had thirty one presents and innumerable letters. She sent us in a tin of biscuits and a lot of grapes for lunch. After school we went and had tea in her room.

October 31st – My tenth brother was born this morning at half past six in the morning – All Hallows Eve. When Lucy Baily was eating her supper she came across a large and corpulent beetle which had been baked in the bread. We did not want any supper after for fear of another being there.

November 16th – I became the poor creature to get an order mark today because my gloves happened to fall off my lap on to the ground (at a church service).

December 12th – Miss Dyas would not allow us to do any work today but made us come into her sitting room for a jolly evening.

– Extracts from the 1891–3 Journal of Lizzie Buckeridge, a Pupil at St Mary's

The Last Years of the Century

School life in those first years appears to have been strict, but the appointment of Miss Dyas as headmistress in 1888 probably marked the start of a more relaxed and comfortable period. She was described as 'motherly, affectionate and kind; someone you could always go to'. She was dedicated to her work and loved and respected by her pupils. She kept a firm hand, however, as can be seen in a journal written by one of her pupils, Lizzie Buckeridge.

Mrs Murray recognised that St Mary's owed Miss Dyas an immense debt of gratitude. She wrote, 'It is largely owing to her great gifts as a teacher, her enthusiasm and her powers of sympathy, by which pupils are turned into life-long friends, that the numbers were soon doubled.'

A pupil of the time, Alice Toops, told how the girls would go for bike rides in the summer, accompanied

and three young sons attended the school. There were also the children of the Heath family, who were bookbinders and stationers; the Maundrells, some of whom ran a foundry while others were farmers; the Pinnigers, who had been a cloth-making family and then coal merchants; the Bridges, the Fells, the Bakers and the Fraylings. Some of these families had further children attending down the generations.

With the addition of the three adjoining houses in 1890, it became possible to extend the boarding facilities during the next few years. The school's custom of giving people's names to the dormitories began at this time with Gabriel, Dunstan, Duncan and Wordsworth, named after Bishop Wordsworth, who had visited the school in 1889 following a Confirmation service.

Although the education was good, the financial position of the school had always been difficult. We get a hint of the underlying concern that this caused Canon Duncan from his speech of 1896. 'Of the good work done in the School, the parents of the pupils are witnesses. St Mary's has done valuable educational work in this town and neighbourhood and is now established as a permanent institution and practically a self-supporting one.'

Both Miss Gabriel and Mrs Murray had covered the deficits since the foundation but Canon Duncan had constant anxiety about how the future of the school would be secured. After Mrs Murray's death the deficit was

by Miss Dyas on her tricycle. She also tells of Sunday evening readings in the sitting room decorated with 'masses of peacock feathers'. She goes on, 'We were then given a sweet each; it was all very homely'. Mary Baker remembered Miss Dyas 'taking her rings off on Ash Wednesday and wearing black throughout Holy Week'.

A report by Miss Pearce, a school examiner, said, 'The School goes forward under Miss Dyas' able leadership. The students are evidently conscientiously and intelligently taught without cramming'.

Miss Dyas founded the forerunner to the Old Girls' Association, when in 1891 she began the St Mary's Guild, members paying a 2s 6d annual subscription and pledging to pray daily for the school and the church in Calne. Members could make use of the school library on the payment of 6d a term.

By the end of the century St Mary's School was providing a well-respected education for the daughters of many families in Calne. Among them were the Buckeridge family, who ran a grocery and wine and spirit business in the High Street. We know that three of their daughters

Left: *Ruth Buckeridge*

Below: *From a school magazine*

on the country's finances and prompted the Efficiency Movement, which demanded a more streamlined use of public funds. Different areas of government were inspected, including education. The review led directly to Balfour's Education Act of 1902, which abolished government-run school boards and handed their duties to the Local Education Authorities. Church schools could receive funding and were given a special status under the arrangement, with local authorities deciding the nature of the religious teaching within their own schools.

Over the previous years the pupil numbers at St Mary's School had gradually risen, and in 1900 there were 45 names on the register but a deficit of £45 14s 1d in the accounts. The continuing shortfall in income was unsustainable, and to Canon Duncan the changes in the education system seemed to provide St Mary's with a lifeline.

He submitted a statement to Wiltshire County Council showing that St Mary's School could serve as the girls' counterpart to John Bentley School for boys nearby on The Green in Calne, something that had been considered by both schools and supported by John Bentley School.

Neither school had reckoned with the nonconformists in the town, however, and a heated debate ensued with lengthy correspondence in the press and discussion at a Church congress in Bristol. The nonconformists in Calne were totally opposed to any state aid for a denominational school. In response to this the County Council opened its own girls' department at John Bentley and Canon Duncan was left to find other means to support St Mary's.

Surprisingly, in time these developments were advantageous to St Mary's. A newspaper report on the prizegiving at the school in 1906 describes how placing the nature and character of religious instruction in the hands of the local authorities had 'aroused Church of England parents to a sense of their responsibility, and applications recently received for admission to St Mary's had been so numerous that accommodation was inadequate to meet them'. The number of boarders had trebled in a year.

Despite the difficulties facing the school, we know that through this period the children continued to receive a sound education under Miss Dyas' able leadership, as can be seen in the inspectors' reports.

Above: *1902 school time-table*

Top: *Miss Dyas and the pupils at the school on The Green*

made up by other members of the community and from a small endowment raised when the school moved site. As the century turned, the three founders had every reason to look back on their work of the previous 27 years with pride and satisfaction. They had provided the high standard of education within the Anglican discipline that they had set out to do. The task now was to give the school the secure financial basis it so desperately needed.

Planning for the Future

At the dawn of the new century, Britain was embroiled in the Second Boer War. This had put significant strains

Left: Canon Duncan's funeral cortege going past the school 1907

Below: Extract from a school magazine

The Death of Canon John Duncan

On 28 January 1907, St Mary's and the wider community were shocked by the sudden and unexpected death of Canon Duncan. Mrs Murray reflected how those at the school's prizegiving that year felt so greatly the loss 'of one who fostered it from its beginnings and who was always the life and soul of those yearly gatherings'. Canon Duncan's vision, diligence and commitment in founding St Mary's were immense, but he was also mourned by the town.

The local paper reported that on the day of the funeral 'every place of business, including the licensed houses, were closed and the shutters put up, the blinds of private houses were drawn, the flags from the towers of the church and the town hall were flying at half-mast'.

John Duncan was remembered by his parishioners with great admiration. He was described as 'the soul of honour and integrity'. They valued his 'fatherly advice in all times of sickness and trouble' and recognised his deep spiritual devotion. One commented that 'Calne will never

In Memoriam.
John Duncan. Vicar of Calne.
January 28ᵗʰ 1907.   R.I.P.

Personal.

Miss Edith Smith, after a good holiday in England, returns to Canada to resume her work as a trained nurse.

Miss Ruth Nuthall goes to Wiesbaden after Easter, to teach and to further her knowledge of German.

Edith Daniell has just gone to Coventry to undertake the work of a Nursery Governess.

We regret to announce that Sissie Anstey is absent through illness, & hope for her speedy recovery.

forget this wise, noble-hearted man, this brave and faithful pastor and priest'. He was an assiduous correspondent, good at figures and an expert chairman of meetings, with a remarkable instinct for the right course of action. The Bishop of Salisbury described Canon Duncan as 'both keenly intellectual and unfeignedly devout, both fearless and tender'. Throughout his life he had remained a keen sportsman, fly-fisherman and horseman and loved to walk in Bowood and over the fields towards Compton.

When those early St Mary's pupils joined other children behind the funeral cortege as it wound slowly round The Green past the school, they must surely have deeply mourned the loss of someone who had had such a strong influence on their young lives.

Moving On

On John Duncan's death, Archdeacon Eric Bodington was appointed as the new Vicar of Calne and Chairman of the Governors of St Mary's School. Born in Staffordshire in 1862, he had matriculated at Brasenose College, Oxford, in 1881. He held the post of domestic chaplain to the Bishop of Salisbury for a time and had worked in South Africa for two years. The Archdeacon was to prove as vital to the St Mary's we see today as the three founders had been before him. It now fell to him to take up the mantle left by John Duncan and he did so with dedication, enthusiasm and vigour.

Charles Gough, who as clerk to the governors knew the Archdeacon well, described him as, 'a liberal, he had an open mind. He was always willing both to talk and listen. I really think he loved people.'

Shortly before his death, Canon Duncan had moved to transfer the responsibility for the running of the school from the Trustees to a Board of Governors under the leadership of the incumbent Vicar. Mrs Murray cited a list of those to be invited, which included 12 members of clergy from the surrounding parishes. Those elected felt that the school buildings on The Green were no longer adequate; numbers needed to increase further and the outside play area was not sufficient.

One of the Archdeacon's first major tasks for the school would have been the launch of the appeal in September 1907 for a building fund. This was to finance a move to

Right: *Archdeacon Eric Bodington*

a new site in order to accommodate the increase in the number of pupils and to further expand the school, in the hope of creating a viable concern. Anticipating the need for such an expansion, Mrs Murray had in 1905 invested £500 as the nucleus of a building fund. In order to draw in further contributions, Eric Bodington described in a letter how a successful appeal would give the school a permanently sound financial basis and how it would offer an 'up to date education in all branches in a Church of England setting'. Boarders' fees were promised to be under £40 and day pupils under £6 per annum.

The governors now set about looking for a suitable property. One of the well-established families in Calne was that of the Goughs. George Gough held the position of town clerk. His son Charles was to be clerk to the governors of St Mary's from 1926 to 1958. The family now offered St Mary's their house, Lansdowne Villa, in Curzon Street. On the procurement of a loan, the school accepted, buying the house, a cottage, coach house, stable, greenhouse and other outbuildings for £1,500. This house forms the nucleus of the school today.

The New School Site: 1908

The school house was described by Charles Gough, who had spent much of his childhood there, as 'a nice family home with seven bedrooms, four reception rooms and the usual offices'. The room that is today the headmistress's study had been added by a previous owner to provide a billiard room. It later functioned as a dining room, a staffroom and then a common room known as Gabriel, for the girls. In his appeal for building funds, Archdeacon Bodington described the house as, 'attractive in appearance as it is sanitary in its position, high and roomy. It will increase the physical and mental sources of happiness in teachers and pupils alike.'

It was necessary from the start to enlarge the building in order to provide dormitory space, classrooms and a chapel. A new prospectus was drawn up and wider advertising planned. Work continued through the summer of 1908 and by the autumn of that year the building was ready for use.

St Mary's has an article entitled 'An Educational Experiment' written by Mrs Murray looking back over this period. She applauds the fact that the Church had in recent decades recognised that it should play a stronger role in providing education for middle-ranking families,

and goes on to tell the story of the foundation of St Mary's. Mrs Murray finishes her paper by describing how sufficient funds had been raised for the move to a new site by the sale of the previous properties, a small endowment fund and a generous donation from the Bishop of Salisbury. Past pupils contributed to the building fund by a sale of their own handiwork.

Above: *Lansdowne Villa and the house today*

Above: *The opening ceremony of St Mary's on its new site 1908*

Top right: *The first addition to School House as it is today*

Bottom right: *A classroom in School House which later became Wordsworth dormitory*

On 24 October 1908 St Mary's celebrated the opening of the school on the new site. It was a grand occasion attended by many people associated with the school, including the Bishop of Salisbury, Mrs Murray and Lady Lansdowne. A procession led by the choir under Mr Pullein's leadership wound through the school. After the first service to be held in the Chapel there were speeches on the lawn followed by prizegiving and tea. It was a happy day, full of hope and optimism for the years ahead.

The School Buildings

The new wing that was built on to the Gough's house provided the school with two dormitories on the top floor which came to be known as Duncan and Murray. Below those were three classrooms and on the ground floor, in addition to the Chapel, were a kitchen, a cloakroom and an area later known as Red Hall, although the floor tiles that gave it its name are now covered. At this time the hall was a small, dark area with rooms leading off it: a kitchen, a scullery with a 'treacherous stone floor', a store cupboard which was 'one of Sister Ash's favourite haunts', and a 'little green passage' leading to what was then the dining room. In 1937 walls were removed, and pillars and skylights added to give greater space. The girls returned in the autumn to find Red Hall panelled in oak and furnished with an oak seat, a gift from the leaving girls, and with a clock presented by the school to the headmistress, Miss Matthews, on her birthday. For many years a large brass gong, given by Susan Walsham in 1958 and used for announcing meal times, hung in Red Hall.

On the top floor of the original house were the headmistress's bedroom, a spare bedroom, matron's room, linen room, bathroom and a small room known as Bee's

Knee. This is remembered as a 'cosy' bedroom next to the headmistress's room where girls who were homesick or needed time out could have a night or two on their own. This was in contrast to the dread with which the fender stool in the headmistress's study is recalled, a place where one sat when rebukes were being handed out. At first Wordsworth dormitory was also in this part of the house, though the name was later used for the large dormitory over the extended Chapel. On the ground floor were the headmistress's sitting room, the girls' sitting room, and the school office.

The Chapel

The newly built Chapel, which in 1908 was still called The Oratory, was an important focus for the day-to-day life of St Mary's. It now houses the fiction library, and as a part of honouring the history of the school is again called The Oratory. The arched stone windows give a hint of its original purpose. Many pupils down the generations knelt against the high-backed chairs, celebrated the great festivals of the year, and listened to inspirational words from their headmistresses. Morning and evening chapel framed the day. It is still to this room that past pupils who knew it are drawn.

The Chapel when first built was smaller than the room we see today, with two small windows in the end wall. It was described by someone who knew it as 'a simple blue room with a picture of the Annunciation over the altar'. Ten years later the Chapel was redecorated with William Morris wallpaper and hangings, with four Medici prints on the walls and a new altar frontal given by the leaving girls. By 1925 the number of pupils had increased significantly and

more major work was undertaken, with an extension to the room and also to Wordsworth dormitory above. The Chapel was now panelled in light-coloured oak, financed by Mr Bodinnar, who was later a governor, and the altar framed in blue hangings.

In 1911, 83 Old Girls and school members contributed to a brass memorial plate to be placed in the Chapel in honour of the three founders of St Mary's. That memorial now hangs in the present Chapel. Later, a banner embroidered with the St Mary's lily crest stood by the altar, and outside the Chapel door hung a brass bell, which was rung by a senior girl to call the pupils to services.

In 1951 the Old Girls' Association presented the school with a silvered bronze cross and two candlesticks in memory of the headmistress, Miss Matthews. These are still used today in the present Chapel which was built for the centenary of St Mary's in 1973. Regular daily worship continues as it did all those years ago when the first Chapel was opened in 1908.

The original Chapel in School House

Inset: *Lily image from the Chapel banner*

The Chapel in later years

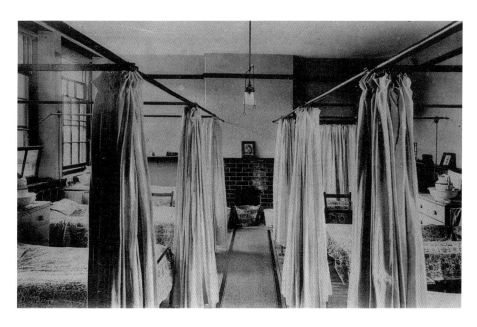

Above: *Wordsworth dormitory in School House before it was extended*

Right: *Extract from the school magazine*

In 1914 two classrooms, one of which doubled as a small gymnasium, were added during the Easter holidays in an annex between the new wing and the cottage. This released more dormitory space for boarders. The smaller room later became a reference library and the larger room was first a dining room and then a sewing room. These two rooms are now LIV Form classrooms.

The Governing Body later accepted Lord Lansdowne's offer to sell an additional cottage to the school at a reduced price as his contribution to the building fund. This cottage became a house for a couple who worked in the school and the garden. An area nearby at first became a tennis court and in 1915 was also used for netball.

We know that in 1912 the pupils played hockey and cricket and held matches against other schools. With limited space on the school grounds, it was arranged that the school should borrow a nearby field on the Hilmarton Road. There is a record that some matches were held at Bowood.

Settling in to School Life at Curzon Street

By the time the school was in its new buildings, Miss Dyas had been headmistress at St Mary's for 20 years. A highly gifted woman, she had nurtured the Christian ethos in the school, supervised the education and welfare of the children, and managed the day to day running of all aspects of school life. In addition to these duties, Miss Dyas had been responsible for handling the main income and expenditure of the school.

A series of hand-written magazines from 1909 to 1911 give us a sense of school life during that period. There are reports on sports fixtures against schools from around the area, records of prizes given, birthdays celebrated and the marriages of past pupils. There were tea-parties and hay-parties; croquet-parties and bike rides; dancing, picnics and bazaars; and outings to lectures and concerts.

Many contributions from pupils include stories and poems in what we would now regard as a highly sentimental vein. There are brain-teasers and jokes which seem dated today. However they also wrote of more weighty matters, such as the pit-dwellers on Salisbury Plain, Tyndale's Bible and a poem written in 1910, 'when the German invasion was most imminent', urging Britain to arm itself for possible future naval attack.

There is a backward look to the royal visit to Calne in 1907 of King Edward VII and Queen Alexandra, and a report on the celebrations in 1911 of the coronation of George V. The summer 1909 edition carries a commentary on the Empire Day events in London.

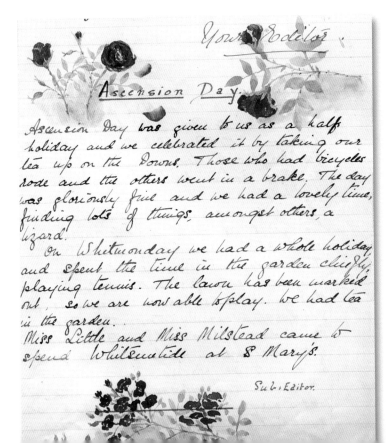

Visits in Britain made during the holidays were written about and include those to many churches around the country. There are also reports on an outing to a cutlery factory in Sheffield, to Tewksbury, Cheddar and to Fountains Abbey.

Old Girls' news came in from around the world: from Gibraltar and South Africa, British Colombia and China, Switzerland and Wiesbaden. There is a wonderful description of a journey to New York on board the *Oceanic*, a ship of the White Star Line, a year before the *Titanic* went down.

These magazines suggest a school that is busy, happy and forward-moving. There is a great sense of community and common interest, where the pupils feel confidence in those shaping their lives.

The End of Miss Dyas' Time at St Mary's

Despite the optimism of the new era, the governors still had the precarious state of the school finances hanging over them. There was some disagreement between the governors, Mrs Murray and Miss Dyas as to the number of staff and the salaries that the school could afford.

On the death of Mrs Murray in 1910, Archdeacon Bodington was the sole person legally responsible for any deficit. To spread the burden, a body of 15 guarantors was set up, each contributing £5. It was decided that the governors should manage the budget and that a housekeeper should be appointed to relieve Miss Dyas of some of her duties.

Florence Dyas was a dedicated headmistress who for 23 years led St Mary's through difficult times with a lightness of spirit. She was loved and respected by her pupils in whom she encouraged kindness and hard work. The changes that were being put in place by the governors led her to take the decision to resign her position. A petition by 76 parents, Guild members and former pupils failed to alter her intention and it was to the great regret of many in the school community that she left in 1911. It was clearly a move that she was sorry to have to make, as can be seen in a letter she wrote to members of the school. Nonetheless she kept in contact with St Mary's and was among the many visitors at the 1923 Jubilee celebrations.

On her death in 1938 a previous pupil described her as a 'great-hearted and gifted woman. Like all high-minded

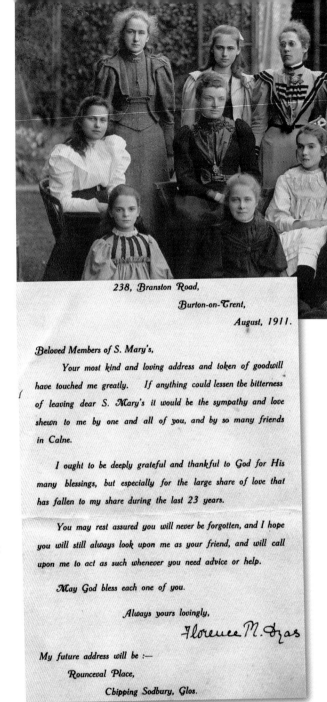

238, Branston Road,
Burton-on-Trent,
August, 1911.

Beloved Members of S. Mary's,

Your most kind and loving address and token of goodwill have touched me greatly.   If anything could lessen the bitterness of leaving dear S. Mary's it would be the sympathy and love shewn to me by one and all of you, and by so many friends in Calne.

I ought to be deeply grateful and thankful to God for His many blessings, but especially for the large share of love that has fallen to my share during the last 23 years.

You may rest assured you will never be forgotten, and I hope you will still always look upon me as your friend, and will call upon me to act as such whenever you need advice or help.

May God bless each one of you.

Always yours lovingly,

Florence M. Dyas

My future address will be :—
Rounceval Place,
Chipping Sodbury, Glos.

Above: *Miss Dyas with the boarders*

Left: *Miss Dyas' letter to the school on her departure*

Right: *Mr Arthur Dunne*

people, Miss Dyas was ahead of her time. She kept the school free from red tape and had no use for restrictions that served no purpose.'

Florence Dyas had succeeded in establishing St Mary's as a school recognised for its sound educational standards. With her pupils she celebrated special occasions in style; she ensured contact with other schools and the wider world; and she brought fun to school life. She had carried St Mary's through the turn of the century, settled it into new

Mr Arthur Dunne KC

Miss Dyas' departure as headmistress came not long after the death of Mrs Murray and the end of her years of support. As with so much in the history of St Mary's, good fortune stepped in when needed. Archdeacon Bodington was devoted to the school and must have constantly worried over the certainty of its future. However, in 1909 he had been joined on the Governing Body by Mr Arthur Dunne, and together they struck up a close friendship which was to prove invaluable to St Mary's. He was to become an extremely generous benefactor to the school and brought with him his considerable negotiating skills.

Arthur Mountjoy Dunne had moved to Calne after serving at the Bar in Calcutta. He continued to have a base in London and practised before the Judicial Committee of the Privy Council. Charles Gough, later clerk to the governors, who worked closely with him, wrote that he was 'one of the ablest men I have been associated with'. Within the town he sat on the local Bench and held the position of warden to the church.

He and his wife lived in Highlands, a house on the Melksham Road that had previously belonged to Mrs Murray. They frequently entertained girls from St Mary's in what is described by Jean Hughes, who wrote about this period at the school, as 'a cultured home where they were treated as adults'. Summer tea parties for the girls were followed by croquet and clock-golf on the lawn. Miss Matthews, who was headmistress when Mr Dunne finally gave up his position as a governor, wrote that 'Nothing was too small, nothing too big for his attention and interest. His personal interest in the girls meant for more than one of them a start in life they could never otherwise have had. To know their need was enough'.

In addition to the small kindnesses of Arthur Dunne, he bestowed on St Mary's a far greater gift of helping to secure its future by personally buying land and property, which in 1929 he gave to the school. Among these acquisitions were the boarding house St Prisca's and parcels of land around it; the area used for playing fields leading to the lime kiln; some cottages on Curzon Street; and the site on which the Medical Centre now stands. It was a truly generous benefaction, without which the school would have been limited as to its future expansion. Arthur Dunne remained on the Governing Body until 1946 and died the following year.

buildings and maintained its strong Anglican foundation. She had been a committed and effective guardian of her little school.

Miss Rachael Donaldson and a Critical Period for the School

After the long tenure of Miss Dyas, St Mary's had to adapt to a new era. The Governing Body chose as headmistress Rachael Donaldson, a person of intelligence and ambition, who was probably the first headmistress with full academic qualifications, having gained a high honours in Classical Moderations and English at St Hilda's College, Oxford. Educated at Cheltenham Ladies' College under Miss Beale, she had taught at Bolton and Carlisle High Schools before arriving at St Mary's in 1911. She was remembered by one of her pupils as 'a breezy open-air type, keen on golf and one who used to go off on the back of the doctor's motorbike'.

St Mary's does not have much documentation from the period when Rachael Donaldson was leading the school but we know that when she moved on to a lectureship at Durham University in 1915, Archdeacon Bodington was warm in his praise of her contribution to St Mary's, speaking of 'the great value of her work'. At prizegiving in 1913 he said that 'What the governors owe to Miss Donaldson no words would ever be able to express.

Miss Rachael Donaldson

'The curriculum is designed with a definite object in view, not immediate utility but ultimate usefulness, not to attain mere results but to produce the highest type of individual. The immediate value of certain subjects may not be apparent, but that is not the point. The question is rather whether that particular branch of study is assisting in the formation of character, broadening the mind and developing the possibilities latent in the child. I believe that the seemingly ambitious study of world history, of which I spoke last year, is already beginning to have its effect. At least it is deeply interesting and will always occupy its right place as long as the curriculum is in my control. And surely never was it so important as it is at this moment for our children to grasp great principles, law of cause and effect and the truth about civilisation. You may rest assured that we are never willingly to lose sight of the true end of education. We shall not be satisfied with imparting information, but endeavour to cultivate in every pupil in the School, in addition to sound churchmanship, breadth of outlook, the habit of independent thought and work, and a sense of proportion.'

— FROM MISS DONALDSON'S SPEECH AT PRIZEGIVING IN 1915

She has been everything that anybody in her position as headmistress could possibly be'. She maintained a high standard of teaching that is well reflected in the results of the public examinations that the pupils undertook.

That Miss Donaldson was a person of keen intellect can be seen in her ideas on the fundamentals of a good education. Her speech on the occasion of prizegiving in 1914 was recorded by the local paper. It gives a picture of a confident, clear-thinking person not afraid to promote her ideas. She soon overcame a perhaps inevitably unsettled period when the school was going through the transition of leadership, and 'the improved discipline among the children' was noted at a governors' meeting in 1912.

Miss Donaldson knew from the time of joining St Mary's that it was struggling financially but she asked that fees should be increased for boarders in order to improve staff salaries. However as 1912 moved into 1913 things became so difficult that the governors voted that the school should close. This could well have been the demise of St Mary's but for the steadfastness of Archdeacon Bodington. He was described by Arthur Dunne as considering it to be 'so grievous a breach of duty on his part and such an utter failure that he would have to leave the parish if the school closed'. He persuaded the governors to change the school from one serving the immediate neighbourhood on low fees to one that could be self-supporting. Despite raised fees and a few more boarders the prospect remained bleak.

*Miss Donaldson,
wearing dark glasses,
as a member of the cast
in a school play*

Some of the very early property conveyances show that Canon Duncan and Ellinor Gabriel believed that St Mary's School should be founded following the principles of the Woodard Society as well as those of the Anglican tradition. It was to the Woodard Society that Archdeacon Bodington now turned, hoping that through their support, St Mary's would have a future and could be drawn into their group of schools. However owing to legal difficulties, this avenue could not provide a solution, so the school struggled on.

Two letters from Miss Donaldson, both dated 1913, survive, one to Archdeacon Bodington and the other to the governors. In these she states her commitment to the school, her own personal ambition and her hopes for a rise in her salary. The outcome is not known but she remained at St Mary's until 1915, when the post at Durham University gave her a chance to advance her career.

We have a photograph taken in 1914 of Miss Donaldson with the whole school of around 40 pupils outside the main school house. There is another wonderful picture of her in full costume taking pride of place among a group of school actors. She was clearly a person of strong character

and though her time at St Mary's was not long she was dedicated to doing her best for the school. For many years the school hymn, 'Consider the Lilies', which she wrote and Mr Pullein set to music, was sung regularly.

Although the St Mary's Guild had been started by Miss Dyas in 1891, there must have been a period when it had lapsed, as in her address to the school at prizegiving in 1915 Miss Donaldson reported on the good response she had received from a letter sent to all past pupils urging them to continue their interest in the school by joining the Guild. She goes on to say, 'It is no longer a dream, but a fact and a flourishing fact, with its officers and committee'. The first News Sheet of 1916 shows Miss Donaldson to be Vice President of the Guild.

Miss Donaldson's final year at St Mary's coincided with a time when events in the outside world were once again to impact on the fortunes of the school. As war swept through Europe, in one small corner of England St Mary's saw an increase in the number of its boarders, as parents sent their children to be away from the Zeppelin attacks in London and the east of the country. The effect of this would in time double the school's income.

CHAPTER TWO

Edith Marcia Matthews 1915–45

The role of the three founders of St Mary's School, John Duncan, Ellinor Gabriel and Penelope Murray, has rightly been recognised and remembered by later generations. Perhaps less well remarked have been the contributions of three more people who could be considered the second founders: Eric Bodington, Arthur Dunne and Marcia Matthews, who was to be the next headmistress. In their time they used their individual skills and resources to give the school the sure foundation it so desperately craved. Without their combined talents the school would probably not have survived. St Mary's owes them a great debt of gratitude.

Above: *Portrait of Miss Marcia Matthews by Ethel Gabain 1946*

Left: *The entrance to School House 1915*

Remembering Miss Matthews

'*She was endowed with a generous love of humanity and an enthusiastic love of life, with great vision, great faith, and extraordinary creative energy. She cultivated the qualities of courage and control, which gave to her work direction, perseverance, and success. Although all her energies were turned outward, one of her favourite quotations was 'Know thyself' and she was very honest to herself. She usually admitted her mistakes and invited criticism, even from her pupils. It is impossible to sum up Miss Matthews' qualities because she was a most unrestricted person. She was so versatile she would not fit into any categories. Her powers of invention were equal to any new occasion; her humour would burst through conventions. Perhaps the most special thing about her was that she was so many-sided and yet so integrated. She combined reverence with jesting, shrewdness with kindness, careful planning with impulsive experiments, broad-mindedness with a clear sense of duty, infinite sympathy and understanding with definite values.*'

– ELIZABETH STAMPER

'*A special tribute must be paid to Archdeacon Bodington, Arthur Mountjoy Dunne KC and Edith Marcia Matthews. These three people were in my judgement the architects of what is known today as St Mary's School Calne. They were a wonderful trio and they worked together in the closest harmony.*'

– CHARLES GOUGH, CLERK TO THE GOVERNORS

The next few decades were the period when St Mary's moved from being a small school providing mostly for the local community to a school with a recognised standing within the country at large. Distinguished national figures associated themselves with the school and the pupils benefited from their contributions.

The St Mary's School of 1915 that Miss Matthews had in her charge was still a very small concern: there were 38 pupils and six resident members of staff, with some subjects having no specialist teacher; the school grounds extended to just over one acre; and war brought shortages and price rises. Developing the school while balancing the budget was going to be a great challenge, but Miss Matthews was well qualified to take on the task.

Miss Edith Marcia Matthews was only 32 years old when she became headmistress of St Mary's, but had come from a strongly educational background. One of a family of ten, her father had been a clergyman and headmaster and she had been brought up in the surroundings of Wellington College and Leeds Grammar School. She became head girl at Godolphin School in Salisbury, which was then under the influential leadership of Miss Douglas. On leaving Godolphin, Marcia Matthews went on to read history at Newnham.

After some years teaching at St Margaret's School, Bushey, where a previous pupil of St Mary's, Julian Boys, was headmistress, Miss Matthews arrived to take up the post of headmistress in Calne. She was to prove an outstanding leader. Matt, as she became affectionately known, was to have a strong influence on the lives of the girls in her care but she is remembered with some mixed feelings by the pupils. She tended to polarise opinion but there is no doubt that her qualities were recognised by those that knew her and it is perhaps best to let their words speak for themselves (*see boxes*).

Miss Matthews recognised the part her own headmistress, Miss Douglas, had played in formulating her thoughts on a rounded education, and she paid tribute to Miss Boys and the quality of the schooling she had received under Miss Dyas. Her ideas on education also echoed those of her predecessor, Rachael Donaldson. Like her, Miss Matthews believed in developing the talents of the individual child in all areas. Reflecting the time they

The staff on Chapel Lawn c. 1915

were in, she said that rather than putting emphasis only on academic achievements, 'a far greater test to my mind of the value of education given here would be a test of the way a St Mary's girl spent her leisure. I think we can hardly hope for more than that she should leave school hungry, with a real desire to continue her own education, that she should have learnt how to work (a really difficult lesson), and lastly that she should leave with a definite idea of service'. As Miss Matthews' years at the school covered both World Wars many of her pupils needed the qualities she instilled.

Early Changes

At first Miss Matthews made few changes to the school routine, but she received support from the parents for her plans to begin afternoon school an hour later, therefore allowing time for games, gardening and walks. Although she valued academic success highly, her desire to take pupils away from their desks into a wider range of activities

led her to introduce lessons in gardening and carpentry. She certainly considered the latter to have wide benefits: 'I value this class very highly for its practical utility and the interest it arouses, but above all for the training in accuracy which it provides. Anything in the nature of slip-shod work is impossible in the carpenter's shop, and the lessons learnt there must surely react on all work, while everyone recognises nowadays how much work of that kind helps to quicken the brain.'

On her arrival Miss Matthews had appointed four new staff members, with only the music mistress, Miss Gutteridge, and the matron, Miss Bailey, remaining from Miss Donaldson's time. Through the first two years, though the number of resident staff did not change, pupil numbers increased considerably. From the initial 38 on the register in 1915, by the end of the summer term in 1917, there were 65. Boarder numbers had risen from 21 to 36. There was no entrance examination for the girls: Miss Matthews chose those she felt suitable for the school. The News

Sheets show they came from Essex to Newport, Exeter to Radnorshire, as well as many local places. A number of the addresses are vicarages and we know that the governors advertised in *The Church Times* and hoped to be able to provide an education for the children of clergy. In 1919 there were sufficient numbers for a netball match to take place between clergy daughters and the rest of the school.

Records of the balance sheets from this time indicate that the school's finances were strengthening. In 1918 there was a surplus for the year of £230 30s 1d, a significant improvement on a few years earlier. The increase in pupil numbers provided the funds for the additional accommodation which was now needed.

So began the first of many acquisitions of property and land for use by the school. We know that many of these early purchases were made by Mr Arthur Dunne. In September 1916 he bought a house, which the school named St Prisca's, at the top of Alma Terrace, overlooking the quarry. It was a tall, narrow building, 'inclined to rock in a high wind'. It provided boarding for a dozen girls, a kitchen for cookery lessons and two rooms for the Kindergarten under Miss Abdy. A verandah made an outside classroom for the summer. In 1928, the father of a pupil, Sir John Hindley, began the funding of a large extension to the

house, adding new dormitories and an enlarged kitchen for domestic science. The main dormitory was to carry Arthur Dunne's name, and a flat roof above provided a place for exercise when the pitches were frozen and for 'sleeping out' in the summer, a practice which Miss Matthews encouraged when the weather was good. The architect for

Above: *The kindergarten outside St Prisca's*

Left: *A cookery class in St Prisca's in the 1920s*

Top right: *The verandah at St Prisca's today*

Bottom right: *Rachel Buck*

this venture was Mr Rudman, who was to oversee future projects for the school. That same year the father of a head girl, Rachel Buck, funded a tennis court for the school next to St Prisca's, known as 'Rachel'. A further court, on ground opposite the house, was called 'Mogle' after Margaret Ogle, another head girl and a talented tennis player.

The Grounds of St Mary's School

It is not easy to imagine how the surroundings of St Mary's would have looked in 1915. The garden at the front of the original schoolhouse next to the road would have been similar to today, although there were four cottages on Curzon Street where the main entrance gate now stands. The garden behind the house was known as Chapel Lawn. A photograph shows it to have been screened by some large trees and to extend to a wall. Part of the lawn was raised on a small bank and for many years this acted as a natural stage for outdoor productions. Beyond the wall, steep banking dropped to a lower level. This banking swept round to below the cottage next to School House where it can still be clearly seen. The present Dining Room and kitchens were later built out from the original Chapel Lawn.

Initially this, along with the lower cottage and the tennis court, was the extent of the grounds, but beyond the limits lay an area with an interesting industrial history that was to offer the school the ability to expand. The nature of the use of this land is suggested by the banks on which the school perched and which can be seen skirting the lower level of the grounds. The lime kiln, standing so prominently in the centre of the school, confirms that much of this area was once a working quarry.

The bedrock under the school consists of a type of limestone composed of petrified coral, known for its rich fossil content. Being easy to cut and of reasonable quality, it made good building stone, and it also provided lime for building and agricultural purposes. There were a number of small quarries in Calne and four lime kilns are recorded, of which only the one at St Mary's still exists.

The site at first contained two quarries which probably began production around 1840. One quarry was owned by the Bowood Estate and the second one belonged to Dr Ogilvie, who lived in Northfield House, now part of one of the school's boarding houses, St Cecilia's.

Ogilvie's Quarry was bought by Lord Lansdowne in 1869 and the two quarries, known as Piece Quarry, were worked together for the following years. It is uncertain when the quarry ceased production, but we know there was a manager, Mark Haines, working here in 1902, only six years before the school moved to the site.

For many years some ponds, which provided a good hunting ground for biology lessons, existed in the farthest corner behind the lime kiln, but being of some danger were filled in during the 1960s. A jungle of vegetation concealing the quarry face was removed and

In front of School House and the cottage c. 1915

Tennis on the Chapel Lawn c. 1915

The lime kiln, today

the ground was levelled, seeded and planted with willows and balsam poplars to help soak up water seeping from the rock. The reclaimed ground was ideal for recreation, and included a croquet lawn.

Ponies, used to transport materials at the quarry, had been housed at the top of the banking, in the area of a small building. It is possible that this building is on the site of the stables as beneath the modern flooring are old cobbles and a drainage gully.

In a paper read by the Vicar of Calne on Prize Day in 1896, he recalls how, when the first school house on The Green in Calne needed an extension, Lord Lansdowne gave the school 'such stone, sand and lime as might be required for enlarging the house and adapting it to its future position'. It seems possible that these materials came from the quarry that would later be part of the current school grounds.

The lime kiln at St Mary's is of a typical construction, with an egg-shaped burning chamber at the top and an air inlet at the base. It remains a feature of the school grounds and is a listed building. Over the years bushes have grown on its grassy banks and repair work has been carried out; it has provided a platform for school events and a hide-away for sun-bathing. Its position in front of the new Sixth Form house brings the school's heritage into sharp focus with the most up-to-date facilities.

Touched by War

The first year of the Great War coincided with the final year of Miss Donaldson's time at St Mary's. In welcoming Field Marshal Lord Methuen, the guest speaker at Prize Day that year, Archdeacon Bodington reflected the preoccupations of the country and the school with the words 'our hearts and minds are full of the war'.

Records show that St Mary's rose to the challenges of the time, supporting a number of charities. A fundraising entertainment was put on in the town hall for the local Patriotic Fund, the younger children performing a play and the older girls and the staff 'a very light comedy'. At the same time pupils continued to follow the routines of school life: examinations were worked for; when possible matches against other schools took place; any girl who wanted a plot of land to garden was given one; and clubs such as the Reading Society, the Newspaper and Magazine Club and the Stamp Club were attended. The gardens were extensively worked to provide vegetables for the school kitchen.

Pupils working in the school garden c. 1915

POST OFFICE TELEGRAPHS.

As the war continued and Miss Matthews joined the school, further involvement with the war effort ensued. Wounded soldiers were given an entertainment of music and recitation. The girls raised 'more than enough money for the tea' and the staff 'provided cigarettes'.

Proceedings at Miss Matthews's first Prize Day were scaled down. She commented later that she 'could not feel it right, when hearts were stricken in so many ways, to have even the usual festive tea'. Looking back that day on the work of Miss Donaldson, Miss Matthews recognised the high standard of work that had been achieved as reflected in the examination results. She was to present the same prizes as previously but was adding one of her own in order to give encouragement to 'observation, general reading and interest in current affairs'. Some of the prizes were in the form of war vouchers.

At the end of the school year in 1916 Miss Matthews urged each pupil to work on the land or help with war work during the summer holidays. She also asked them all to prepare an essay on some kind of war work.

The following term it was announced that St Mary's was to 'adopt' a prisoner of war, a Lance Corporal from the 4th Hampshire Regiment, who was imprisoned at Kut al Amara near Baghdad. He received letters from the school and later parcels. 1918 saw the school raise funds for the Wiltshire Prisoners of War Fund.

In the spring of 1917 a group of staff and girls visited Yatesbury Camp to see the 'fighting machines', including 'one of the new ones in which the gunner sits in front of the pilot'. They also saw the German prisoners' encampment in which 'they appeared to be very comfortably housed in two long rows of huts with neat little gardens in between'.

As the country moved into the final year of the war, St Mary's was still hard at work. A sale of the needlework that the girls had been producing over the previous year raised money for a number of charities, including the Officers' Families' Fund. In response to an appeal 418 hospital bags were made in ten days and the staff funded a war shrine in Curzon Street.

Finally Armistice Day arrived. The school first became aware of the event when it was noticed that a man was standing precariously on top of a partially completed chimney stack on Harris' newly built factory waving a Union Jack. The prefects were allowed to go to the post office to receive a telegram confirming the fact. On their return, 'The whole school, hatless and coatless, broke bounds and rushed excitedly down to the town'. Later the girls gathered to sing the National Anthem and then sat on the front wall by the road and sang songs while the staff went into Calne to buy flags, tin trumpets and red, white and blue ribbons.

That afternoon the pupils marched in a procession to a service of thanksgiving on The Strand in the town and in the evening a 'magnificent' supper was laid on by the staff in St Prisca's. The following night St Mary's celebrated further with a bonfire and songs.

Although Europe had been in turmoil, within the confines of the school Matt had done all she could to provide as normal a life as possible. Societies and entertainments had flourished and outside speakers had illustrated talks with lantern slide shows. Outings had taken place and the library had begun to accumulate an extensive collection of books. The Literary and Debating Society had debated the motion 'That the position of women has been improved by the war'.

St Mary's Expands its Horizons

With war over St Mary's found itself with healthy finances, ever-increasing pupil numbers and a growing self-confidence. In 1924 Archdeacon Bodington presented the governors with a suggested scheme for the 'Government of the School'. He proposed that as vacancies occurred among life-governors, representative governors should be elected by the Archbishop of Canterbury, The University of Oxford and The University of Cambridge. The outcome is not recorded but it indicates his ambitions.

Miss Matthews' interests spread far and, in addition to her work within St Mary's, she built strong links with

Top right: From the 1915 to 1919 photograph album

Bottom right: A letter to Anne Durst, grand-daughter of Canon Duncan, from the Archbishop of Canterbury

the town of Calne. She sat on the Bench as a magistrate and chaired several committees. Her wider connections brought eminent visitors, particularly from the world of education and the Church, to lecture and preach. The Archbishop of Canterbury took a close interest in St Mary's, gifting a divinity prize to the school; Miss Douglas from

'At the beginning of the Christmas term we began a new hobby, plumbing. The first thing we did was to put new washers on taps. We all repaired to the cloakroom for this and practised on the taps there. Another very interesting lesson was upon the way in which fresh panes of glass are put into windows. We experimented upon the windows in Murray and Duncan. We have also learnt about gas, pumps and cisterns, and how to solder leaking tins. The solder went on beautifully when Mr Gunning did it, but when we tried to do it, it suddenly became most desperately obstinate.'

– EXTRACT FROM 1922 NEWS SHEET: PLUMBING

Godolphin School gave support and advice; and a games mistress from St Paul's School, an international lacrosse player, spent an afternoon on the pitch with the girls.

The speaker at prizegiving in 1919 was Dr Spooner, the Warden of New College, Oxford. After presenting the prizes, he talked to the girls about the importance of using well the education that they were receiving. He said that the education of women had acquired a new and special interest and importance as the war had revealed to women that many careers were now possible. Also, women had been put in a position of great trust, some having been granted the vote which would 'largely determine the happiness, prosperity and future of their country'.

Distinguished visitors from the art world made memorable visits to the school. Among them was Miss Dorothy Green (of the New Shakespeare Company), who on three occasions stayed at the school for a few days at a time to read several plays, thrilling the girls with her ability to take on numerous characters. From this association many very successful visits were made to Stratford by groups of pupils.

This was an exciting time for the school. The Board of Education gave official recognition to the standard of teaching and learning that St Mary's had achieved; the first pupils were entered for the Cambridge Higher Examination and two girls were accepted at Lady Margaret Hall in Oxford. Dorothy Morrison and Jean Sorsbie were the first to tread the path to Oxford and Cambridge that many later St Mary's pupils followed. Jean Sorsbie had won a major open scholarship and the governors supplemented this with a grant of £3 towards her books. The first St Mary's girl to go to any university was Margaret Randolph, who went to study French at the Sorbonne in 1920.

Above: *Cricket in the 1920s with School House in the background*

Left: *The 1929 school tennis team*

Top right: *The Sixth Form outside Hut Passage after lunch 1930*

Bottom right: *The gymnasium in Hut Passage*

Miss Ethel Alexander

In the year leading up to the 50th anniversary of St Mary's in 1923 the deputy headmistress, Miss Alexander, stood in for Matt for a term as she recovered from a serious operation. Again, in 1938 she deputised for a term. Ethel Alexander, known by everyone as Alex, was described in a tribute by Miss Matthews as being 'the backbone of the staff'. She praised the quality of her teaching, which led to a number of pupils gaining scholarships and exhibitions to Oxbridge, and for her great organisational skills. The two of them formed a remarkable partnership which continued until Miss Alexander's retirement in 1940. In addition to her teaching commitments, she ran the library, cared for the Chapel and supervised the school's charitable endeavours.

Alex was renowned for the notes that she would post on the boards, one reading, 'Will those who are such bad shots please stop aiming at the waste paper basket'.

Miss Alexander died in 1961. A tribute from the time said that 'It was the solid, practical wisdom and the goodness of Ethel Maud Alexander that guided Miss Matthews' meteoric energy and kept it down to earth'. Her great legacy to St Mary's is a series of diaries that she wrote throughout her time at the school. They record the day-by-day events and are a wonderful window into life at St Mary's during that time. On her retirement Alex maintained strong links with the school through her work with the Old Girls' Association.

Stepping into the gap left by Miss Alexander as senior mistress came Miss Margaret Thouless. She proved to be exceptionally loyal to the school and a great support to the headmistresses she worked with. A notable scholar, she taught English and some German and infused the naturalists among the pupils with her love of birds. Kay Stedmond, who wrote the history of St Mary's up to 1986, remembered her keen intellect and her kindly generosity. She recalled, 'The neat suits, the immaculate handwriting, the tidy desk and the quiet air of competence'. An Old Girl described her as 'strong and quiet'. Her career at St Mary's was to span 18 years and when she left, the headmistress wrote, 'Her complete integrity, unswerving loyalty and the high standard of her scholarship have been of inestimable value'.

While the wider world swung into the 'Roaring Twenties', St Mary's gained its first gramophone as 'a helpful way of teaching music'.

New Ground

As the school started to look ahead, hoping for more settled times, its physical horizons began to extend. Arthur Dunne bought four acres of allotment land which covered ground leading to just beyond the lime kiln. The girls helped prepare the area for use as a games pitch by pulling thistles. The acquisition of this land made a huge difference to St Mary's. Tennis courts were established and lacrosse

St Mary's School's Golden Jubilee

At the end of 1922 Miss Matthews announced to the school community that with the 50th anniversary of the foundation of St Mary's coming in the following year, she would like to have ideas as to how to celebrate the occasion. She also asked for reminiscences from Old Girls. The school archive has some of the letters she received which are invaluable in giving a pupil's perspective on their time at the school from the earliest days.

A dream of Miss Matthews had been that the school should have a specific room for teaching science. By the summer term of 1923 Matt was back from her convalescence and able to see five pupils lay foundation stones for the Jubilee Building. It would provide an art studio, three small music rooms, a room for woodwork and the longed-for science laboratory.

Jubilee Building stood on the lower level of the school grounds close to where the Music School now stands. Opened by Lady Lansdowne at the Jubilee celebrations later that term, it was a valuable addition to the school and very much fitted the educational ideal to which Miss Matthews' aspired. The Jubilee Building was adapted to

different requirements in the years that followed until it was dismantled in 1988. Its construction and the consequent widening of the curriculum was a fitting way to mark the 50 years since the foundation of St Mary's.

The new building was finished on the Friday night of the Jubilee weekend. The studio was temporarily converted into a sitting room for over 80 Old Girls and other visitors, including two previous headmistresses. They were wonderfully entertained over three days, beginning with a production of *Much Ado about Nothing* on Saturday evening in the garden. After supper on Sunday the girls put on a concert. Monday began with a service in the church conducted by the Bishop of Salisbury. Lunch in a marquee on the cricket field was followed by prizegiving, speeches and the opening of the Jubilee Building, before a further performance of the play in the evening. The weekend had brought together the different generations of St Mary's and celebrated a great milestone on the journey the school was taking. It was a particularly meaningful occasion for Archdeacon Bodington, who had placed such faith in the future of St Mary's.

Above: *The science room in Jubilee Building*

Above left: *A drawing of the Jubilee Building which accompanied a fundraising letter*

Left: *Looking towards Jubilee Building with the Marcia Matthews Building on the right*

Above: *The Sixth Form during Sunday afternoon letter writing 1929*

Right: *Pupils in 1928*

and cricket were now played within the school grounds. In 1923 shrubs and trees were planted around this area.

The year 1920 became a significant one when the school acquired an ex-YMCA hut from Yatesbury Camp. This gave considerable extra space, with three classrooms, a large room that provided a hall and gym and a small Sixth Form room heated by a stove, in what had been the camp bar. Some years later the school also had use of a cottage nearby for piano lessons. Pupils from that time remember how the Sixth Form used the upstairs room for parties, helped out by lardy cake from Maslen's bakery, and smoking out of the window.

Moving classrooms out of School House released room for additional dormitories and the school's first library. Hut Passage, as it became known, lay on land alongside today's main entrance drive, where the school Chapel now stands, and it was connected to Red Hall by a narrow, sloping wooden passage, later lined with school photographs. It was intended to be for temporary use but continued as the main centre of teaching until the Plumer Wing was built in 1954. Even after that the gym was still used and cloakrooms took over the form rooms. Hut Passage was eventually demolished in 1963.

Arthur Dunne's legal skills became vital to St Mary's when in 1922 it faced a threat to its future. Miss Matthews told the governors that there was a problem with the

behaviour of people using a track across the quarry as a short cut. In seeking to close the route, the school faced some opposition which led to public meetings. It had been suggested that a road by-passing the town centre should follow this route. Much correspondence followed the issue and without the right resolution the outcome could have led to the closure of the school. Mr Dunne asked several local people who had worked the quarry from the middle of the 19th century to state whether it had originally been a right-of-way. Their affidavits make fascinating reading, giving information that would otherwise have been lost. Happily the dispute was resolved in favour of the school.

1923 The Need for More Boarding Space

As St Mary's said goodbye to its Jubilee visitors and the school year drew to a close, the governors took possession of Congresbury House on Market Hill in Calne. This fine building with old oak panelling belonged to the Buckeridge family, many of whose members had been pupils at the school. At first the house, which the school called St Bridget's, was rented from the family for £50 a year. However in 1929 the school was able to buy the property outright, and it remained in the ownership of St Mary's

blessed with running water at this time, a benefit of which St Prisca's could only dream.

In 1926, School House too was to have a taste of a new way of life, recorded in the following extract from the school diary: 'Those who have experienced the dismalness of Calne gas will easily believe that our greatest joy is our newly-installed electric light. We no longer have to grope our way through dark passages and cloakrooms but find switches and a flood of light wherever we need them. Some of us can even turn off our lights from our beds.'

Five years after St Bridget's was acquired, a second house, St Faith's, standing at the lower end of Alma Terrace and described later as 'gaunt and gloomy', was at first rented by the school and then bought. Named after one of the original school houses on The Green, it was suitably fitted out and in the summer term of 1928 six girls and two staff members moved in. St Faith's remained a boarding house for St Mary's until 1960, when it was sold.

Events in Calne

During the 1920s and 1930s Calne provided Miss Matthews with wonderful opportunities to give her pupils contact with events in the wider world. When she came to St Mary's, she had worried that they would be too far from centres of culture. However a very active musical society brought well-recognised musicians to the town for recitals and concerts which the pupils were able to attend.

Of course the parish church was very familiar to the girls, who attended weekly services and the many excellent concerts held there. As a church school, with the vicars having such a close interest in the welfare of St Mary's, the bond remained strong down the decades, although in

until 1967, when a new boarding house in the grounds meant St Bridget's could be sold.

The house provided accommodation for nine girls, three mistresses and the housemistress, and the pupils appreciated having the opportunity to live there, despite the need for the accompanied walk in groups down the slicket in the evening. St Bridget's was at that time run by Miss Cates, who created an exceptionally homely atmosphere and was renowned for the wonderful cooked breakfasts that she produced every morning. She was, however, a stickler for tidiness and kept the house immaculately polished; so shiny were the wooden stairs in fact that it was essential to hang on tightly to the bannisters to avoid a fast descent to the bottom. St Bridget's was also

Above: *A Greek dance 1926*

Left: Much Ado About Nothing *1923*

Right: *The audience on Chapel Lawn watching a production of* As you Like It *in 1933*

future years the Vicar no longer sat on the Governing Body and the school had their own chaplain.

A programme of public lectures in the Town Hall was another wonderful widening experience for the pupils, with talks on such subjects as 'An Expeditionary Force in Russia', 'Flying over East Africa', 'John Bull and Uncle Sam', 'Devastated Areas of France' and 'Scene shifting in China'.

The League of Nations Union, with its promotion of world peace, had a high profile at this time, with a very active local branch which received some distinguished speakers from their headquarters. St Mary's was a keen supporter, with girls going weekly to meetings in Calne, and sometimes the speakers visited the school.

Events Further Afield

In May 1926, as St Mary's began a new term, the concern was on events outside. The General Strike was sweeping the country and it was unclear where this would lead. Bulletins which were being posted in the town after news was broadcast were sent up to the school by the mayor, and the staff were asked by the mayoress to help run a canteen for lorry drivers. Post was delayed and newspapers limited and restricted in size. Miss Matthews, who wanted the girls to be well-informed, invited a speaker with a close knowledge of the mining industry to tell the pupils of the working conditions of the coal mines and the events that had led to the crisis.

In 1929, during the Great Depression, the country was asked to support the mining areas. St Mary's was coupled with an elementary school in Aberdare, South Wales. Of the 400 pupils, a third were children from families suffering unemployment. The need for support was

immense. St Mary's responded by collecting and making clothes and providing other necessities which were sent to Aberdare on a regular basis. At the same time clothes for younger children were sent to a Friends' settlement in the Rhondda Valley, to which the English teacher at St Mary's had moved to become a social worker.

Companies

In the spring of 1917 the school began its Company system. Initially its primary purpose was to promote tidiness in the cloakrooms and the gym but soon its remit spread further. Each term the pupils were divided into three groups headed by senior girls, being first given the name of the leader and soon after also the names A, B and C Company. Red points could be won by the Company or by individuals for such things as deportment, gaining honour points or winning matches. Black points would be deducted. An entertainment was staged each Saturday by one of the Companies. In time more ambitious productions were being performed and sports matches between the Companies were regular events.

In order to delegate some of the decisions regarding the running of the school to the pupils, a Manners and

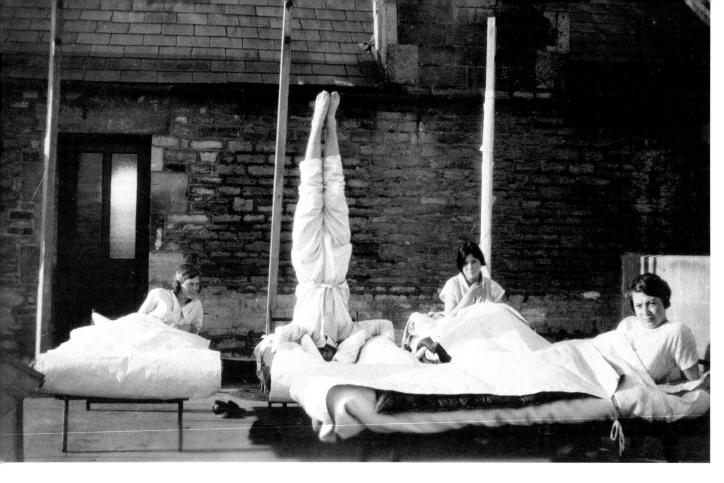

Sleeping out on the roof of St Prisca's 1929

Responsibilities Committee had been formed in 1922. Miss Matthews chaired this with representatives from the staff and each class present. In 1924 they decided that the Company system in the school should become more formal, instilling a greater sense of pride and competition. At first the boarders were divided into four Companies named Poore, Grosstete, Osmund and Moberly, with the day girls in Edmund Rich. All were named after people who had been historically connected with the Diocese. Later each of the five Companies had its own group of day girls included in it.

In 1942 Miss Matthews felt that with the number of pupils in the school increasing, the Companies should become similar to the house system of other schools. Three members of staff were allocated to each Company and a new enthusiasm for Company activities was born, including each working its own allotment area.

Archdeacons Bodington and Coulter

Archdeacon Bodington had the satisfaction in 1927 of seeing the number of pupils in the school creep to over 100, and perhaps this was a fitting way to round off his time in Calne. He moved to a post in Dorset, and the next Vicar of Calne chaired the governors of St Mary's. To the school's delight Archdeacon Bodington agreed to remain on the Governing Body; however he had been in his new post for scarcely two years when his death was announced.

To the school this was a very great sorrow and he was deeply mourned. Miss Matthews said of him, 'I know of no school where the Chairman of the Governors was also chaplain, father and grandfather to us all'. It was to him that the school owes its continued existence. A minute book bears witness to 'the continual struggle he had, to fan into life the feeble flame that was so often all that served to show that the School was still alive'. His persistence was rewarded and he brought to St Mary's a sensitivity that coloured his dealings with the pupils. His love of beauty in the written word, in nature and in holiness was conveyed to the girls. As one said, 'He was always so gentle and courteous'. In 1932 a fiction library was created from two rooms in School House, opening onto Red Hall, and fittingly it was given the name the Bodington Memorial Library. A 'beautiful' door given by the leaving girls of 1933 led into the library.

'Calne will feel the loss of her Vicar for many a day and deeply. No worker so earnest and so good in heart and mind can have laboured as he has done, for all these years without gaining the warm affection for those for whom and among whom he has worked.

'His work for St Mary's will live for all time after him. He has remained at his post to see its growth from the very humblest beginning through trying and anxious times to a successful vitality far beyond anything that one could ever have counted on, or even hoped for in those early days. His devotion to, and belief in the School was absolute always, he loved it.'

– FROM A LETTER WRITTEN TO MISS MATTHEWS IN 1926 BY ARTHUR DUNNE ON THE OCCASION OF ARCHDEACON BODINGTON LEAVING THE POST OF VICAR OF CALNE

Above: *Archdeacon Joseph Coulter*

Below: *The Bodington Memorial Library in School House*

Towards the end of Archdeacon Bodington's time as chairman, the governors had moved to change the constitution of the Governing Body. Of the original group of trustees who held the property in the name of the school, only three remained. A company, St Mary's School (Calne), was formed under the management of a new Governing Body. Also at this time Arthur Dunne transferred the properties which had been in his name. As the school had been able to afford it, he had received some reimbursement for his purchases, but it is highly unlikely that he ever sought, or received, full settlement. His generosity was immense.

The new Archdeacon of Wiltshire and Vicar of Calne, Archdeacon Joseph William Coulter, became Chairman of the Governors. Sitting with him and Archdeacon Bodington were the Marquess and Marchioness of Lansdowne, Mr Arthur Dunne, Mr J.F. Bodinnar JP, Lord Warrington of Clyffe (who was a friend of Archdeacon Bodington and who gave invaluable legal advice in connection with the new trust) and the headmistress. Archdeacon Bodington's death was announced on the day that the governors met to confirm that the legal transfer of the government of the school to the new company was complete. The minutes record profound gratitude for his great contribution to St Mary's School.

Archdeacon Coulter, born in Ireland in 1867, was educated at Trinity College Dublin, representing them in rugby. After his ordination he worked for five years in County Wexford before transferring to the Salisbury Diocese. He moved to different positions in the Diocese until his appointment to Calne. He was described as having a 'huge fount of humour' and 'a merry smile', and as well as being popular among his parishioners, he was held in high esteem by the non-conformists of Calne, who recognised him as the 'spiritual head of the town'. He was to remain at Calne and as Chairman of the Governors at St Mary's for 24 years.

The Governing Body in 1928

Throughout his chairmanship, Archdeacon Coulter was supported by many distinguished men and women. Until the end of the 1920s the governors had mostly come from among notable local people, including Lord and Lady Lansdowne and the Mayor of Calne, Mr John Bodinnar, later to be knighted. St Mary's now began to draw from a wider sphere.

On Archdeacon Bodington's death Sir Ernest Gowers KGB, who had a daughter at St Mary's, was invited to join the governors. He was chairman of the board of the Inland Revenue and became known for his books on English language, including *The Complete Plain Words*, which he wrote at the invitation of HM Treasury.

After the death of Lord Lansdowne in 1936, Miss Ethel Steel OBE took up a post as governor. Miss Steel was headmistress of The Royal School in Bath, and St Mary's knew her well, as the two schools played matches against each other. In 1933 she had invited St Mary's to join five other schools in an annual Music Festival that she had initiated in Bath.

Miss Steel became a good friend and mentor to Elizabeth Gibbins, who later became headmistress. She said of Miss Steel, 'I could not have had a kinder or better guide'. After Miss Steel ceased to be a governor, Miss Gibbins often saw her and always came away 'with the knowledge that she had given me an undefinable kind of spiritual strength'. Miss Steel died in 1959.

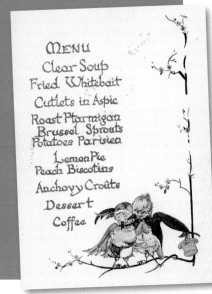

MENU
Clear Soup
Fried Whitebait
Cutlets in Aspic
Roast Ptarmigan
Brussel Sprouts
Potatoes Parisien
Lemon Pie
Peach Biscotins
Anchovy Croûts
Dessert
Coffee

A menu for a dinner given by the pupils for visitors

Into the 1930s

Despite the difficult time the country was going through, the strong leadership of St Mary's governors led to some important decisions being made in the acquisition of further land and property, and the investment in building projects. The minutes of the governors' meetings show their persistence in pursuing funding through loans, grants, gifts and internal fundraising.

Miss Matthews thought it essential that St Mary's retain its family atmosphere and did not become too large. The governors decided for the present not to allow the number of boarders to rise above 100. In 1934 the headmistress reported that they were having to turn away 'four or five times as many as are admitted'. The school was aware of the sacrifices that many families were making in order to give their daughters a private education and on many occasions they gave financial help. Girls going on to university were assisted with a fund raised by all the pupils through sales of their work. Help was also given to staff members who had time off through illness, or as a gratuity for long service.

The girls were continuing to receive a wide-ranging education which provided so much outside the academic curriculum. On the death of George V in 1936 St Mary's bought its first wireless. In one particular year the many lectures included one by Elizabeth Kitson, an Old Girl, who had carried out archaeological work with Louis Leakey in Kenya; a visit by a Native American chief; a demonstration of water divining; and a lecture at Marlborough College on evolution. Other visits to Marlborough were to hear the Poet Laureate, John Masefield, give a recital and to attend a lecture by Professor Julian Huxley. Later school lectures included Italian art, Molière, fungi and brewing.

Walks held a special place in the memories of pupils from this time. The youngest girls walked with the staff in crocodiles but they could soon gain privileges which allowed them to go independently in fours or twos. One girl remembered a walk in Bowood, where she 'sat on a stile and watched hares and partridges so tame that they came to within a few feet'. She continues, 'Many were the discussions we had, on religion, on art, on everything'. The

Above: *The prefects' tea 1930*

Right: *A late 1930s school postcard*

The Lansdowne Family

A name that has been closely associated with St Mary's since the very early days on The Green in the centre of Calne is that of the Lansdowne family from Bowood, just outside the town. The Marquess of Lansdowne owned much of the land around the area, including most of that on which the school now stands. Over the years the estate has sold parcels of land to St Mary's, often at favourable prices.

The family has also had a more personal connection to St Mary's, with members serving on the Governing Body, and daughters within the school. Lady Lansdowne opened St Mary's on the present site in 1908 and later generations of the family have presented prizes and opened additional new buildings, right up to the opening of the Sixth Form Centre in 2008 (later named the Helen Wright House). Their generosity and involvement have been greatly valued, and on Prize Day at the start of World War I, Lord Methuen said of the then Lord Lansdowne, 'There is no man in England with a clearer head or a kinder heart'.

The girls of St Mary's have often been made welcome at Bowood. It was a favourite destination for walks over many years and during the hard winters of 1929, 1940, 1947 and 1963, when the lake at Bowood froze, the girls were able to use it for skating.

highways and by-ways around Calne became familiar to this generation at a time when visits home were infrequent and the freedom to go further afield was restricted. They thought nothing of walking many miles, and once they became prefects they could explore further afield on bikes.

Skating on Bowood Lake 1940

The Workhouse

The Workhouse

Some of the old photographs of St Mary's show pupils going about their daily lives with the towering presence of the Victorian workhouse in the background. Built in Jacobean Revival style around a courtyard, the building had a main three-storey block with two-storey flanking wings. This imposing structure stood to the north of the main school buildings on a site which now houses the school's Sports Centre. At one time the workhouse was home to 60 elderly men and women, and records show that from 1929 until its closure, the pupils entertained the residents with carol singing and dancing. With the introduction of social security schemes in the early 20th century, the workhouse gradually became redundant, and in 1932 it closed. Two years later the school bought it for £650.

At this time St Mary's was offered the opportunity of buying 11.5 acres of land called Northfields from Lord Lansdowne. This took in the back of the quarry and ran north, covering an area which became games pitches but had previously been allotments. What became known as Upper Field provided a large pitch for lacrosse matches and rounders, and a smaller one for lacrosse and cricket practice. The girls were greatly impressed when the Archdeacon opened Upper Field by taking a wicket with the first ball. On Lord Lansdowne's death the area was renamed after him. Later a further pitch, Lansdowne II, was made out of an allotment area to the left of the main field, and which the girls spent two terms clearing of stones. To celebrate the coronation of King George VI in 1937, an avenue of lime trees was planted along the path dividing the two games fields.

The Religious Dimension of St Mary's School

The foundation of St Mary's School by Canon Duncan, the incumbent Vicar of Calne in 1873, was based on the guiding principles of the Church of England. The school carries the name of the parish church and in the early days drew pupils from the Anglican families in the town and surrounding villages and farms.

Church and chapel worship structured the school day, week and year, providing a moral framework for the young lives. Quotes from biblical texts were written around the walls of the first school room, and each pupil was given an illuminated copy of the motto that the school held at the time, taken up after Bishop Wordsworth visited the school: 'Whatsoever he shall say unto you, do it.'

When St Mary's moved to its present site, much care went into creating the Chapel, and it became an important focus of the school community. It was stipulated that the headmistress should be a practising member of the Church of England. As well as being a committed Christian, Miss Matthews had the gift of communicating her beliefs and instructing her pupils in religious teaching. Her sermons made a deep impression and stayed with many pupils for years after they left the school: 'How the words went home'. Groups of pupils would listen to her talks on Sunday evening and some girls took up the option of learning lengthy sections of selected texts from the Bible and Prayer Book in order to earn their Lilies. At first the reward was a silver cross, later a card carrying the Lilies and later still a Lily badge on a silk ribbon.

Those involved in the day-to-day running of the school received strong support from the clergy. Until Archdeacon Coulter retired, the Vicar chaired the school governors and was a familiar figure in the pupils' lives. The Bishop of Salisbury acted as Visitor to the school and for many years the Bishop of Sherborne was a governor. The school diaries show that many clergy, both from local parishes and further afield, visited St Mary's to preach.

Every year one of the Bishops visited Calne for the Confirmation service. This usually took place in the parish church but occasionally, such as during epidemics, the service would be in the school Chapel. Miss Matthews prepared pupils for Confirmation.

A cardboard cross from Canon Duncan's time

The Health of the Pupils

St Mary's had managed to escape the great flu outbreak of 1918 and was praised by inspectors for the care it took with the pupils' health. Periodic epidemics broke into the routine, with girls either isolated from other pupils or sent home. Attendance at church services was abandoned or changed to another parish if Calne was known to have an outbreak. The first Sanatorium was a house known as 'Gazelle' opposite the school in Curzon Street.

For many years Dr Ede, one of the doctors from the town, visited the school. His commitment extended far beyond the purely medical, and he judged and presented the school reading prize each year. He and his wife became firm friends of St Mary's and frequently invited girls to tea. His time as school doctor spanned the same 30 years as Miss Matthews', and on his retirement in 1945 she spoke with gratitude of his friendship, skill and integrity.

As the school grew, additional medical beds were required, so in March 1925 land was bought by Arthur Dunne from Lord Lansdowne and by the end of the year the school had what in Miss Matthews' words was 'a model sanatorium'. However, the school diary of July 1926 records that, 'Much to our regret Nurse Mooney is leaving us because we are too healthy! She has only had two cases since the new sanatorium was opened'.

When larger epidemics struck the school, dormitories were commandeered and additional nurses brought in. The spring term of 1931 became known as the 'measles term', in which half the pupils went down with the infection. The situation was exacerbated by the teaching and domestic staff being stricken by flu. For three weeks all the girls who were not affected contributed to keeping the school running, doing domestic work and helping with meals. As the patients began to recover, they went for extra walks and were given singing exercises to 'strengthen their lungs'.

After this, central heating was added to the largest dormitory, but was only to be used at times of illness. The matron of School House had a room to treat the more minor complaints of the girls and it was here that quinine was regularly spooned out to ward off colds. The Sanatorium is still used as the Medical Centre today.

On the west, the new land ran beside the boundary wall of the town cemetery. The workhouse stood on a site surrounded by this area. It made sense for the school to take over the workhouse and they considered making use of it, but owing to cost and its position it was decided that the main building should be demolished and the stone used for building work in the school. The workhouse lodge and laundry survived the demolition and are now used as offices and for storage. Both are listed buildings.

Land lying between the workhouse site and the Sanatorium was levelled using unemployed labour and made into a garden of roses, grass walks, herbaceous borders and vegetable beds. The last provided an 'unceasing supply' to the kitchen, which was particularly valued during the Second World War, thanks to the hard work put in by the pupils. A competition for the girls was held each year to learn the name of the flowers and Old Girl Laura Barlee (Attlee) says that she still remembers many she learnt while at school. At that time bees, hens and ducks were kept in the garden, the ducks making good use of the quarry ponds. Throughout the war supplies of coal, bought in the summer for the boilers, were stacked on the old workhouse site.

The rose garden behind the San

Charity and Social Services

Miss Matthews regarded a sense of service as an important part of the wider responsibilities to society. At the end of the First World War the emphasis of charity work within the school shifted and St Mary's began a long-running connection through the United Girls' Schools Mission with a parish in Camberwell in London. Collections were made through the year to support their work in caring for the health and welfare of families and children in an area that was suffering great deprivation, and every summer two young boys stayed at the school for a two-week holiday. The highlight of St Mary's year in this regard was the annual Health Festival which for many years took place on St Luke's Day. Each class was allocated a window in the Chapel, which they decorated with items they had made, collected or bought and which could be useful to the Mission.

Collections made at the Chapel service on Tuesdays went to the many local, national and international causes that St Mary's supported. The pupils were generous in their efforts to back organisations that were brought to their attention.

In 1933, with the Depression deepening, it was felt that more should be done within the school to help suffering communities. The Freewill Offering Fund was set up in which the girls decided at the beginning of each term what contributions they would give. They also responded to an appeal for clothing for families of the unemployed by collecting what they could and sending off regular parcels. A knitting campaign produced a supply of clothes and blankets.

Each year some of the senior girls took part in Social Services week, when they spent time at a United Girls' Schools settlement in Peckham. In 1933 the pupils who went learnt of the life of a 'working girl' by visiting trade schools, factories, a laundry and employment exchanges. On returning to St Mary's they gave a talk about their experiences.

The Academic Life of the School

Miss Matthews's Speech Day report in 1924 stated the standards she expected of St Mary's girls: 'pride in exact scholarship, a widespread desire for accuracy, a refusal to tolerate anything slipshod or mediocre and a growing

'At lunch on a sunny Sunday in high summer, Matt would stand up and announce 'long rest' today. This meant that for two or perhaps three hours we all lay on rugs in the grounds in profound silence. In May 1999 I have had time to lie in our Sussex garden and have recaptured the feelings of a 13-year-old during long rest: the harmony with nature, the peace and the timelessness'.

– Written by Anne Norris (Brown) in the OGA magazine, 1999

realisation of intellectual responsibility'. These objectives led to some outstanding academic achievements. She also knew, however, that some girls needed to apply these standards to a more practical programme of work, and these girls were accordingly placed in the 'Arts and Crafts' stream. She was extremely supportive of the less able pupils and went out of her way to see that they fulfilled their potential. Every girl in the school had her own timetable and Miss Matthews discussed each one with the girl's form mistress and parents.

Miss Matthews had a particular interest in getting the pupils to read as much as possible. Each class held a record

Above: *A classroom in Hut Passage*

Right: *A picnic on the downs c. 1918*

High Days, Holy Days and Holidays

Past pupils have mentioned Miss Matthews' breadth of vision, impulsiveness and sense of fun. She was able to break out of routine and spring surprises on the school. This meant that sometimes schoolwork was put to one side and the afternoon would be spent having a picnic, going for walks, blackberrying or just having free time. Such a 'frolic' was given in response to the announcement that the first pupils had received places at Oxford.

Matt's birthday was always celebrated with a party, games, fancy dress or dancing. Sometimes she would arrange a competition such as guessing the number of tiles on the roof of the new building, or learning the speech from Shakespeare's *Henry V* on the eve of the Battle of Agincourt. On other occasions she hired the cinema in Calne.

Some of the church festivals were marked with holidays. Each Ascension Day the service in the church was followed by a general knowledge paper and a free afternoon. A picnic might be arranged in the garden of the George Inn at Sandy Lane or on the White Horse. Other times trips were made to local sites such as Avebury, Lacock or Maud Heath's monument. If Easter fell early it might be within the fixed Lent Term, so the pupils remained at school. Matt arranged for flowers, Easter eggs and cards to be on the breakfast tables and entertainments were put on by the staff and girls.

Summer half terms began with a father-daughter cricket match before the girls went out with their parents or home if they lived locally, and the autumn half term began with prizegiving. There were, however, always pupils who could not return home at half term. They were entertained royally with visits, perhaps to Oxford, Bath or Longleat.

Each term a 'maidless day' was held when the domestic staff had Saturday off and the girls produced the meals and cleaned the rooms. In 1929 there was a 'staffless day', when the Sixth Form carried out the teaching.

of the books that the girls had read, which acted as a great incentive even, as one Old Girl remembers, if it meant going for the slimmest volume, such as (in her case) a book about Elizabeth Fry.

The School Inspectors' visits were positive, though on one occasion they felt there were too many staff. The inspectors of 1930 commented, 'We were all unanimous in our opinion of your happy, charming and self-reliant girls'.

Public examinations had been introduced into the school by Canon Duncan, and in 1917 some of Miss Matthews' pupils began to take the Cambridge School Certificate in the Fifth Form, the top class. The following year she started a Sixth Form which gave two years of more specialist work and allowed the girls to work towards university entrance. External examinations in French and for the Institute of Hygiene were also undertaken. A number of the early Oxbridge candidates took degrees in languages. Mademoiselle Antoine was a long-serving member of staff who left St Mary's in 1957 after 27 years of teaching at the school. She was described by Kay Stedmond as 'a person of great dignity and charm', but she was also 'terrifyingly rigorous in her demands'. Each term finished with Mark Reading, when results of the term's achievements were read to the school and awards given.

Science teaching during Miss Matthews' time was very popular, mainly because there was a great deal of practical work and 'exciting new apparatus' introduced, such as the spectroscope for studying light and a microprojector which allowed the pupils to study small living organisms, and to project the images onto a screen. Many live creatures found their way into the laboratory, some collected from Bowood Lake, the quarry pond and the nearby canal. Worms and frogs were dissected and in 1934 the pupils returned to find the 'fresh skulls of horses, pigs, sheep and rats' to study. The interest in science led to a number of girls studying medicine at university.

Music at St Mary's during Miss Matthews' Time

Music has run like a thread through the life of St Mary's from the earliest days. It is an aspect of the school often commented upon by Old Girls and remembered with affection as the foundation of a life-long interest. From the start the pupils had been given every opportunity to hear music of a high standard and to learn an instrument of their own. School choirs and musicians gave frequent performances both within the school and to a wider audience.

Under Miss Matthews' leadership the musical life of the school flourished. Her director of music, Miss Jennings, spent 18 years at St Mary's until 1939. Known as Jenny, she saw the music staff treble in number, started an orchestra, and developed the choral work. She was remembered for her 'black hair and flashing violet eyes' along with her flowing clothes and enthusiasm: her piano playing had 'passion and great aplomb'. Miss Jennings lived to be 101. In addition to the many concerts, operas and recitals that the pupils heard both in and outside school, they were able to sing with other schools and groups and take part in musical competitions within the school. Musical appreciation was part of the curriculum and each spring term some pupils would study a particular composer and give a concert of that composer's work.

Pupils remember how on Sunday evenings the girls would sometimes be treated to listening to recorded music in the hall. These were no light-weight occasions, as complete symphonies would be on the programme.

In 1924 St Mary's was very privileged to have Miss Fanny Davis, a distinguished pianist, give an informal assessment of the musical standard of the school and to entertain the pupils with a recital on her Steinway grand piano, which 'preceded her to the School'. Over the years the girls attended concerts in Bath by performers such as Backhaus, Kreisler and Elizabeth Schumann. One Old Girl, Anne Wood, a professional singer, made frequent visits to perform at the school.

The Music Festival in Bath was always a highlight of the musical year. Usually, under the baton of Dr Reginald Jacques, the girls had the opportunity to sing in a choir of 400 with an orchestra of 50. The six-school festival had to be abandoned on the outbreak of war but St Mary's

continued to sing with Westonbirt School when they were evacuated to Bowood. After the war St Mary's held its own annual Music Festival, with all the girls taking part. Also at this time the nerve-wracking ordeal of solo-playing began, with each music pupil having to play termly in front of her form and all the music staff.

Mr Pullein, who had been organist at the church since 1886, retired as visiting music master to St Mary's in

Above: HMS Pinafore – *summer 1938*

Top: *The school orchestra* c. *1937*

1943. Since the earliest days of the school he had taught generations of girls to sing and play the piano, some of whom went on to become concert pianists. As a composer and a fine musician, he made a huge contribution to music at the school. His 57 years with St Mary's makes him the school's longest-serving teacher.

Miss Matthews' Building Projects

By 1934 Miss Matthews had been at St Mary's for nearly 20 years. Her determination to push the school forward and continue to provide a modern, wide-ranging education for her pupils was as strong as ever. She was quick to point out to the governors the areas in which greater investment was required and they gave her the support she needed.

Following the demolition of the workhouse, construction began on an extension to the original school building. A wing was thrown out from Gabriel, the common room off Red Hall, providing two additional classrooms downstairs and a dormitory, known as Bodinnar, and staff bedrooms above. The extension was designed to blend with the original house and was built using workhouse stone.

At Prize Day in 1934 the addition of the new wing was welcomed, but Miss Matthews and the governors were continuing to look ahead. The audience were told that

Right: *The art studio in Jubilee Building 1940*

Below: *Ascension Day picnic at Sandy Lane 1930*

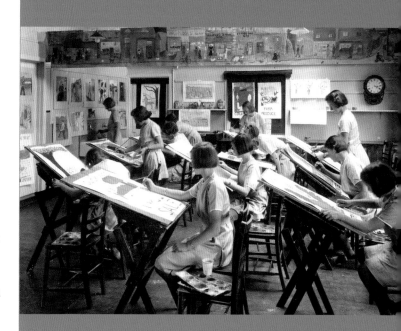

Art

As part of her desire for the girls to have a wide cultural education, Miss Matthews had from her arrival given St Mary's prints of well-known art works. These were hung round the school and each acquisition was recorded in the diaries. They were greatly appreciated by the pupils and indeed they often gave Miss Matthews further prints for her birthday. A competition naming the artists was held annually.

In 1933 pictures were loaned from the Wertheim Gallery, which displayed works of artists in their 20s, and later from the Victoria and Albert Museum. In 1938 an organisation began providing new prints every three months to fit into a series of frames that the school held.

The art studio in the Jubilee Building became a centre of activity, with an exhibition of work being displayed at the end of each year. The pupils had the opportunity to experiment with many different media, and hobbies in the studio on Thursday nights extended this further into such activities as book-binding, glass-painting, glove-making and photography. Some years, work was entered into the Wiltshire Arts and Crafts Exhibition.

'The idea of embellishing the building with the low relief work originated with Miss Matthews who expressed a wish that representations of the three patron saints of the School, St Bridget, St Faith and St Prisca, should be placed on the wall. The architecture of the building however required four such carvings and since the hall on which they are put is to be a music room, St Cecilia, the patron saint of music, was added.

'St Bridget was a fifth-century saint in Ireland. She lived in the woods and the relief shows her by the great oak of Kildare preaching to the wolves. St Prisca, one of the saints martyred by the Romans, was so good that when she was given to the lions they licked her feet. The design shows this incident in her life. St Faith, 13-year-old Princess of Agen in France, was another saint martyred by the Romans and the carving depicts her in the wilderness. The fourth saint, St Cecilia, is shown with a stringed instrument.'

— A DESCRIPTION OF THE DETAIL ON THE NEWLY BUILT HALL AND DINING
    ROOM IN 1936

the school was in great need of a larger assembly hall and a new dining room and kitchen. In November 1935 Lady Lansdowne laid the foundation stone, 'performing her duties most carefully with a special trowel, mallet and spirit-level'. Under the stone in two sealed bottles were the names of all those in the school, the coins of the year and a Jubilee crown.

A number of different plans had been drawn up that included extensive accommodation for teaching and domestic staff, with the chosen design being one that put the assembly hall over the dining room. The whole project was to cost £20,000, a large sum that would be financed through loans and fundraising among the parents and friends of St Mary's. Seventy per cent of the building stone was to come from the workhouse.

The buildings were to stand in the garden behind the main school, connected by a passageway from near the cottage. It meant the loss of an orchard, a summer house and a belt of fir trees below the Sanatorium. The only regret expressed at the position of the buildings was that they would also cover the natural garden stage, the site of many a summer performance. An exploratory bore hole had not hinted at any likely difficulties in the position, but when work began it was discovered that some of the ground had been made up with rubble during the time of the quarry and so it was necessary first to fill the area with concrete to secure the foundations.

The imposing main entrance to the hall and dining room was approached by a new driveway from

Above: *The reliefs on the side of Marcia Matthews Building*

Below: *A stained-glass lily emblem over the main entrance to the Marcia Matthews Building*

Above: *Marcia Matthews Building*

Right: *From the* Wiltshire Gazette

Curzon Street. The building stood proudly above the lower grounds and was described as having a 'gracious simplicity'. Windows had been faced with Bath stone and four low-relief carvings graced the north-facing wall. Designed by a resident of Compton Bassett, Mrs Birnstirgl, and carved by Mr Osborne of Pickwick near Corsham, the reliefs depicted the saints associated with St Mary's.

It was a project on a large scale for St Mary's, and the details of the statistics were recorded in the *Wiltshire Gazette* after the opening ceremony in October 1936. It talks of quantities in terms of tons of roof tiles, acres of plaster and paint, and cart-loads of stone. The electric installations were notable in that it had taken nearly three miles of cable and was the first scheme in Calne to be wired for AC supply. Dedication of the new buildings was carried out by the Bishop of Salisbury, with the Mistress of Girton and Lady Lansdowne in attendance. In 1955 the hall and dining room were named the Marcia Matthews Building.

One can imagine the great impact that such an addition had on the school. However, from the start the buildings were seen as being 'nothing new, nothing upstart; they are mellow, dignified and at the same time friendly'. It was felt that they provided a sense of permanence and gave recognition to the fact that St Mary's was now a school widely recognised as providing a first-rate education. They could look ahead with pride.

The Isolation Hospital

No sooner had the new land at Northfields and the workhouse site become part of the school then Calne's isolation hospital, which lay beside the north boundary of St Mary's, was put up for sale. The governors were keen to buy this, and Miss Matthews felt it would grant an opportunity to extend the teaching of science in the school and to provide its own place of isolation during epidemics.

Built of brick, the hospital was on a site that belonged to the Bowood estate and allowed accommodation for 20 patients. It was made up of four wards with a detached lodge for the matron.

In 1937 the sale went through, but with another war looming, conversion was deemed too expensive, and on consideration it was felt that the science teaching should be nearer the main school. The governors had to find money to provide air raid shelters and called upon the parents for some of the costs. At first it was considered digging these in the banks of earth which lay beneath the Sanatorium and St Prisca's, but the expense led instead to the reinforcement of cellars under some of the school buildings.

Although the hospital could not be used as intended, it was not neglected. Miss Matthews, ever innovative, had decided the girls should know about the workings of a combustion engine. Under the guidance of Mr Cooper, an ex-Mayor of Calne who had donated an ancient Fiat, the Sixth Form had lectures and practical sessions on the construction and operation of the car.

At the height of the Munich crisis in 1938 some children from a London school were temporarily housed in the old hospital. Following in the school's tradition, the building was named after a saint, Margaret of Scotland, and the

ensured that a series of interesting lecturers had talked to the school on the situation in the world. They covered an extraordinarily wide range of subjects. The most outstanding of these speakers had been a Mr Donald Grant, who had visited St Mary's regularly for a few days at a time and given a series of lectures on subjects such as 'The present dangerous state of Europe', 'The Pacific – A New Civilization?', 'Austria and the Danube' and 'The Changing World'. He was described as asking 'a great deal of his audience. We really have to use our brains'. A lecture by the Lieutenant-governor of Malta straight from the front line of battle brought the immediacy of the situation to the school.

In 1933 the pupils had received a lecture which divided opinion in the school. They had been told of the rise of Nazism from the first-hand knowledge of a Mr Peter Matthews. As events unfolded, views changed. In 1943 the pupils had a visit from Pastor Karle, who had experienced the concentration camps and the Nazi suppression of Christianity in Germany. He spoke about the need to rebuild both the Church and the churches in that country.

A diary entry of 26 September 1938 reflected the anxiety within the country at this time as to the possibility of war. 'We listened in to every broadcast and on Wednesday our own men with five others started digging trenches over by St Prisca's'. Miss Matthews sent a letter home to the parents saying that all the girls had been provided with gas

Left: *The Isolation Hospital*

St Mary's girls worked hard to make it welcoming to the newcomers. Later in the war, schools evacuated from other parts of the country took up residence and some space was lent to the Women's Voluntary Service to be used as a depot for supplies sent to the county by women in America. To extend the science facilities in the school it was decided to relocate the carpentry workshop from Jubilee Building to the old hospital, and in 1940 the junior department moved to St Margaret's, where it has remained ever since.

War

With storm clouds gathering over Europe, the girls had had the privilege of being well-informed on international affairs. Since the middle of the 1930s Miss Matthews had

'As the supporter of politics as a desirable theme for a lecture, Mr Peter Matthews told us of his experiences in Nazi Germany. As he himself is, or was at the time, an ardent Nazi, we were enabled to look at the problem from an especially interesting angle. The comments afterwards were also interesting. Some diehards had refused to give the Hitler salute, and others were, for a week or so at any rate, enthusiastic Nazis who saluted everyone they met. Politics reached a high-point of popularity.'

– An extract from the News Sheet of 1933

Above: *The St Mary's and Marlborough College Rustics cricket teams – 1930s*

Right: Twelfth Night *1937 in front of the kitchen wing before the flat roof extension was added*

masks. On the Thursday the school welcomed 40 pupils, evacuated from Lady Margaret School in Cricklewood, to the old hospital. The tension abated with the news that the immediate crisis had passed, and the evacuees left. However by December preparations were being made for a black-out in Calne: 'Curtains were lined with newspaper, chinks stuffed with rags and candles provided for dormitories'.

The situation eased again over the next few months but in September of 1939 Miss Matthews added an insert into the News Sheet to her Old Girls commenting on the situation they were all facing. How sorely she must have felt the responsibility of guiding the school through another war, while at the same time knowing that her pupils that had left would be confronted with more direct involvement in the hostilities.

St Mary's felt fortunate that they were able to stay within their school grounds unlike Westonbirt School, whose girls were evacuated to Bowood and Corsham. Their closer proximity did mean that more contact between the two schools was possible in a time of petrol rationing, and the older pupils received tuition in advanced biology from the Westonbirt staff. Regular matches were held and in the winter of 1940 the two schools skated together on the lake at Bowood. Contact was also maintained with Marlborough College, Dauntsey's School and Chippenham Secondary School.

'The School has responded well to calls made upon it to help in the War Effort. The "Dig for Victory" campaign entails many hours of hard work, both in the School grounds and in answer to calls made upon us from our neighbours. Such disagreeable jobs as cutting and drying nettles have been shouldered all through the summer by public-spirited volunteers. First-rate work has been put into the knitting for the Merchant Navy. The "Wings for Victory" Week meant a tremendous effort for the School: to our amazement we found we had collected £2,043.'

–THE SCHOOL'S CONTRIBUTION TO THE WAR EFFORT FROM THE NEWS SHEET, 1943

Through 1940 St Mary's was aware of the contrast between the world outside and the 'peaceful almost normal world within' the school. The calendar for the year was as busy as usual with concerts, lectures, matches, plays and outings. This did not however mean that the school was not doing its part towards the war effort. During the summer term nearly 1,000 bags were made for the Red

Drama up to 1945

Anyone who has been a pupil at St Mary's School is deeply familiar with the language of Shakespeare. From the time the school was on The Green in Calne the girls listened to readings of the plays, were able to take part in productions, and experienced professional performances. Form Shakespeare became as much a part of the school year as examinations and Founders' Day.

As a competition each autumn term, Form Shakespeare allowed the girls to produce chosen scenes from different plays and to experience the full process of staging a performance. The text and any music were chosen, parts allocated and rehearsed, scenery built and costumes created from the school uniform using no stitching. It gave opportunities for freedom of interpretation and creativity. Each year the News Sheet contained detailed critiques of these productions.

From 1932 two or three visits were made by the older girls each summer to Stratford, where they saw actors such as John Gielgud and Donald Wolfit in leading roles. Other visits took the girls to Bradfield and Dauntsey's schools and to French plays by Les Comédiens de Paris in Bath. Visiting actors from Oxford University, the RAF and the WAAF entertained the pupils in the school.

Around 1930 the St Mary's Repertory Company was set up, producing plays in the summer term, and every year a great deal of time and commitment went into the Company plays.

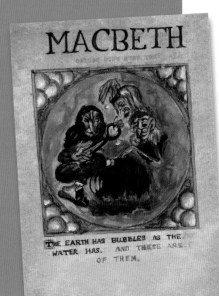

MACBETH

THE EARTH HAS BUBBLES AS THE WATER HAS. AND THESE ARE OF THEM.

Cross to distribute to wounded soldiers to hold their belongings.

Meal times were transformed when the girls were allowed to knit for the Merchant Navy as they waited, turning out items such as socks. Parcels of clothing were sent to the Finns, help was given with hay-making and caterpillar-picking on local farms, and all the pupils helped in the garden. Parties of girls assisted with the distribution of ration books in the Food Office in Calne. Members of staff regularly helped at the RAF canteen at Yatesbury and with the CAB in Calne.

Among those working in the kitchen and cleaning the classrooms, was a 14-year-old Margaret Gee from Derry Hill. Starting work at 6.30am each day, she lived in one of the new bedrooms for the staff. There are descendants of Margaret working at St Mary's today.

The inclusion in the News Sheet of 1939 of a Roll of Honour of fathers and brothers who had lost their lives in the call of duty, sadly became a regular feature for the following five years.

Adapting to the Changes

Throughout these years the school was living under black-out conditions, and one Old Girl remembers how those walking to St Bridget's each night were issued with white bands to make them visible to others. The mornings began with 'twenty minutes violent PT' and the pupils started lessons in first aid and home nursing. In 1940 Miss Matthews wrote to the parents reassuring them that school life was continuing as normally as possible: that the prefects were able to listen to the news and the rest of the school had access to newspapers and were told particular news as it occurred. She asked whether, in line with general advice, they could provide an identification disc for their daughters in the form of a bracelet.

S. Mary's Roll of Honour.
(THIRD LIST)
1942
KILLED IN ACTION

BRAGG. Wing Commander. Peter Hugh Bragg, in December. (husband of Felicity Bradford.)

BRIDGMAN. Sergeant Gunner Francis Harley Bridgman, R.A.F. missing since April, 1941, now officially presumed killed. (Brother of Joan O'Hara and Hannah Bridgman.)

BROOME. Stewart Broome, R.A.F., in Canada, March. (Only brother of Miss Broome.)

BULMER. Paul Bulmer, R.N., in May, missing, believed killed, from H.M.S. Olympus. (Brother of Betty Goodden Crane.)

CHADWICK. Capt. Hector G. Chadwick, Hussars, R.A.C. in October. (Brother of Beryl.)

CHARSLEY. Lieut. Commander John Hough Charsley, R.N., Fleet Air Arm, in June. (Brother of Meriel.)

EVANS-LAWRENCE. Capt. John Evans-Lawrence, R.A. in July. (only brother of Stephanie.)

HERBERT. A.B. Martin Owen Beauchamp Herbert, M.N. (only son of Captain (E) S. J. Herbert, R.N. lost in H.M.S. Hood, and brother of Penelope.)

JARRETT. Peter William Jarrett, R A.F. in October, 1941, (Brother of Cicely.)

MACKENZIE. Major Robert Mackenzie, R.A. in November, 1941, (husband of Peggy Reade.)

SADLEIR. Lieut Michael Thomas Carey Sadleir, R.N.V.R. in October, (brother of Anne Hornby.)

SHERWOOD. Humphrey Sherwood, R.A.F. (Brother of Maureen.)

MISSING

MITCHELL. 2nd Lieut. W. S. Mitchell, R.A.S.C. (Brother of Barbara.)

ROBINSON. Captain J. F. Robinson (Husband of Ursula Robins.)

ROOME. Midshipman David Gordon Roome, R.N. (Brother of Lois.)

PRISONERS OF WAR

BURKE. Graham (Brother of Amy Murland and Doreen Burke.)

DRAYSON. Capt. Burnaby Drayson (Husband of Winifred Heath.)

DUTHIE. John Duthie (Husband of Dandy Levesen.)

GAY ROBERTS. Major Alan Gay Roberts. (Brother of Althea.)

FLETCHER. Lieut. Richard Fletcher, wounded (Brother of Audrey.)

MEAD. Major H. C. H. Mead (Brother of April Zinovieff.)

SCOTT. Lieut. Col. T. A. R. Scott (Husband of Margery Parker.)

Above: From the News Sheet

Left: A Form Shakespeare programme 1930

Above: *The school maids in the 1930s with Margaret Gee front right*

Right: *A letter from General de Gaulle to Cecily Jarrett*

The shortage of staff led to the girls being given some of the domestic duties. In 1943 these were allocated to the Companies, which meant that every five weeks one Company took responsibility. Even in the holidays the staff duties continued as the school was turned over to a youth week, a course for Wiltshire teachers, Auxiliary Territorial Service officers and boys from Rugby School who were working on local farms.

Miss Matthews Keeps Moving Forward

The position that St Mary's School now held in the wider arena was illustrated in a meeting convened by the headmistresses of the Girls Public Boarding Schools to establish an association of governors. Sir Ernest Gowers became deputy chairman and both Miss Steel and Miss Matthews were on the committee until Miss Matthews was replaced in order to give more schools representation.

In 1940 Miss Matthews ran a competition within the school to write a letter in French in support of the Free French in London. The winning entry by Cecily Jarrett was considered 'suitable for a general' and so was sent to their headquarters. The school was delighted when Cecily received a reply signed by General de Gaulle.

Letters were sent home on matters relating to food and clothes rationing, the need for the girls to bring toiletries to school and the suggestion of the school doctor that the pupils take vitamins during the holidays.

War came closer to home in the autumn of 1940 when air raid warnings interrupted the routine, as planes flew overhead on their way to the Midlands. The school had a night watchman on duty and the girls often moved to the cellars for periods of time. From time to time distant gunfire and explosions could be heard. Regulations restricting building maintenance came into force and in 1941 the iron railings were requisitioned from the front of the headmistress's garden.

St Mary's frequently made mention at this time of the high value they placed on those running the domestic side of school life. Miss Jackson, in her role as housekeeper and cook, managed to work with the rations to produce meals and picnics that were often marvelled at. A comment from 1942 states that 'The summer term has been marked by an abundance of strawberries and oranges, and since Mr Robinson's ton of honey ran out we have had marmalade every day.'

Miss Greenwood and Miss Weetman, matron and housekeeper, among their myriad of duties eked out the uniforms by patching and mending, enabling them to be handed down from one girl to the next many times.

ST. STEPHEN'S HOUSE,
Victoria Embankment,
Westminster, S.W.1.
Tél: ABBEY 1384.

Londres, le 18 juillet, 1940.

Mademoiselle,

Les sentiments que m'exprime la lettre que vous avez bien voulu me transmettre au nom de votre collège me sont un précieux encouragement. Je vous en remercie toutes très chaleureusement.

Dans ces heures tragiques de l'histoire du monde, tous ceux qui en ont encore la liberté doivent s'unir avec résolution pour résister et pour vaincre.

Veuillez agréer, Mademoiselle, l'expression de ma considération très distinguée.

Général de Gaulle.

Miss C. Jarrett,
St. Mary's School,
Calne. Wilts.

Boundaries were pushed further when in 1941 Miss Matthews instigated a Greek week within the school, when all lessons and activities were themed to the subject. These included lectures, plays and readings where each form studied a different aspect of Greek culture, life and literature. The following year a French week and a Housing and Town Planning week were held, and all featured in *The Times Educational Supplement* as being an imaginative addition to the curriculum. The year 1943 saw a Local Government week within the school with pupils attending a County Council meeting and having lectures on health, education and finance from council leaders.

The diary shows that the Sixth Form had a civilian day introduced into their timetable every week for a term in order to give them practical experience in specialised work such as teaching, farming, laboratory work and as librarians in a camp hospital.

Military and naval victories were celebrated by the 'frolics', or holidays, that Matt was so fond of giving the girls. These became especially valued as half terms away for the more local girls were no longer possible.

Important milestones, such as the celebration of St Mary's 70th anniversary in 1943, provided opportunities for parents and Old Girls to visit. A service in the parish church was taken by the Bishop of Sherborne. Wreaths of roses and laurel were laid in front of the memorials to Canon Duncan and Archdeacon Bodington and the church was decorated with lilies. The occasion was particularly remembered as the time Matt held up the British army in order to get her girls over the road. The service was followed by tea and a Shakespeare performance at the school.

The Visit of Queen Mary

One of the greatest thrills for the girls at this time was Queen Mary's visit to the school on 28 September 1943. The News Sheet describes the visit as 'the coping stone to our 70th year and a wonderful stimulus to the beginning of a new decade in the history of St Mary's'. The morning was spent making the school spotless, 'as we knew that the Queen looks not only at things, but

into them'. On her arrival in the afternoon she was greeted by Miss Matthews, Miss Thouless and the two head girls, before making a tour of the school, visiting lessons, the hall, dining room, kitchens, sewing room and staffrooms. She spoke in French to Mademoiselle and met the other staff in the library. She was then given a rousing send-off by the whole school.

Following her visit the school received a signed copy of The Book of the Queen's Dolls' House for the library.

Above: *The Governing Body at the opening of the Matthews Building 1935. Back row l–r Mr Dunne, Miss Matthews, The Bishop of Salisbury, Sir Ernest Gowers, Miss Steel, Mr Bodinnar. Front row l–r Lady Lansdowne, Archdeacon Coulter, The Mistress of Girton who was a visitor*

Above: *The Upper Sixth 1943*

Far left: *From the school diary*

Left: *The inscription at the front of The Book of the Queen's Dolls' House*

Right: *St Cecilia's*

Changes in the Governing Body

In 1942 St Mary's had to say goodbye to two of its governors, Sir Ernest Gowers and Mr John Bodinnar, both called to senior administrative posts in the wartime government. They were replaced by Mr Arthur fforde, a solicitor with a role in the Ministry of Supply, and Mr W.G. Phillips from Quemerford near Calne, both of whom had first come into contact with the school as parents. It was at this point that the governors changed the time of their meetings to enable them to join the pupils for lunch, therefore making them a more familiar presence around the school.

In May 1940 Mr H.U. Willink MC KC MP was invited to join the governors, becoming a generous benefactor. When he was later promoted to the Cabinet as Minister of Health and Mr fforde became Temporary Under-Secretary to the Treasury in 1944, the school marked the occasions with a further holiday.

The Acquisition of St Cecilia's

For many years the school had known that one day the Hut Passage would have to be replaced. With greater pupil numbers, it was becoming increasingly necessary for other building projects to include new classrooms, and in time a gymnasium. The architects looked at possible sites and it was decided that the most suitable was near the Jubilee Building. This however required extending into land that belonged to Northfield House. The owner, Mr Redman, had some years previously offered the property to the school and so the governors approached him again with a view to purchase.

In 1943 they announced that the school was to buy Northfield House on Curzon Street, and the garden behind it, which was surrounded by a wall that extended to between the Jubilee Building and St Prisca's. This property had been known to the school as Naboth's Vineyard, as its beauty had been much admired and envied. Once the wall was demolished, the school had access to this wonderful area.

Northfield House was one half of a building which is described as 'a good example of a mid 18th-century early semi-detached house'. The school was to acquire the other half a few years later. It was called St Cecilia's by St Mary's and in time provided boarding space for many girls. In the 19th century the house had belonged to Dr Ogilvie, who used it 'as an asylum for nervous patients' and grew opium poppies on some of his land behind 'to sooth the patients'.

1929 tennis stars

The News Sheets leading up to the Second World War report extensively the progress of sport through each school year. The successes and failures of matches, the advance or otherwise of individuals and teams and how improvements could be made are all recorded in detail. St Mary's had settled into a pattern of sports that saw mainly lacrosse and netball in the autumn and spring terms and cricket and tennis in the summer.

The increase in the land available for sport had led to significantly improved sporting facilities, and the school embraced the opportunities. The arrival of hard tennis courts, generously donated by friends of St Mary's, was enthusiastically welcomed and these, along with the grass courts, allowed more pupils to play regularly.

Team, Form and Company matches were part of school life, and sometimes staff and mothers took part. Fathers' cricket matches were held every summer, with some success for the girls. In 1943 the BBC visited the school while researching for a broadcast comparing boys' and girls' cricket.

The year 1929 saw the introduction of Umpire Coaches. Selected pupils received tuition in netball and lacrosse, in order for them to be able to coach ordinary games and to umpire matches. This released time for the games staff and was considered an honour for the girls, who received a U badge as recognition. Badges with other signifying letters were allocated for different sporting achievements.

Since early on, St Mary's practised a type of gymnastics known as Swedish Drill, the object of which was 'to make you think all the time'. This had been a strong activity at Godolphin School, which Miss Matthews knew well, and she promoted competitions between the two schools and within St Mary's. Drill made use of the gym equipment, such as the vaulting horse and ropes, but it also included free-standing work, marching and team work. The routines were conducted under the commands of a pupil acting as sergeant. The examiners commented on the carriage, rhythm, lightness and balancing abilities of the participants.

Reporting of sporting progress in the News Sheets was reduced when war broke out, owing to the shortage of paper; however the enthusiasm for sport continued, albeit on a more limited scale. The school had until this time played matches against schools and county ladies' clubs from around the wider area. With the arrival of war they had to restrict their travelling. Having Westonbirt at Bowood was greatly welcomed, and St Mary's girls were still able to play against Chippenham Secondary School and a Women's Auxiliary Air Force team, and had tennis and cricket matches against some of the Marlborough College house teams. Such a cricket match in 1943 saw, once again, the tradition of a ball being hit into the quarry pond. Whether this led to a shortage of cricket balls is not recorded, but certainly that year the school was low on tennis balls.

In addition to the restrictions of war, the weather sometimes interrupted normal sporting life. The school saw this as a challenge. When grounds were too hard for games, St Prisca's flat roof was cleared of any snow in order for skipping to be practised. Skipping competitions became annual events for some years and expanded to include team work and musical accompaniments.

Occasionally dancing demonstrations would be put on to raise funds. In 1932 a display of national, country and Greek dancing raised money for the Scholarship Fund. At the time of Miss Matthews's retirement, the governors had ambitions for a further expansion of the sporting facilities, including a new gym and a swimming pool.

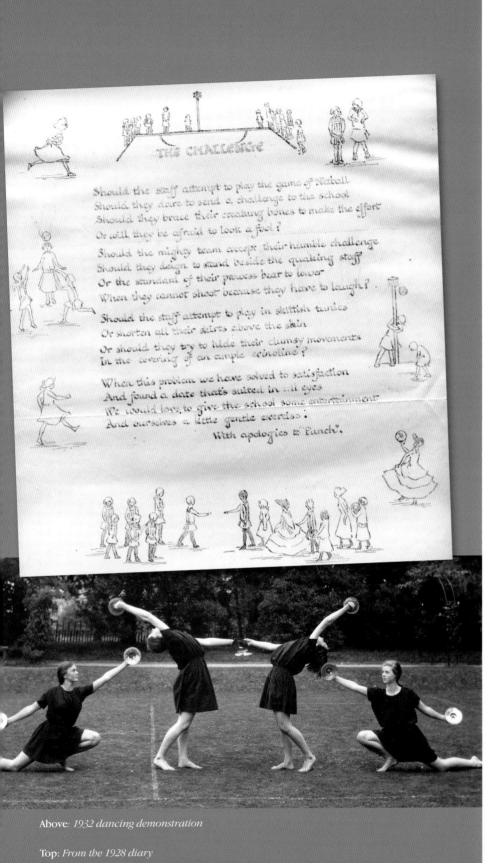

THE CHALLENGE

Should the staff attempt to play the game of Netball
Should they dare to send a challenge to the school
Should they brace their creaking bones to make the effort
Or will they be afraid to look a fool?

Should the mighty team accept their humble challenge
Should they deign to stand beside the quaking staff
Or the standard of their prowess bear to lower
When they cannot shoot because they have to laugh?

Should the staff attempt to play in skittish tunics
Or shorten all their skirts above the skin
Or should they try to hide their clumsy movements
In the covering of an ample crinoline?

When this problem we have solved to satisfaction
And found a date that's suited in all eyes
We would love to give the school some entertainment
And ourselves a little gentle exercise.

With apologies to 'Punch'.

Above: *1932 dancing demonstration*

Top: *From the 1928 diary*

Moving towards a Conclusion

As the war moved into its final year St Mary's continued to record and honour those family members who had been killed in action, declared missing or were prisoners-of-war. The personal toll had been high. Also recorded were the positions Old Girls had taken up in the forces, the Civil Service, in professional careers, business and universities. Oxbridge entrances continued, with five listed in 1944.

In November of that year Miss Matthews announced that she would be retiring the following summer. It was right that she should oversee the celebrations of VE Day within the school as her time at St Mary's neared its end. Wars had framed her headship and it had been with a sure hand that she had guided the school through those many difficult years and seen it prosper and provide a fine education for a generation of pupils. St Mary's had much for which to be thankful.

Before the farewells of Founders' Day and the July reunion were the celebrations of VE Day on 8 May, reflecting those of the country at large. Miss Matthews made the announcement of the end of hostilities to the school in the Chapel, where so many prayers had been offered up over those anxious years. The next day flags were strung from the windows of the boarding houses and the school joined the crowds on The Strand in Calne for a short thanksgiving service.

A 'victory dinner' in the evening saw the whole school in fancy dress, and toasts to the King, the Prime Minister and the forces were drunk (with orangeade). It was then a change back into school cotton dresses for two hours of dancing on the cricket pitch which had been thrown open to the public, interrupted only by listening to the King's speech. The evening finished with a huge bonfire topped by straw effigies of Hitler and Mussolini on the workhouse site and singing conducted by a self-appointed master of ceremonies, a Scots airman.

Despite the imminent departure of Miss Matthews, St Mary's saw this period as a time of optimism and for looking forward. They recognised that the school had come through the war 'so safely and with so much vigour', and that Matt had earned time for herself in retirement.

The school community said goodbye to Miss Matthews on Founders' Day that summer with a service conducted by

the Archdeacon and a sermon by the Bishop of Rochester. The pupils performed a ballet in the evening. The reunion at the end of July allowed the Old Girls to give Matt a fine send-off. Nearly 200 people attended the first reunion held at the school since before the war.

Among the gifts Miss Matthews received was a quilt made by many of the Old Girls picturing scenes from school life. It was accompanied by an entertainment relating to the story behind it. The quilt was a wonderful memorial to her time at St Mary's and now hangs within the school.

Miss Matthews received many words of appreciation. One Old Girl wrote, 'For thirty years she has devoted all the gifts of her rich personality, all her intellectual power, and above all her immense spiritual strength, to preparing her girls for life.' She is remembered for her leadership, her teaching, her moral fortitude and the concern and support for each of her pupils. 'Miss Matthews never forgot; she always knew when one had put one's heart into one's work. What a thrill was an "Excellent" from her, not half-hidden in a corner, but given like everything she gives, in full measure, and scrawled half across the page'.

The tributes went on and she should have had years of happy and fulfilled retirement ahead of her, but in the October of the following year she died. A memorial service was held in the parish church in Calne. Miss Matthews' legacy lived on through a Bursary Fund set up in her name by the governors and the Old Girls' Association. It provided funding for the daughters of Old Girls and so formed a link between her pupils and those following.

In 1940 an article in the News Sheet at the time of the 25th anniversary of the arrival of Miss Matthews and Miss Alexander at St Mary's, included a comment on how together they had given St Mary's a lead in girls' education in this country: 'It has been a quarter of a century of great progress in all educational practice and St Mary's has been kept in the very forefront of the advance. Two wise and sometimes adventurous minds have guided it from the narrow curriculum and close supervision of "then" to the wide training and character-building of "now", and we look forward eagerly to what "tomorrow" may bring.'

Far left: *Miss Matthews*

Left: *Upper Sixth in the summer of 1944*

Right: *Miss Matthews' quilt made for her by the Old Girls*

Miss Joyce Field

Through the twists and turns of the history of St Mary's School there had been times of confidence and times of anxiety, times when the school was on a rise and seemed set for the future and other times when it paused and questioned the way ahead. Such a period now returned. After the years of Miss Matthews, the new headmistress was inevitably going to face particular challenges, and for Miss Field they proved overwhelming.

Miss Matthews had been pleased with the appointment of Miss Joyce Field, and in her letter inviting the Old Girls to the reunion in July of 1945 she told them that Miss Field hoped to join them for some of the weekend. Perhaps apprehensions began early when she failed to arrive.

Joyce Field had had an interesting and varied career prior to arriving at St Mary's. Educated at St Paul's Girls' School, where she was head girl, she had gone on to take a degree in Economics at London University. She spent six months in 1920 doing relief work in Belgrade and then began five years teaching. In 1925 she went up to Oxford to read History, and gained her degree before returning to her career in education. She was a successful headmistress at both Trowbridge,

and the Cambridge and County High Schools. During the period she worked in Cambridge she found time to study Divinity and in 1945 obtained the Archbishop's Diploma in Theology. She did not, however, have experience of boarding school life, and Kay Stedmond, in her history of St Mary's, speculated that perhaps she underestimated the demands of such a school. Girls who were present during this transition period remember that she found weekends particularly difficult.

The regular visits of Miss Matthew could not have helped the situation, but maybe Miss Field did not have the authority to make her own mark. Another Old Girl remarked that 'She made no impression on us and we felt no connection with her'. It became obvious that she could not cope, and she began to withdraw from contact with staff and pupils.

In February 1946, following a meeting with some of the governors, Miss Field tendered her resignation with the intention of leaving at the end of the Lent term. The governors recognised that she was not the right person to lead the school and asked the senior mistress, Miss Thouless, who had been keeping the school running through this time, to continue as acting headmistress.

CHAPTER THREE

Elizabeth M. Gibbins.

Elizabeth Gibbins
1946–72

After the long period of stability that St Mary's had enjoyed, the school community was now faced with an uncertain future. Yet, as an Old Girl from that time understood, it was also a blessing. Those two terms that saw the school adrift meant that the next headmistress, Elizabeth Gibbins, who had recently returned from abroad, was available to take the helm and guide St Mary's into calm waters. In her unique manner she was to prove as sure a leader as Miss Matthews.

Above: *Portrait of Miss Elizabeth Gibbins by Egerton Cooper*

Left: *Pupils returning from lacrosse practice 1955*

The handwritten record shows:

St Brandon's Clergy Daughters School Bristol 1.	Independent	History Mistress	1935	1938 Nov
Diocesan Girls School Hong Kong.	Grant -in-Aid	Head Mistress	1938 Dec	1945 Sept. 1942 — 45.
[Interned in Stanley mshtan Internment Camp in Japanese hands.				
City of Bath Girls School	Maintained	Senior History Mistress	Jan 1946	June 1946
St Mary's, Calne Wilts	Independent	Head Mistress	June 1946	

Like Matt, Miss G (as she was known by the girls) had a steadfast faith, both being described by an Old Girl who knew them well as 'sound religious souls'. As with Miss Matthews, the pupils were mixed in their devotion to Miss Gibbins. She evoked strong responses, but one could not fail to recognise her outstanding qualities: 'She looked exciting and sailed into the School with confidence'.

Born in 1911, Elizabeth Gibbins had had what she described as 'a very Edwardian upbringing'. Her father, a doctor practising in Dorset, died when she was six. She and her brother Guy, who became a Catholic priest, were at first taught by a governess, with Betty later going to Sandecotes School. Having gained a first in history from Westfield College, she went to Cambridge to take a DipEd. After three years teaching she was invited in 1938 by the Bishop of Hong Kong to take on the headship of the Diocesan School there. The occupation of Hong Kong by the Japanese led to her internment in Stanley Camp, where, under exceedingly difficult conditions, she ran the senior school and the adult education programme for over three and a half years.

Elizabeth Gibbins had witnessed times while interned that the girls of St Mary's could never have imagined. The extreme deprivation and maltreatment she experienced during this period, and the strength she found to carry out her work there, were to inform her future life. One Old Girl described her as 'truly a saint'. In his address at her funeral in 1992, the Revd Marsden-Jones commented on her bluff exterior hiding a complex person of great sensitivity and deep humility. How familiar to the girls was the resonant chuckle, the voice booming down the school corridors, and the steady plod as she made her way into Chapel.

After her appointment Miss Gibbins got to know St Mary's through weekend visits, and was present at St Mary's for the first day of the summer term to take prayers and welcome the new staff and pupils. She was able to take up her post full time in the middle of June 1946. She quickly gained the respect of the staff and struck up an immediate rapport with the Old Girls, writing to them of the welcome she had received. Like Miss Matthews, she recognised the importance of nurturing the link with past pupils.

Above: *A record of Miss Gibbins' teaching career*

Far left: *Ascension Day picnic at Sandy Lane with Miss Gibbins standing in the centre*

Post-war Changes in the Governing Body

Elizabeth Gibbins had the strong backing of the governors although in the years immediately following the war they had many changes. That old friend, Mr Arthur Dunne, resigned in 1946 after so many years of service to St Mary's. Miss Matthews paid him a fitting tribute and commented on how, as a generous benefactor of the school, 'He was behind every forward step.' The governors were soon joined by Sir Granville Ram. The following year the Bishop of Sherborne died and the Bishop of Salisbury was welcomed the year after. Also in 1948 Archdeacon Coulter, who had been a cheerful presence at St Mary's for 21 years, stepped down to become deputy chairman, with his place being taken by Henry Willink, who was now Master of Magdalene College, Cambridge. The school was delighted to welcome back Sir Ernest Gowers after his wartime duties but had to say goodbye to Mr O.S. Cleverley after many years and also to Sir Arthur fforde, who became Headmaster of Rugby School. In 1949 the first Old Girl to become a governor, Margaret Maclean (Randolph) was appointed at the same time as the Headmaster of Westminster School, Mr John Christie, who later became Principal of Jesus College, Oxford.

Ill health meant that The Right Hon. Henry Willink was forced to resign in 1950. Looking back on his ten years on the Board of Governors, he regretted that war and its immediate aftermath had limited any building at the school, but recognised that the reputation of St Mary's was 'as high as ever'.

Building Development in the Post-war Years

The lack of new building had indeed been significant to the progress of St Mary's, and the school looked to make up for lost time. The urgent requirement for a larger kitchen area, more staff and pupil accommodation and new classrooms to replace those in Hut Passage led to plans being drawn up by the architect, Mr Christopher Green.

By the autumn of 1945 St Cecilia's boarding house was ready for use after building alterations had been carried out. This helped with the accommodation shortage by providing room for seven girls and three staff members. It also gave the Sixth Form a sitting room 'with a fire, easy chairs and a gramophone': a room which the girls considered to be a perfect place for parties. The following term a physics laboratory was fitted out in the kitchen of the house.

With the acquisition of St Cecilia's had come The Mews, a low building of stables and garages. By October 1947 work had started on some of this area to raise the roof level for additional staff housing. It was not long after that the authorities allowed for some of the planned new

Above: *1955 A new classroom in Plumer Wing*

Right: *St Cecilia's in the 1960s*

Miss Gibbins Settles In

At 34 years old, Miss Gibbins had taken on great responsibilities, and she was lucky to have the wise advice of Miss Steel, who knew St Mary's so well. Reaching out from the beginning to parents and past pupils, and by creating a caring, relaxed environment based on a Christian faith that did not force religion onto the girls, she soon gained the support of those around her. The staff worked closely with her and the day-to-day administrative side of the school was ably run by one of those first appointed by Miss Gibbins, Mrs Peggy Hart, who was to become a dear friend to Miss G. She was later joined by an accounts secretary, Betty Shepherd.

The continuity of the Matt years is apparent from the News Sheet reports. The traditions of school life continued and, as the limitations of the war years receded, St Mary's girls were once again able to travel further afield for match fixtures, concerts and to Stratford-upon-Avon for the much-loved summer treat of seeing professional Shakespeare productions.

An early change that Miss Gibbins did initiate was to move the date of the School Certificate Examinations from November to the previous summer term, in line with many other schools. Miss Matthews had always valued having a summer free from the pressure of examinations, but the change allowed for a full two years of study before the Higher Certificate was taken.

Left: *Miss Gibbins presenting prizes in 1952*

Below: *A letter to the parents from Miss Matthews*

building to proceed. The News Sheet of 1948 describes being surrounded by bricks and workmen as the extension of the main kitchen area was carried out. When the Marcia Matthews building had been put up in 1936, the kitchen wing had included a 'gloriously sunny corridor' which ran down its length with stone mullioned windows overlooking the Chapel Lawn. This passage was now absorbed into the kitchen and staffroom, and a single-storey, flat-roofed extension was thrown out to include the wide Long Passage which now leads to the Dining Room, and adjoining rooms which were at first used as classrooms. In 1957 the Curved Passage link to Red Hall was added; before this, there had been no convenient way to School House.

Miss Gibbins' letter to the Old Girls in 1950 told them of the appeal that had recently been launched for a building fund. This was the beginning of the next programme of expansion for St Mary's. Like Miss Matthews, Miss Gibbins was a great correspondent, and it was largely down to her personal letters that accompanied the more formal appeals that the fund began to grow.

NATIONAL HEALTH SERVICE ACT

St. Mary's School
Calne.

Dear Sir/Madam,

Under the arrangements for the National Health Service pupils at Boarding Schools can, like everyone else, receive medical attention without charge if they so wish. This applies to general medical care, to treatment in hospitals which forms part of that Service, and to the service of specialists when required. It will still be possible, however, by paying private fees to use the services of specialists other than those immediately available under the Service.

The provisions of the Act entitle persons to choose for general medical care any Doctor taking part in the Service within the area where they live assuming the Doctor is willing to accept them. Parent or Guardians or other persons in charge choose the Doctor for children under 16. Since considerably more time is spent at School than at home in the case of Boarders, it appears to be proper that the Doctors chose for Boarders should be in the School rather than the Home district, an in the opinion of the Ministry of Health this arrangement is administratively convenient.

The School Doctor will be taking part in the new Service. der the provisions of the Act a parent is free, as has been indicated,

St Mary's under Miss Gibbins continued to flourish academically with frequent Oxbridge successes being rewarded with a holiday for the pupils. Miss G's flexible entrance policy allowed for girls who had done less well in the Common Entrance examination to gain a place in the school, and often achieve significant success later.

The post-war foundation of the welfare state led to a number of initiatives which impacted on St Mary's. At this time the Board of Education, through the Fleming Scheme, was offering bursaries for children from state primary schools for places in independent secondary schools. In 1947 Miss Gibbins was actively involved in pursuing the possibility of offering places to girls under the scheme, leading to some such admissions.

In 1948 she sent a letter to the parents of pupils, explaining the process for them registering their daughters with Dr James, the school doctor, as part of the newly formed National Health Service.

With no significant endowments to back the financial position of St Mary's, the governors were forced in 1948 to raise the school fees to 60 guineas a term. It was a step taken reluctantly but the rise in salaries and costs meant that the school was running at a loss. As always the governors were sympathetic to cases of hardship.

Meanwhile the pupils worked to raise money for particular items. Founders' Day of 1949 saw St Cecilia's garden being transformed into a fairground with stalls, bran tubs and a treasure island. A long line of pennies ran along the Putney to Mortlake boat-race course laid out on the lawn. The £115 raised provided a new carpet for the Chapel.

Into the 1950s

The General Election of 1950 stimulated great interest in politics within St Mary's and transformed the Sixth Form Discussion Group into the Social and Political Society. Miss Gibbins gave an introductory talk and the girls were able to discuss the issues with the Mayoress of Calne representing the Conservatives, and the Alderman of Chippenham for the Labour Party. Election broadcasts were listened to and pamphlets, books and cuttings made available.

Polling day, described in the diary as 'a day of much excitement and interest', also heralded the start of a major

flu epidemic in the school. More than 100 pupils took to their beds, form rooms were converted into sickrooms, the staff took on nursing duties and timetables were severely disrupted.

The governors were now functioning under a change to the constitution made in 1948. This stated that there should be 12 on the Governing Body, eight Association members and four elected members each to serve a four year term. The elected members could be re-elected or become members of the Association. This allowed for new appointments from time to time.

1951 saw several retirements from the Governing Body of St Mary's, and the arrival of The Hon. Eleanor Plumer, Principal of St Anne's College, Oxford; Miss Gwen Kirby, Matron of Great Ormond Street Hospital and a past pupil of the school; and the Vicar of Calne, The Revd W.D. O'Hanlon. The following year, Mr Stephen Lloyd joined, and Mr J.A. Keevil and Mr A.A. Martineau the year after.

Miss Plumer was to become Chairman of the Governors in 1955 and like Miss Steel was a great support to Miss Gibbins. She became a familiar face in the school and particularly got to know the staff and senior girls. Miss Gibbins wrote of her, 'She enhanced the quality of life at St Mary's by her scholarship, her keen interest in everything, her almost legendary travels and, of course, by her wit.'

Right: Founders' Day ballet 1950

The New Building Projects

The year 1953 was a significant year for the country and for St Mary's. The coronation of Queen Elizabeth II was celebrated by the school with a five-day exeat, when many girls joined the crowds on the streets of London. A few weeks later St Mary's marked its 80th birthday. This provided the occasion for a special appeal for further contributions towards the building fund. It was planned that the building of the classroom block and a swimming pool would begin the following year.

The foundation of the new classroom wing built of Bath stone was celebrated in the autumn of 1954, a year before it was ready for use. The Bishop of Salisbury dedicated a carving over the east door bearing the seal of the bishopric, and the two Miss Barton sisters, who had been pupils when St Mary's was still on The Green, were among the guests. A passageway knocked through the staffroom area provided access over a bridge to the nine classrooms, the Coulter Library holding the fiction section, an art studio and sleeping accommodation for 28 girls and two members of staff. The building was named Plumer Wing in 1964.

Miss Gibbins had proposed that the new dormitories should carry the names Christie, Willink and Alexander, in recognition of the contribution those three had made to St Mary's. A portrait of Elizabeth Gibbins painted by

Egerton Cooper and given to St Mary's by the Old Girls was hung in the library. Over the years part of the building has seen changes of use, housing individual bed-sits, a reference library and IT suites, but the classrooms still remain two generations later.

By June of 1955 the 75ft x 30ft open-air swimming pool was in use. Positioned in Chivers Field on the top of the cliff above the quarry pond, this was to become an equally loved and dreaded addition. The pool was unheated and caught the winds blowing across Calne. The changing huts were a cold run across the games pitch. However, despite the drawbacks, the pool provided many hours of lessons and competition, and when the weather was good, much relaxation and fun. It became the focus for annual Company events, with spectators gathered on the surrounding grass banking. In the 1970s a generous donor gave funding for the pool to be heated, surely a much-appreciated addition.

Above: *Architect's drawing of Plumer Wing 1956*

Left: *The Plumer Wing*

Above: *Rest after lunch in Gabriel 1955*

Top: *'Flip Flap' in the hall 1955*

Right: *Red Hall 1955*

The governors were always mindful of the need to look ahead and provide the necessary facilities for a school of St Mary's position. They had now been joined by Mr (soon to be Sir) Edmund Compton and Mr Horace West. When in 1956 the opportunity to buy Curzon House adjoining St Cecilia's arose, they took the decision to combine the houses. The two houses are an early example of semi-detached dwellings. In the 19th century Curzon House had belonged to a Mrs Guthrie, who used it as a training school for domestic servants. The house has some fine 17th-century linen-fold panelling added to one of the rooms and the walled garden behind was kept as a private garden for the school staff. The space in Curzon House meant that St Faith's was no longer needed by the school, and for a time it was rented out.

With this new acquisition came additional land and it prompted the governors to make an assessment of all the school grounds, including the derelict and unsightly corners. This identified the need for screening to prevent dumping in the quarry area; levelling and tree planting; dealing with the workhouse site; and improving the car park below School House. When the present site had been bought it came with a cottage opposite Red Hall steps, which for years was used as the school laundry. The car park area had been strung with clothes lines all this time and did not make for a good entrance to that side of the school. In 1960 two sisters, the Miss Wheelers, both deaf-mutes who had been the school laundresses for 42 years, retired. Their long service was recognised by the governors with the present of a television. An outside laundry was then used and the cottage became a pottery studio. It was later the school shop.

75

Left: *A school outing to Castle Combe in the early 1950s*

Far left: *Miss Lancaster taking an English lesson 1955*

School Life in the 1950s

Throughout the Matt years a tradition at Christmas of 'Tea and Speeches' had been a light-hearted occasion in which various members of the staff and girls gave humorous renditions, often including the staff ghost, who spoke through an interpreter. In 1952 this tradition was eventually replaced by 'supper and tests', which were in fact a series of quizzes, so rounding off the autumn term.

Pupils who knew St Mary's through Miss Matthews's years and on into the 1960s have described the school as being 'very egalitarian'. Individual achievements were not as a matter of course acknowledged, and Miss Matthews decided to stop presenting prizes before the Second World War. This approach ran even to sharing solo parts in concerts and continued to some degree under Miss Gibbins.

St Mary's had maintained strong contacts with Marlborough College over the years. Annual cricket or tennis matches and choral singing brought the pupils together and Miss Gibbins now arranged for dances for the Sixth Forms with a formal programme. Dresses were acquired, the hall was decorated and food was prepared.

Lectures of these years were regular and incredibly varied, covering subjects relating to world affairs, charities, historical research, natural history, careers, art, scientific

topics, religion and many other subjects. Despite the limitations of school life compared to today, the girls had exposure to events in the wider world and their eyes were open to the opportunities they offered.

A trip in 1959 took four girls to Paris with 1,400 pupils from around Britain. Mornings were taken up with advanced-level lectures at the Sorbonne, afternoons with sight-seeing trips and evenings with outings to the theatre or, as one girl described, 'We were free, according to taste, to sit and eat hot chestnuts, dance or drink coffee'.

In 1946, Miss Barkley had arrived at St Mary's as the PE teacher. She found a place in the hearts of the pupils, staying for 15 years. Her influence spread beyond the sports field. She was instrumental in devising dance dramas which the girls performed on Founders' Day, and for a few years she took a group of St Mary's girls to Sweden to run a two-week holiday boarding school for 60 Swedish girls. Outside English lessons, they were introduced to Company sports, Scottish dancing, and songs including the Hokey-Cokey.

St Mary's link with the diocese had always been strong and in 1958 some of the girls joined 70 other schools for the 700th anniversary of the consecration of Salisbury Cathedral.

Art and Drama

Arms and the Man *1967*

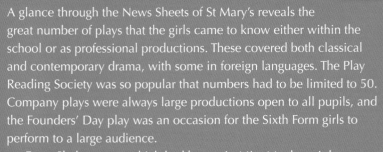

Romeo and Juliet *1951 (above) and a Form Shakespeare programme*
1949 (inset)

A glance through the News Sheets of St Mary's reveals the great number of plays that the girls came to know either within the school or as professional productions. These covered both classical and contemporary drama, with some in foreign languages. The Play Reading Society was so popular that numbers had to be limited to 50. Company plays were always large productions open to all pupils, and the Founders' Day play was an occasion for the Sixth Form girls to perform to a large audience.

Form Shakespeare, which had begun in Miss Matthews' days, continued throughout Miss Gibbins' time. Today this might seem an outdated concept, but it allowed all pupils to be involved in a production process and provided a wonderful focus for each form. The opportunity to produce innovative and experimental staging was there for the taking, and some of the performances were outstanding. The requirement for costumes to be made out of school clothing prompted some inspired creations such as delicate dresses from handkerchiefs, and it is known that at least one pupil from this period went on to follow a career in costume design.

The Art Department (along with its various off-shoots, including the pottery room and the darkroom) was a magnet for some of the girls, and associated clubs were very popular. Miss Stannard, a free spirit who came down from London for a few days each week, headed the department. In her report to the governors in 1968 she stated her aim

in teaching art was to educate 'the senses and feelings in order to strengthen the imagination and to guide the expression of emotion'. She described in the News Sheet of 1957 the outraged reaction to prints of modern masters such as Matisse, Gauguin and Bracque which she hung on the walls; painters whom she knew 'had not been considered avant garde within the last thirty years'. She clearly felt she had ground to make up, and she had time, as she did not retire from St Mary's until 1977, 30 years after her arrival. It was Miss Stannard who introduced History of Art to St Mary's.

Miss Stannard, together with Miss Nesbitt, from the Music Department, suggested to the governors in 1968 the value of a joint music, art and cultural room with an exhibition space, a library and a record player. There was a need for more space devoted to the arts, but the school would have to wait a bit longer.

The new Art Studio 1955

The Science Laboratories

Among the pressing necessities for the school at the end of the 1950s was that of up-to-date science facilities. There was a keen interest in science among the pupils and St Mary's had a good academic record in this area. With the promise of a bank loan, plans were drawn up and work began.

Miss Windsor-Aubrey, who had studied Natural Sciences at Newnham, had arrived at St Mary's in 1938. She was described by Kay Stedmond as 'a true scientist and a person of transparent sincerity and kindly humour', inspiring many pupils to follow a scientific career. A much-loved but absent-minded and slightly eccentric member of staff, she was known as Sparrow. It was not unusual for her to retire to bed when others were rising, after nights spent hunting biology specimens by torchlight. When it came to designing the science building, Miss Windsor-Aubrey was assiduous in visiting new laboratories and investigating the latest equipment. She was to remain at St Mary's for 27 years.

The new science block was a T-shaped building with a copper roof, sited on one of the old tennis courts. It provided a range of rooms that took science teaching at St Mary's to a different level. In addition to the laboratories for the three main subjects, there was a balance room, a darkroom and a double fume-cupboard so that 'if something starts to fume unpleasantly it can be transferred to the second half and be left to fume undisturbed'. The Bishop of Sherborne dedicated the building in 1961.

Since wartime, pupils taking advanced physics had been taught by Mr Leacy of the John Bentley School. His place was taken in 1964 by Rodney Davis, who became the full-time physics master until his retirement in 1998, and in 1965 Charles Crawford, who became a valued member of the senior staff team, was employed to teach chemistry.

New Buildings in the Early 1960s

The collapse of a large part of the lime kiln ushered in the 1960s at St Mary's; it was soon rebuilt, however, and was back to being the landmark in the centre of the school grounds.

In the News Sheet of 1962 Miss Gibbins remarked on the governors' 'courage and forethought in a continued policy of making our buildings really first-rate'. The school were soon to hear of plans for a new gymnasium, the old gym in Hut Passage being beyond repair. Built of stone and red cedar weather-boarding, the new gym was in use by the end of 1963. It provided a wonderful space for exercise and became invaluable as an examination hall during the summer term. An unforeseen echo was cured with the addition of an acoustic ceiling.

Hut Passage, which had been intended as a temporary building, had had its day, and it was with mixed emotions that it was demolished. The area near the main gate where it had stood since 1920 was now laid down with gardens. Sixty pupils shared small plots where they grew flowers, vegetables and soft fruit which usefully supplemented a slightly uninspiring daily diet. Meanwhile the main school garden continued to provide a significant quantity of fruit and vegetables for the kitchen. Every year the governors'

Above: *Sixth Form pupils in 1968*

Right: *The old swimming pool*

minutes recorded its contribution to the budget with, for example, £691 worth of produce in 1961.

In 1963 the governors, who were beginning to look ahead to the centenary, had identified areas for further development, including a new boarding house. However with fewer girls leaving early further up the school, Elizabeth Gibbins reported that there was a bulge in the number of pupils. They needed to move quickly and Mr Sampson Lloyd, the new architect, suggested in the interim an extension to The Mews, which when completed provided accommodation for eight girls, a member of staff and a family house for the new geography master, John Bieneman.

School Days during the 'Swinging Sixties'
Boarding school life in the years following the war had been austere. The food was mostly unexciting, the dormitories were spartan and the possibilities of following popular culture limited. With the outside world beginning to let its hair down and the focus shifting to the younger

generation, St Mary's felt the pressure to ease some of the restrictions. The advent of study bedrooms for some allowed for greater privacy and the freedom to put up pictures and posters.

This was the era of Radio Caroline, when pop music was beamed in from the North Sea and the small portable transistor radios newly available meant that St Mary's girls could listen to music illegally under the bed-clothes.

The school rented a television in 1964 but, as the minutes state, 'for a limited number of programmes authorised by a small committee'. These included Wimbledon, election broadcasts and the Olympic Games. How exciting it was when the weekly showing of *Top of the Pops* was included. The girls squeezed into a room off Long Passage, some standing on tables in order to get a view from the back. A film projector given by the Old Girls was a hugely appreciated asset and saw regular use, with showings of films such as *Genevieve* and *Appointment with Venus*. The sounds and sights of the 1960s drifting in from

'In St Bridget's some of us woke in the mornings to find our flannels stiff with ice. But the cold weather did bring pleasures. One Saturday the whole school, clad in thick sweaters and trousers went to Bowood and spent the morning on the frozen lake, which held two hundred of us quite easily. As long as the snow lasted we were allowed to wear trousers. This was a great innovation, and we think we must be one of the most emancipated schools in the country.'

– EXTRACT FROM THE NEWS SHEET OF 1963

outside coloured the school days of that generation of girls, although within the school boundaries life was still constrained.

In a further nod to the times, the restrictions on wearing mufti were gradually eased and an Old Girl commented in 1970 that 'the girls, dressed in high boots, long skirts and gypsy blouses made a very gay picture'.

Everyday Life

The severe winter of 1962/3 had really tested the hardiness of the pupils. Despite the fact that Mr Thomas, the caretaker, was praised for his success in keeping the water pipes free, the school was extremely cold. As tankers were only able to make infrequent deliveries, an extra oil tank was fitted. Sports pitches were frozen for weeks, so games times were sometimes spent at Bowood skating on the lake. The Junior Bird Club did its best to help the wildlife survive the harsh conditions. The economic cost of the cold weather to St Mary's was considerable but Miss Gibbins reported that there was virtually no illness that winter.

Since the end of the First World War St Mary's had supported the United Girls' School Mission in Peckham. By 1966 it was decided that, with changing times, it was appropriate that the girls should be more involved with

local charities. The Sixth Formers began weekly visits to elderly residents of Calne and others made Sunday visits to the nearby Cheshire Home. Funds were raised for national and international charities and for the school, through competitions, fetes, an Indian market on Founders' Day one year and a country fair on another occasion.

Those who knew Miss Gibbins recognised her strong faith and her ability to convey the importance of carrying

Above: *The Indian market 1969*

Left: *Outside Marcia Matthews Building in 1967. Julia Buckingham became a governor of St Mary's many years later*

Above: *Relaxing on the lime kiln in the 1960s*

Right: *1968 pupils by St Cecilia's pond*

Christian values into daily life. Her lessons, brief noteless sermons and the evening Bible study discussions in her sitting room known as 'Lections' were memorable, while a more formal framework of worship marked the week with the possibility of attending up to five services some Sundays. For a few years in the 1960s groups of Sixth Formers went on retreat to St Agnes House in Bristol, and the Dinton Conference in Salisbury offered a chance to meet others for interdenominational debates.

For many, many years St Mary's girls had arrived at school via the steam train from Paddington Station, trunks having preceded them. From Chippenham they took the branch line to Calne. Now, under Dr Beeching's review, this line was to close. St Mary's made a valiant effort to reverse the decision by writing a letter of protest and asking if a special train could be run for the school, but to no avail. No longer would the 5.30am walk to the station at the end of term be taken, nor would it be possible to have old pennies flattened by a passing steam engine.

The lecture programmes of these years were, as in the past, extremely wide ranging and often reflected concerns or events of the time. Examples are the Common Market, computers, devaluation, nuclear research, mental health, drug addiction, thalidomide and the 1968 students' revolt in France.

Field courses took pupils to The Weald, Flatford Mill, Slapton and a marine ecology centre in Pembrokeshire where a wet week on the seashore was made worthwhile later by a related A Level question.

Societies flourished, and attendance at political meetings in the run up to the General Election, debates and foreign visits all featured in the life of the school through these years. Around 1967 the members of the Debating Society were invited to visit the House of Lords by Michael Richardson, the father of Vicky, a pupil at that time. The girls were then entertained to lunch in the House of Commons by Robert Maxwell MP. In 1969 a group of girls spent the Easter holidays on an educational cruise to the Mediterranean, winning a prize for the best kept logbook but coming second in the tidy dormitory prize to the Germans, who won because they washed the door. Closer to home, some pupils began to attend meetings of the Calne Civic Society, which was set up in response to the diversion of the A4 through some of the old buildings of the town.

The younger girls in the school had a variety of clubs to join and, after one attempted to smuggle two white mice into Wordsworth dormitory, arrangements were made for an area for pets. Soon doves, hamsters, guinea-pigs and an increasing number of rabbits found a home by the science laboratories.

Music During Miss Gibbins' Years

Barbara Nesbitt's name will be fondly remembered by many of the generations of girls who knew her. A quietly capable person, she joined the music staff in 1940 as a pianist and to teach elocution. She had briefly taught at the school a few years earlier and was to have a long and successful career at St Mary's, retiring in 1975. A fine musician, her wide contacts in the musical world brought many notable performers to the school. She was to take on numerous other roles within the school, including producing the annual school play; as housemistress at St Bridget's; and senior mistress after Miss Thouless retired.

As the tradition of music-making continued, it was Miss Nesbitt who drove the day-to-day musical life of St Mary's. However she had the backing of some very distinguished musical directors. From 1944 Christopher Le Fleming, a composer and professional pianist, held this position. In the ten years following his departure in 1948, two organists of Salisbury Cathedral, who were great friends, and whose careers mirrored each other in an extraordinary way, took up the role in succession, visiting St Mary's weekly. David Willcocks is remembered for his contribution to improving the standard of singing in the school, and for training pupils for big occasions including the Music Festival. An organ scholar of King's College, Cambridge, he would later become its musical director.

Stepping into David Willcocks' place, Douglas Guest joined St Mary's staff in 1950. His daughter, Sue Garrett-Cox, who became a pupil at the school, remembers how much he enjoyed his visits and how highly he thought of Miss G, joining her at the high table for lunch. He composed works for the school choir, including carols and (as Sue recalls) a small prayer in three parts which was sung in evening Chapel. Douglas Guest left in 1957 and later became the organist at Westminster Abbey. Mr Clifford Harker, organist at Bristol Cathedral, replaced him at St Mary's.

One of the highlights of the musical year had been the annual choral concert performed by the Sixth Form with Marlborough College. This event had begun during Miss Matthews' time and after a seven-year break the tradition was renewed in 1947, to continue all through Miss Gibbins' years and beyond. In line with Miss Nesbitt's beliefs, all the girls in the Sixth Form, however musical, were able to take part, so all experienced the exhilaration of singing in a large choir.

Throughout these years the girls had wonderful opportunities to attend many concerts by first-class orchestras such as the Royal Philharmonic Orchestra conducted by Sir Thomas Beecham and the Hallé Orchestra under Sir John Barbirolli. They heard innumerable fine performers including Yehudi Menuhin and Frederick Grinke, who on several occasions played with the school orchestra. Particularly thrilling was the presence of Sir Michael Tippett at the Marlborough choral performance of *A Child of our Time* in the spring of 1967. Music continued to weave its way through the fabric of life at St Mary's, be it in Chapel, choirs, orchestras or individual tuition.

Above: *Barbara Nesbitt*

Left: *Miss Nesbitt taking a singing lesson in 1955*

Above: Pupils in St Cecilia's garden c.1966

Below: Kay Stedmond

Many past pupils will remember traditions that persisted, some of them strange and unexplained: using only a fork at mealtimes; waiting to be offered things at the table rather than asking for them, even if it meant going without; or services for the whole school in the Hall, on Mondays facing the stage and on Saturdays facing the concert end. Hair washing was once a week, Wiltshire lardy cake was warmed up on the radiators and shopping in Calne was not allowed until the UV Form.

Weekday life was busy but as yet there were no morning lessons on Saturday. Some pupils were involved in matches, and occasionally outings were arranged, however the weekends were at this time mostly free for pupils to pass as they wished. Increasingly girls who were able to do so would go home, while those left at school had hours to fill. On warm summer days there were plenty of places within the grounds to while away the time. In the winter it was not so easy. Looking back to the end of the 1960s there is a sense that for some the restrictions of boarding school life hung heavily.

Academic Life under Miss Gibbins

St Mary's has been blessed through its time with some dedicated teaching staff. Many have devoted a large part of their careers to the school.

Language teaching at St Mary's had for many years held a strong place in the curriculum and was well represented on university placements. Classics had been taught by Miss Wood since 1954 and she provided a full programme for the Classical Society, with interesting lecture programmes and outings to museums, excavations, archaeological sites and theatrical performances.

Foreign trips became more regular and the 1968 News Sheet reported on a trip to Russia by three of the girls who were the first pupils to study the language at St Mary's. They were taught by Mrs Olga Lawrence, a person with an interesting history, her mother having been Lady-in-Waiting to the last Tsarina. In an interview for the pupils' in-house magazine in 1982 she described her family's escape from Russia during the Revolution. When she retired from St Mary's in 1980, the headmistress, Mrs

history of St Mary's up to that year. At her leaving party, Kay Stedmond, making reference to her many years at the school, talked of her support of the Benedictine principle of stability: staying and giving.

Teaching patterns at this time still tended to reflect the old-school methods of factual learning, but the girls were beginning to look for more opportunities to question and discuss. One former pupil commented that Miss Washer, an English teacher, stood out as someone who 'made you think'. Janet Washer, who had a wide love of literature and languages, died young, and at her memorial service at the school in 1982 a colleague reflected on 'the meticulous care she took to share her knowledge and perception'. Her extensive library was left to the school.

The Challenges of the Time

The winds of change blowing through society in the 1960s put mounting pressure on girls' boarding schools, particularly small ones like St Mary's. Increasingly pupils had the option of transferring for A Levels to sixth-form colleges or to independent co-educational schools. With

Left: LIV Form pupils in 1963

Below: The Ascension Day general knowledge paper

Walters, commented, 'Life will be greyer without her. We will miss her kindness, learning and wit'.

Among those members of staff who stand out in the annals of St Mary's is Kay Stedmond. A graduate of St Hugh's College, Oxford, she arrived at the school in 1947 to teach history and divinity. In 1970 she had a well-earned sabbatical on a round-the-world trip to New Zealand visiting places en route, of which she said the historical connections 'brought alive many of the topics which come up in lessons'.

In addition to her teaching Miss Stedmond carried administrative responsibilities in the school and became a senior mistress when Barbara Nesbitt retired. She had a deep knowledge of St Mary's and supported and advised those around her in her calm, practical way. She has been described as taking on a 'union role' in particularly supporting the interests of the staff. She remained until her retirement in 1986 and then went on to chronicle the

ST. MARY'S SCHOOL, CALNE

GENERAL KNOWLEDGE PAPER

Ascension Day, 1966

N.B.—Parents may consult each other; no other help, or books, allowed.

I Who is speaking in these remarks taken from the New Testament (N.E.B.):
 1 I am not the Messiah. *John the Baptist*
 2 Are you the King of the Jews? *Pontius Pilate*
 3 I am ready to go with you to prison and death. *Peter*
 4 I appeal to Caesar. *St. Paul*
 5 Here and now, sir, I give half my possessions to charity. *Zacchaeus*

II Choose the word which correctly matches each of the following definitions:
 Haran Nisan Qumran Ramadan Sanhedrin
 1 A Jewish Court. *Sanhedrin*
 2 A Jewish Month. *Nisan*
 3 A Moslem Fast. *Ramadan*
 4 Part of Canaan known to Jacob. *Haran*
 5 Place where the Dead Sea Scrolls were found. *Qumran*

III 1 From which Epistle are the words of the Grace, with which Morning Prayer ends, taken? *1 Corinthians*
 2 From which Gospel is the Nunc Dimittis taken? *St. Luke*
 3 Give one word to signify an instruction occurring in an order of service—often printed in italics. *Rubric*
 4 Give one word to signify a sequence of short prayers with a simple congregational response. *Litany*
 5 Name the Church Festival which has the subtitle " The Manifestation of Christ to the Gentiles." *Epiphany*
 6 Name the Sunday next before Lent. *Quinquagesima*
 7 Give the date of All Saints' Day. *Nov. 1*
 8 Complete the statement "The Prayer Book has services for the

and Nuffield Science. Although this was not an easy time, Miss Gibbins made every effort to rise to the demands, introducing a vestigial tutorial system run by the Company staff, to give the girls advice on O and A Levels.

After the election of the Labour party in 1964, there were changes afoot in the educational world. The government began to research how it might integrate public schools within a comprehensive state system. Along with other girls' schools, St Mary's looked into the implications for the school, considering such issues as whether it was prepared to be wholly non-selective and the impact on the career development of women teachers.

In the event the threat passed, as did the possibility of a road running through St Cecilia's garden to bypass the bottleneck on Curzon Street. In 1968 the layout of the centre of Calne was greatly altered by a new road cutting down past St Bridget's, which had by now been sold as the school had adequate boarding accommodation on site.

This period of transition, when young people were seeking more independence and no longer accepting the status quo, was a challenge to all authorities. The traditional boarding school structure was no longer adequate and over the coming years greater changes would prove necessary.

Above: *Charles Crawford taking a chemistry lesson in the 1970s*

Right: *The Gibbins House plaque put up when a common room and study bedrooms were added*

their greater pupil numbers they were often able to offer a wider curriculum and better facilities. Towards the end of the 1960s St Mary's was losing a significant number of girls at this stage of their education. Miss Gibbins attempted to stem the flow by inviting the parents of girls in the middle school to a meeting with staff where she outlined her belief in the value of continuing into the school's Sixth Form.

The curriculum requirements of the new universities of the period were an added pressure, with Miss Gibbins fearing that a rounded education would be compromised. Members of staff were asked to present subject reports to the governors outlining their plans for the future, and how, for example, they were incorporating Modern Mathematics

Looking Towards the Centenary of St Mary's School

As the decade moved forward, St Mary's was looking ahead and ambitions were huge. Throughout 1967 the Plumer Wing classrooms made a perfect viewing spot for building work on a new boarding house, which was later named Gibbins House. This gave accommodation for members of staff and for 59 girls, in single rooms and study bedrooms. The building was dedicated by the Bishop of Salisbury, an event partly recorded in a 35mm film of the period. The school housekeeper, Miss Gibbs, who took the recording,

OPENED BY ELIZABETH GIBBINS FOUNDERS DAY 1979

Left: *The Bodington Library in Plumer Wing 1973*

was recognised by the governors for the work she and her staff put into getting the building ready on time. Also thanked were Mr Wood and Mr Taylor from the Maintenance Department, who worked throughout that summer holiday. Geoff Taylor, known by the girls as Golly, was employed at St Mary's for 37 years and his wife worked in the kitchens for 43 years.

With the opening of New House, space was released in Plumer Wing for additional classrooms, the Bodington Library and eight study bedrooms. A further consequence of the rearrangement of rooms was the opportunity to extend the reception and headmistress's quarters. Miss Gibbins had to leave for her holiday in good time that summer so that work could be completed for the autumn term. By September the girls were in New House and all the other changes had been effected.

Amid all these projects, however, the beacon on the horizon was 1973, the school's centenary, when the hope was that a new Chapel and a link building to Red Hall would be completed. Miss Gibbins wrote, 'It is thrilling that having provided for all the essential educational needs we are now in the position to raise funds for the new Chapel'. The governors looked to loans, and the funding from this was supported by a centenary fund set up in 1963 and which had steadily grown, thanks to Miss G's hard work. Now the Old Girls' Association offered to arrange a ball at The Dorchester Hotel: a glittering event which raised

£1,000 for the Chapel. It was soon possible for plans to be drawn up.

Events moved fast and the date for the dedication of the new Chapel, 19 February 1972, was decided at the same governors' meeting that Miss Gibbins announced her retirement. The following year was going to be hugely significant for St Mary's. Building work began in the autumn term of 1971, uncovering the foundations of Hut Passage in the process, and the Chapel was ready on time.

Miss Elizabeth Gibbins Retires

Miss Gibbins's work at St Mary's was now drawing to a conclusion. She had spent much of her career at the school and her strong personality had marked the school and influenced the girls under her care. She had carried St Mary's through a period of expansion that had given much improved accommodation for study and boarding and she had nurtured the spiritual life of those within it. Perhaps recognising the increasing pressures from the outside world, her humility led her to question if she had achieved enough for the school.

On her retirement, and after her death in 1992, many remembrances of Elizabeth Gibbins were recorded. Her forthright manner, which sometimes bordered on bluntness, could be intimidating to those who did not know her, but a quick perception and deep humanity shone through. She listened, was kind and wise and had a caring concern for those around her. She was perhaps drawn to those girls who were more of a challenge, recognising and appreciating their individual natures.

Sir Edmund Compton, Chairman of the Governors for many years, spoke on Founders' Day in 1972 of her qualities:

A whole generation of St Mary's has been blessed with a headmistress who is both great and good. Greatness is rare. So is goodness. The two together are pretty well unique. In Betty Gibbins we do indeed recognise, and recognise at once, a unique personality. Dedicated to her profession and superbly equipped for it, she applies her talents without a trace of self and with Christian drive and love. There is nothing derivative in her speech

The Chapel

How fitting it was that Elizabeth Gibbins' retirement should coincide with a new Chapel for St Mary's. Her life was shaped by her faith, and the new space allowed the whole school to worship as one. It was a bold leap in design by Mr Sampson Lloyd the architect, for which he won a commendation at a Royal Academy Exhibition.

The Chapel was described by an admiring Old Girl that summer as 'a great welcoming, light semi-circle with wide open doors; a place to go in and come out of freely, where one is not excluded'. There was some severity in its detail, however, which did not appeal to all, with exposed girders and grey block walls. Behind the altar hung a striking reredos both designed and painted by Mr Lloyd. Light shafted onto it from a towering window, and the wide-spanned roof sloped down to further windows at ground level. In alluding at the dedication of the Chapel to the design, Bishop Joseph Fison of Salisbury urged the school to 'use its tent well'.

Pupils of that time who had watched the walls rising came to appreciate the part it would play in the life of St Mary's, and talked of their pride in the Chapel, and how it had become 'completely part of the school and harmonious with it, yet remaining a building unique in itself'. A memorial to the three founders of St Mary's was placed in the Chapel along with other treasures and important furnishings from the old Chapel, so providing continuity with the past.

As part of the project a link from the Chapel to Red Hall gave further rooms to that part of the school. A reading room opened out from the Chapel and could take additional seating for services if need be, and a Sixth Form sitting room led off the corridor from Red Hall; the corridor itself was used as an exhibition space for the girls' art work.

In later years, as ideas changed, the interior of the Chapel was softened with light-coloured rendering on the walls, and chairs replaced the hard bench seats. The silvered-bronze cross that the Old Girls had presented to St Mary's in memory of Miss Matthews now stands against the wall with the candlesticks on the altar in front. Pupils' artwork and some of the kneelers from the old Chapel adorn the new. It is a welcoming space that continues to act as a central focus for school life.

Middle: *The cross and candlesticks from the old Chapel are used today*

Right: *The school Chapel prayer book used from the 1920s to the 1970s*

St Mary's Chapel built in 1972

Vouchsafe we beseech Thee, Merciful Father to prosper with Thy blessing the work of this school. Grant that those who serve Thee here may set Thy holy will ever before them, and do that which is pleasing in Thy sight, and persevere in Thy service unto the end, through Jesus Christ our Lord. Amen.

We give Thee thanks O Lord, for all Thy mercies to us this day. Thy hand has guarded us, Thy love has protected us;

make us ever to love Thee and do Thy will, and do Thou bring us at last to the eternal rest which remaineth for the people of GOD through Jesus Christ our Lord. Amen.

Lighten our darkness we beseech Thee, O Lord; and by Thy great mercy defend us from all perils and dangers of this night; for the love of Thy only Son, our Saviour Jesus Christ. Amen.

The Lord bless us and keep us; the Lord make his

Sport

Throughout the 1950s and 1960s lacrosse continued to be the primary winter sport, with the highlight of each year being a three-day tournament at Merton Abbey in London. In 1950 the St Mary's team, one of 20, drew in the final against Newbury County School in an extremely exciting match. The school always received enthusiastic support on the sidelines from family and friends. Two of the games mistresses from the 1950s were members of the England lacrosse team.

Tennis also featured large in the school calendar, and as more hard courts were added, practice was spread throughout the year. As well as tournaments against other schools, friendly matches were played with parents, staff and the 'Casuals' and 'Rustics' teams from Marlborough College. Visits to Wimbledon inspired the girls, and the introduction of the Nestlé ladder was very much enjoyed, with the winner going on to play in the main tournament.

The arrival of the new gym allowed for badminton, and when the swimming pool was built summer sport gained a new dimension, although the lack of heating meant that in some years it was hardly used. However, life-saving certificates were gained regularly.

In a 1968 drive to extend the activities open to the girls, the sports staff introduced putting, volleyball, hockey and quoits in school, and squash at the Devizes courts. A couple of years later a fencing coach was brought in.

The 1950s lacrosse team representing St Mary's at the Merton tournament

Form Tennis 1966

and action, always original, always practical. Utterly sincere in herself, she will always respond to sincerity in others.

She was given a wonderful send-off by the staff, the girls and their parents and later by her Old Girls at that summer's reunion.

Those who knew Miss Gibbins throughout her later years can testify to the fact that she was profoundly affected by her wartime experiences. She went out to Hong Kong for a short time after she left St Mary's and then returned to village life, where she was active in the Church and the community. One past pupil commented, 'We still hold her up as an example of how to face up to any challenge to the very best of one's abilities and to the highest standards.'

Miss Gibbins once remarked that when she arrived at St Mary's she found the ethos similar to her own. A visiting Old Girl sensed a familiar unity and purpose in the school. That spirit, engendered by the founders and which had through unspoken attitudes been passed from one generation of girls to the next, was well tended during Elizabeth Gibbins' headship and was once again to be recognised and commented on by her successor, Mrs Joyce Bailey.

Right: *Miss Gibbins at her final Founders' Day in 1972 with Sir Edmund Compton and Mr Gordon-Clarke*

'Children in trouble? Oh, they could always come and see me. Mind you they didn't always say what the problem was and sometimes the atmosphere was so good in the School that their friend would come first and ask me to send for her on some other pretext. The children used to come during the day and the staff at night, and I expect people wondered why I wandered about the School late at night, but there was always someone who needed keeping an eye on. There were all sorts of problems of course and sometimes one was more in a position to help because being a head meant that one was neutral'.

– Miss Gibbins on her time at St Mary's, taken from an interview given to Sue Rotherham in 1990

'Miss Elizabeth Gibbins wishes to retire in a year's time after 25 years as headmistress of St Mary's School Calne. It is in character that she should have said so in personal letters to over 200 parents, in which she says nothing of her own achievements and everything about the strength and spirit of the School that her successor will take over from her. If St Mary's has a unique reputation among girls' Independent Schools, that reputation flows from the personal work of this dedicated and Christian individualist. Self-effacing in many other matters, she is confident she has built to last. Her confidence confirms not only the quality of her words but also her standing as a great headmistress.'

– Press notice on Miss Gibbins' retirement released by the governors

CHAPTER FOUR

Joyce Walters

Joyce Bailey (later Walters) 1972–85

As 1972 drew to a close St Mary's Calne stood at the dawn of its second century. From the handful of pupils at its foundation in 1873, it now had over 230. It had much to celebrate and that responsibility fell to its new headmistress, Joyce Bailey. Years later, in 2012, Mrs Bailey, who by then was Mrs Joyce Lynn, described how surprised she was to be appointed as headmistress of St Mary's, and the privilege she felt at having the opportunity to lead the school. As a Classics teacher at Badminton School in Bristol, she had applied for the position, not for a moment expecting to be successful, but thinking the experience at interview would be valuable. To her astonishment she was offered the post, and so St Mary's took a stride into a new era.

Above: *Mrs Joyce Bailey*

Left: *The UV Form outside the Dining Room 1977*

her as having a 'huge presence' and being an 'inspirational role model'. Another remembers her kindness when she scooped up a tearful, homesick junior and took her to her room for toast, hot chocolate and a chat in front of her fire.

Mrs Bailey's Aims for the School

It was clear to Joyce Bailey from the time of her arrival that some aspects of school life needed to be reviewed. High on her list was the desire to improve the O and A Level results. She felt strongly that many of the pupils in each group were unnecessarily young in comparison to other schools, and were not intellectually mature enough for the demands of the curriculum. She raised with the governors the possibility of adding an extra year group to the school. This had huge ramifications and it was not until 1976 that it could be put into place.

An additional year would also mean more time to fulfil Mrs Bailey's wish of promoting music, drama, art and other extracurricular activities for the girls, 'so that their school lives might be rich and fully rounded'. She immediately added riding, squash and judo to the sports on offer. By the beginning of 1974 the younger pupils could choose from drama, orienteering, sailing theory, oil-painting, pottery, brass-rubbing, crafts, Red Cross and ballet as activities for a Thursday afternoon.

Joyce Bailey was a graduate of St Anne's College, Oxford. Still under 40, she brought a new perspective to St Mary's which both delighted and ruffled the school community. Having been a non-resident member of staff at Badminton, she was unfamiliar with boarding school life, but this proved to be an advantage, as she was able to bring fresh ideas as to what teenage girls might appreciate for their lives to be more comfortable. Despite the changes that had been made in the preceding few years, she found St Mary's 'a spartan place'.

This was not an easy appointment for Mrs Bailey, and she was shocked as she began to realise what a deep effect it would have on her family life. The demands on the headmistress at this time were all encompassing, and she related later how at night she often had to patrol the school grounds checking for intruders. However, she tackled the job with energy and an acute clear-sightedness, and was later told by a governor that she had 'dragged the school screaming into the 20th century'.

She quickly established a rapport with the girls, amazing them with the speed at which she learnt their names and ways, 'both good and bad'; she felt strongly that she wanted to have a relationship with the girls in which they felt they could discuss anything with her. Pupils from that time plainly liked and respected Mrs Bailey. One spoke of

Top left: *Mrs Walters with pupils*

Left: *Pupils in the art studio in 1970*

The Centenary of St Mary's School

Mrs Bailey clearly enjoyed a party, considering it to be a valuable way to draw the community together. In time she was to initiate social gatherings at drama productions, large school events, teas for the new girls and their parents and buffet lunches for the leavers and their families. The school's centenary was a particularly good opportunity for everyone to celebrate, and soon a committee was charged with putting together the programme.

The occasion was to be combined with Founders' Day towards the end of the summer term of 1973. An account in the News Sheet of that year by two of the girls describes the events of the weekend. A wine and cheese party on Friday night was followed by a performance of *St Joan* by the Sixth Form. On Saturday the Bishop of Salisbury led a service of thanksgiving in the parish church, with the Marlborough College trumpeters playing a fanfare. After picnic lunches a medley of activities was offered to visitors, including PE demonstrations, a French market, international cookery and an exhibition of St Mary's history. Parents were able to participate in science experiments including being tested for colour blindness and having their blood group determined.

Meanwhile 100 books were on sale which could be donated to the school library. Along with exhibitions, a tree planting ceremony near St Prisca's took place and the orchestra gave a concert. Tea and birthday cake, a second performance of the play and a service conducted by the OGA rounded off the day. It was a memorable event drawing together many friends of St Mary's, including Miss Gibbins and Elsie Rutherford, who had been a pupil in the 1890s. Mrs Bailey admitted to apprehension at hosting such an occasion but saw it as having had 'a great unifying effect on the School, linking past, present, and future and encouraging me to feel that I now really belong'.

The OGA marked the anniversary with a ball at The Dorchester in London to raise funds for a centenary bursary fund and a brief history of St Mary's was compiled by Miss Thouless and Jean Hughes.

Top: *The Bishop of Salisbury arriving at Calne Parish Church for the centenary service*

Above: *Old Girl Elsie Rutherford unveiling the Centenary Tree plaque*

Inset: *The Centenary Ball programme*

Hand in hand with her drive for better results, she hoped to encourage the girls to be academically ambitious and pursue rewarding careers, while at the same time being stylish and feminine. Many parents were supportive of her stance but she faced some resistance, and recalls being warned by one father that 'too much education was likely to make his daughter unmarriageable'. She was undeterred, however, and before her first term was over she had put career information into the anteroom of the office which had been created from the old Chapel. A few years later, Miss Cummings became the careers mistress in the school and St Mary's became part of the Independent Schools Careers Organisation (ISCO), which gave careers advice to the girls.

As a further move to improve standards, Mrs Bailey placed less emphasis on engaging staff willing to live in school, and more on their academic ability. The accommodation for staff had been very modest and she saw the need to provide more self-contained flats for housemistresses and to increase their pay. In return, with the help of assistants, they would assume greater responsibility for the girls' leisure time.

The comfort of the girls was also of concern to Joyce Bailey. She had been struck by the bleakness of Wordsworth dormitory in School House, likening it to a Victorian hospital ward. She worried that the girls were not able to go to their houses until 8pm, and so their time after supper was spent in either their classrooms or the rather limited school sitting rooms. She proposed that each house

should have its own common room where the girls could spend the evenings. The changes that were envisaged would mean some substantial reorganisation.

A Time of Austerity

Beside the internal demands of the school, this was a difficult economic time in the country at large. Industrial disputes and the oil crisis led to a three-day working week, power cuts and rising prices. The winter of 1973/4 was a particularly grim period, and St Mary's was not immune from the disruption. In January 1974 the school's quota of fuel was 30 per cent below the normal consumption. Heating was only on for a period in the mornings and evenings and every effort was made to economise on lighting.

Mrs Bailey's arrival at St Mary's coincided with that of a bursar, Mr R.C. Wilkins. His reports in the minutes over the next few years show how raging inflation was making it extremely hard to predict expenditure. Time and again estimates for costs were revised, particularly for food, fuel and electricity: 'Uncertainty builds upon uncertainty and the figures must be regarded as highly speculative.'

Above: *The UV Form in front of the San in 1977*

Left: *Centenary celebrations by the lime kiln*

Right: *Gabriel common room 1973*

94

Additional salary costs were incurred with the Houghton Award to teachers. School fees had to increase. In January 1973 the termly cost of boarding was £257. Three years later it was £450, and by the end of the decade it was £800. Some parents were forced to withdraw their daughters from the school while others were given remission in fees.

In 1975 Joyce Bailey felt that she had to anticipate a future drop in numbers and so allocated places to a greater number of children. In the event, no more pupils left, and with some would-be leavers further up the school deciding to remain, the school was over-booked. Accommodation would have to be found urgently.

Change of Room Use

In the spring of 1973 Mrs Bailey mentioned to the governors that the Dining Room was overcrowded and perhaps the school would have to begin two sittings. Mealtimes had always been considered an opportunity for girls of all ages to mix. For many years at lunchtime a painted Formica square received at the door indicated which seat to take for that particular meal, with the staff sitting at the heads of the tables. The UVI Form usually sat with the headmistress at the high table.

For a time there were two sittings, but by the autumn of 1976 the kitchens were updated and a cafeteria system was introduced. This allowed for a choice of food and may have been partly prompted by Mrs Bailey's opinion

of the school food. She certainly commented on the spam fritters, 'an austerity dish dating from World War II', which were served regularly on Monday lunchtimes. To compensate for the more casual mealtimes, annual formal candle-lit Company dinners were begun, occasionally with guest speakers.

In order to begin to make the changes necessary for boarding house common rooms, staff bedrooms in the kitchen wing were made into study bedrooms for Sixth Form girls, and became known as The Penthouse. By the summer of 1974, St Prisca's had its common room. However, its use was brief, as in order to manage the number bulge, it had to once again revert to a dormitory.

Mews House was the next to be converted to make rooms for five pupils and one member of staff. This absorbed the increasing numbers created by girls staying on for Oxbridge entrance but the issue of further common rooms still had to be addressed. With Mrs Bailey relinquishing some of her rooms, better accommodation was provided for the new housemistress in School House who succeeded the matron Miss Payne. For a time, Joyce Bailey slept in the cottage and retained rooms in School House for use during the day and for entertaining.

Further conversion work was carried out on garages and a trunk store in The Mews and by the autumn of 1976 it became a Sixth Form house, with 22 study bedrooms and a small common room. Joyce Bailey declared, 'It is very popular with the UVI Form who live there in great comfort and style!'

At long last it was possible for the girls in St Prisca's and St Cecilia's to have common rooms in which to spend the evenings. Televisions were bought with the profits from the tuck shop. Mrs Bailey was edging towards her vision of a comfortable, stimulating environment for all the girls, but she had not yet finished.

As room use was considered, the need for suitable accommodation for Mrs Bailey was pressing. At first the cottage by School House was suggested, and then the San, but eventually it was decided that School House was probably the most convenient. During the summer holidays of 1977 various changes were made to provide a private flat. Common rooms and offices were reallocated with the UV Form moving into the partitioned old Chapel.

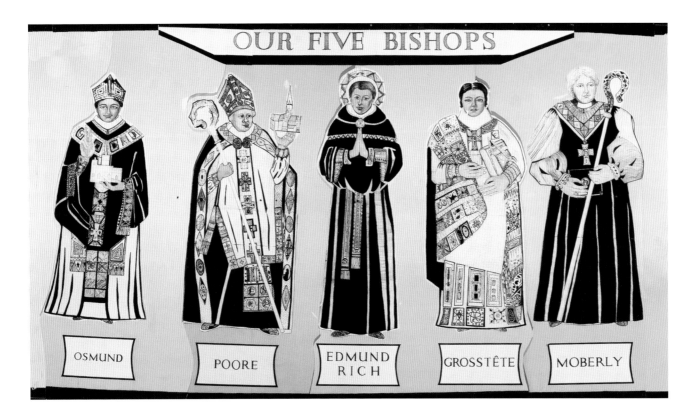

OUR FIVE BISHOPS

OSMUND   POORE   EDMUND RICH   GROSSTÊTE   MOBERLY

Mrs Bailey and her Staff

Joyce Bailey had soon come to understand the huge commitment of heading a school such as St Mary's. With no resident chaplain, one of her duties was to preach at the Sunday evening service, when there were often parents present, an experience which was new to her. Kay Stedmond commented, 'She put forward undogmatically, yet earnestly, the great ethical principles of discipline, kindness, honesty and truth'.

Teaching did come naturally to Mrs Bailey, and she keenly maintained a role in the Classics Department, giving the younger pupils a good grounding in grammar. Greek studies flourished and the older girls benefited from her enthusiasm, scholarship and rigour.

Finding herself having to supervise the girls' evening meal after many of the other staff had left, she felt unable to fully focus on her main responsibilities, and so suggested to the governors that two deputy heads should be appointed: one academic, and one acting as senior housemistress to help with pastoral work and to oversee evenings, exeats, the junior girls' free time and some weekends.

The weekends had always presented a problem, with boredom not unusual. Two members of the academic staff would be expected to be present but as the governors'

minutes state, 'They can do little more than keep the School ticking over'. Mrs Bailey now suggested that extra staff should be brought in to give tuition in activities such as craft, cookery and dressmaking. The upgraded housemistresses and their assistants would replace the two resident staff that each house had at the weekends. However this proved harder to achieve than she expected.

By October 1977 the difficulty of providing the necessary house staff for evenings and weekends had come to a head, and Mrs Bailey told the governors that she considered the situation might be the most serious threat facing the school. It was important to improve salaries, accommodation and working conditions in order to hire the right quality of staff.

On Miss Nesbitt's retirement there was no member of staff able to take over all her responsibilities as senior mistress, so her duties were divided between four: Kay Stedmond, Charles Crawford, Janet Washer and the head of PE, Miss M. Turner. Mrs Bailey later praised the support and kindness Kay had shown in helping her to settle into St Mary's. Also of great help to Mrs Bailey was the bursar at the time, Commander Henry Harwood. From a naval background, he was instrumental in ensuring the smooth day-to-day running of the school. He worked closely with

Above: *Part of a mural made for the Centenary showing the five bishops after whom the St Mary's Companies are named*

Right: *The governors with the Bishop on Founders' Day 1973*

Back l–r Mr Henly, Mr Lloyd, The Bishop of Salisbury, Sir Edmund Compton, Sir Oliver Millar, Canon Witcomb.

Front l–r Miss Kirby, Mrs Wilkinson, Mrs Bailey, Mrs McCrum, Lady Brooke of Cumnor

The Governors

When Mrs Bailey arrived at St Mary's Sir Edmund Compton headed the school governors. A distinguished civil servant, Sir Edmund was elected as the first Parliamentary Commissioner by Harold Wilson in 1967, the same year that he followed Miss Plumer as chairman at St Mary's. He had had daughters in the school, and had a keen interest in music. Sir Edmund guided St Mary's for many years, and gave a moving address at the retirement of Miss Gibbins in 1972. He oversaw the building of the Chapel and on his retirement from the Governing Body in 1976 a cross was placed on the apex of the Chapel roof as recognition of his place in the school's history. In 1983, when the area was redesigned to include two junior classrooms, Sir Edmund unveiled a plaque at the entrance to the Chapel.

Lady Trend followed Sir Edmund as Chairman of the Governors. Commander Harwood said of her that 'She was a real professional; the best admiral I served under'. It was during her leadership in 1978 that the Articles of Association of the Governing Body were revised to state that it was desirable, but no longer necessary, for all members to be communicants of the Church of England, provided that the majority were. In addition it was decided that all governors would be subject to re-election after a four-year term apart from the Vicar, who would remain ex-officio.

Towards the end of 1973, Mr A.A. Martineau retired after 20 years as a governor. He was well known for taking the early train from London in order to walk from Chippenham to Calne for the governors' meetings.

There were other changes around this time. Dr Bremner Cameron arrived, soon followed by Mrs Ellis, wife of the Master of Marlborough College, and by Mrs Sue Rotherham, who as chairman of the Old Girls' Association knew St Mary's well.

the governors, particularly Lord Farnham, who chaired the finance committee and, though on a tight budget was always keen to keep a cap on the fees when possible. He remembers the trepidation among the governors when the fees reached £1,000 a term.

The Future of St Mary's School

A study into population trends had predicted that birth levels were likely to fall during the 1980s. Mrs Bailey was asked by the governors to produce a paper on the future of St Mary's, and it was agreed that, true to its foundation, the school should continue to uphold a high academic standard within a Christian tradition. In order to maintain numbers, a thriving Sixth Form would be essential, and it might be necessary to increase the number of day pupils to fill spaces.

Joyce Bailey felt that in addition to a more attractive environment for the Sixth Form, there should be a further improvement in the recreational, leisure and pastoral facilities, and also in those of science, art and music. She proposed a residential husband-and-wife team to run a house and supervise extra-curricular activities.

The changes that would be necessary were the motivation behind a new appeal. In order to manage this appeal effectively, a professional firm was employed, and Captain Daniel Hunt spent time at St Mary's. Throughout 1978, with the help of Miss Gibbins, more than 1,000 parents and Old Girls received letters asking for their support and Captain Hunt toured the country visiting many of these people. A total of £260,000 was raised, well over the sum envisaged. Mrs Bailey received many messages of support for her plans and the school felt it had the full support of its parents behind it.

The Next Phase of Building Development

With a successful appeal underway, the governors were eager to start the first phase of the new building programme. A staff family house and a large common room with study bedrooms above were added to Gibbins House. It was thought that in time these might be part of a self-contained Sixth Form Centre. By February 1979, despite heavy snow, an oil shortage and a lorry drivers' strike, the study bedrooms were ready for use, and in the

Perhaps the most exciting addition was the Art Centre, a new extension on the north side of Plumer Wing. The old art room was divided into a History of Art room, a Sixth Form studio and an office. The new room was in two parts, for art and craft, divided by a glass screen, and part of the Jubilee Building was transformed at first into a pottery, and later into a mixed-media studio.

The official opening was by Sir Oliver Millar, Surveyor of the Queen's Pictures and one of the St Mary's governors. Soon the studios were busy with lessons, during evenings and at weekends. It proved a fine investment and was welcomed by parents who had lobbied for it.

The building work of this period had been planned in phases, and the last of these was to provide a larger common room for The Mews with views over St Cecilia's garden. It was named Lloyds after Stephen Lloyd, who had been a governor for 27 years, and his nephew, Sam, architect for the school.

Above: *The art studio in the 1970s*

Top left: *Miss Gibbins at the opening of the new Sixth Form common room in 1979*

Bottom left: *A Gatsby party in the 1970s*

summer term the girls were enjoying parties and birthday dinners. The novelty of receiving direct incoming calls was welcome; they felt they had a certain amount of independence from the rest of the school.

Significant alterations to Plumer Wing created two new classrooms from study bedrooms and a fourth laboratory. There was now room in Long Passage for the offices to be moved more centrally in the school.

Drama

As the 1970s moved on into the 1980s, drama productions at St Mary's became more ambitious. The Sixth Form began a Junior Drama Club teaching the younger girls acting techniques. The musical *Oliver* brought the music and drama together with huge success, and a highly ambitious production of *Murder in the Cathedral* was performed in the Chapel. It was clearly powerful, with its use of strobe lighting and recorded voices echoing around the lofty roof space, and was said to have 'enthralled the audience'. The setting provided an alternative location to the main hall where the limitations of the stage were beginning to be felt.

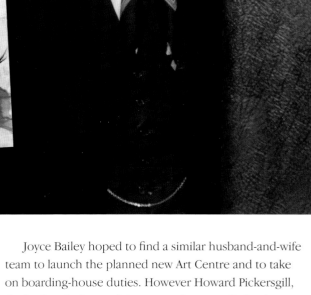

Fiona McAndrew as Robert Southey in The Parable of Talents *1983*

Extra-curricular Activities

Mrs Bailey's early vision of how St Mary's could be moved to its next stage of development was gradually being implemented. It was clearly important to her that the issue of how the girls spent their spare time was resolved, and this involved some structural changes within the school.

In order to draw the school community together within a comfortable and dynamic environment she now advertised for the people she required to fulfil the role. She found just those she was looking for in Colin and Ulla Carter. He was head of English at Badminton School and worked for the Cambridge Examination Board. They arrived in 1978 and, when it was ready, moved into the new staff house linked to Gibbins House. Ulla Carter soon became matron in Gibbins House. Colin Carter was to hold a part-time teaching position and to organise weekend and evening activities for the senior girls. The arrangement was perfect and before long a marked improvement could be seen in the areas they covered. Among the activities they introduced were monthly trips to a field study centre in the Mendips, which necessitated the school's first minibus.

Joyce Bailey hoped to find a similar husband-and-wife team to launch the planned new Art Centre and to take on boarding-house duties. However Howard Pickersgill, the husband of one of the art teachers, applied to become Director of Art Studies on a temporary basis. He was supremely qualified. He had taught art for many years and was a lecturer in Art History and Appreciation at the University of Surrey. He had travelled extensively and had spent a term studying art in Italy. Highly recommended, he was employed initially for one year but in fact stayed until 1983. The Pickersgills oversaw the design of the new studio.

With their improved conditions, house staff were willing to take on extra duties, and so the lives of the girls at the weekends were beginning, as planned, to shift from the school to the houses.

Many societies were now available for the girls and a 'Programme of Achievement' was introduced for the Fourth Form, in which each girl was expected to gain points in areas of sport, arts and crafts and in community life and service.

Along with all the changes taking place in the school, Joyce Bailey's personal life was taking a new direction. She remarried in the summer of 1979 and returned to the school as Mrs Walters.

Day-by-day

A glance at the calendar for each term through this period suggests a busy timetable that brought interesting speakers to St Mary's, took the girls round the country for sports fixtures, concerts, plays, films, exhibitions and on educational and recreational visits. There were many trips abroad: Switzerland, Florence, Venice, Moscow, Normandy, a regular exchange to Toulouse – and the list goes on.

Among the many charitable enterprises, the girls regularly joined the annual Wessex Sponsored Walk. In 1980 St Mary's started to raise money to support the education of an Indian girl for five years and in 1981, the Year of the Disabled, a 'mediaeval fair' on Founders' Day raised money for Stoke Mandeville Hospital.

The school's involvement with the Calne Civic Society began at its inception in response to the A4 slicing through a large section of the town centre in 1968, with pupils regularly attending meetings. Girls also took part in the

Calne Festival and joined John Bentley School for musical events, quizzes and debates.

The Queen's Silver Jubilee Year, 1977, was celebrated at St Mary's by an Elizabethan evening when 700 people were entertained with madrigals, dancing, music and fireworks, and feasted at a banquet of boar's head, suckling pig, syllabub and other Elizabethan dishes.

Top left: *The choir on tour in 1979*

Bottom left: *The kitchen staff dressed for the Elizabethan evening*

100

Changes in the Classroom

Mrs Walter's conviction that St Mary's would serve its pupils far better if the O Level course was extended by a year became reality in 1976, when a Middle Fourth Form was added to the school, with the logistical difficulties it threw up being absorbed into the accommodation alterations of that time.

Saturday morning school proved more controversial, particularly among the staff and the parents of day girls. For some years Joyce Walters had pushed for the innovation, in order to manage the weekend problem of keeping the girls occupied and easing the pressure on the weekday timetable. By 1982 her tenacity paid off and she was given the go-ahead to make the changes for the following September. The staff were assured they would get a full day off during the week and that teaching hours would not increase.

Once introduced, Mrs Walters reported that there was a 'calm, serious and purposeful atmosphere', and that day girls attended 'regularly and without complaint'. There had been some reorganisation of weekday school, with lessons and prep ending earlier for the Fourth Form, giving them more time for other activities. The governors praised Joyce Walters for her persistence in fighting through the issue.

A few months later, Mrs Walters, in collaboration with her staff, decided that the UVI Form boarders should have Saturday mornings for private study with day girls of that form not being required to come in. The boarders would continue to have four long exeats a term rather than the two granted to the rest of the school.

The Curriculum

'I feel it is time that the School had a computer', said Mrs Walters in 1980. St Mary's was offered one on loan for half a term to see 'how the girls react to it'. It was obviously a success because a term later the school had bought a second-hand computer and Mrs Langridge, the head of mathematics, went on a computer course. Over the next few months other members of staff followed in her footsteps. By the end of 1981 a multi-terminal computer system was installed and its integration into the curriculum was being considered. St Mary's soon had a computer club and the Sixth Form had the option of studying computer science as part of a general studies course. Before long computer use was becoming incorporated into many subjects throughout the year groups.

'You really have transformed the School and it is lovely to come back and find such an air of dedication, enthusiasm and success throughout St Mary's, with so much on offer in every field. As you know, I love St Mary's and think you, the governors and the staff are doing it proud'.

— Extract from a letter written to Mrs Walters by an Old Girl, 1982

work during the holidays. The pupils were now receiving more support through tutorials.

Steadily O and A Level results improved, and the number of girls going to university increased, including many to Oxbridge. The innovations within the curriculum and the focus on hard work and independent study were paying off. Many girls were achieving good results and were equipped to aim high at the end of their school careers.

Above: *A geography class in 1983*

Left: *An early computer user*

Decisions to be Made

In 1982 the governors were faced with a dilemma. As a consequence of the introduction of an extra year, a greater number of pupils were leaving after O Levels. The numbers in the school would have to increase in order to maintain a viable Sixth Form and also to help cover rising costs. However they did not want to lose the small and intimate atmosphere which had always been the strength of St Mary's. The choice was between retrenching at just below 300 and continuing the expansion to 330.

In either event, it was decided that two new classrooms should be built on Chapel Lawn for the LIV Form so that they could be more closely integrated within the School House area. These went ahead on two levels by the Chapel, and in the autumn of the following year Joyce Walters commented on how pleasant they were for staff and pupils alike, with fewer incidents of home-sickness among the new girls.

Mrs Walters had a keen eye for keeping subject options relevant to the changes in society at large and to the demands of further education. O Level candidates were offered a wider range of modern languages and all the girls were required to do separate science subjects, which led more to take science at A Level.

Over the years she introduced further AO courses for the Sixth Form and a general course which included business studies, current affairs and economics, the last of these becoming an A Level choice. All A Level courses were allocated eight periods a week, and parents and pupils alike were reminded of the need for girls to put time into their

Music

The retirement of Miss Nesbitt in 1975 was inevitably hugely significant for the Music Department. The years of experience that she brought were over, but the change opened the opportunity for new ideas to be explored. The following year, and for years after, St Mary's entered pupils into the Mid-Somerset Music Festival, a competition in which they had considerable success. Among the first entrants were Nicola and Alexandra Bibby; the same year Alexandra won a BBC award for the most talented young musician in the West of England. A couple of years later, Nicola joined the Kensington Philharmonic Orchestra as soloist in a performance of Greig's *Piano Concerto in A Minor*.

Now began a period when St Mary's took its music to a far wider audience. Under the auspices of the director of music, Mr Cowley, the Consort of Voices began an annual series of tours to cathedrals around the country, beginning with a visit to Chester Cathedral and Beverley and York Minsters. Subsequent years took them to Wales, the South West and the South coast area.

New music-making groups appeared, among them a madrigal ensemble; the Schola Cantorum, in which pupils joined with local male singers; girls were part of the Wansdyke Sinfonietta; and solo singing lessons began. The many choirs and instrumental groups performed in local churches and schools, in competitions and for occasions within St Mary's. A highlight of the spring term had been the chamber music competition, for many years judged by Dr Still. In 1972 the family of Cecilia James (Livingstone) gave a generous award in her memory, with the competition subsequently carrying her name.

The Music Department was thriving under the directorship of Mr Cowley with the help of some able musicians including Martin Bochmann, a cellist, who for many years conducted the orchestras, challenging and inspiring them with some demanding works. Helping to weave musical magic through school life were the inspirational talents of three sets of sisters: the Bibbys, the Laidlays and the Stows.

Although the musical tradition of the school was as strong as ever, staff and pupils were not working under the easiest of conditions. Practice rooms were small and scattered, teaching rooms were inadequate and pianos needed refurbishment or replacing. In 1982, Mr Cowley's successor brought all these matters to the attention of the governors. Perhaps the conditions began to have an effect on the morale of the department, as it is clear from the records that for a time a decline in enthusiasm for music set in.

The choir in the Chapel 1980s

It was at this time that more generous Sixth Form scholarships were introduced, first for science and mathematics and later for English and modern languages.

By June 1983 St Mary's was on a high. Excellent examination results the previous year and a record number of applications led the governors to comment that 'they must ensure that the momentum is maintained', describing the situation as, 'a personal triumph for the headmistress'. This was the endorsement that was needed to move ahead with expansion. In addition to the necessary improvements to the fabric of the school, they aimed to have more live-in academic house staff and to engage a chaplain.

The need for an appealing Sixth Form chimed with Joyce Walters' long-held desire to give the Sixth Form more independence and privileges. She had already allowed them to forgo uniform; now was the time to build a separate boarding house. By the end of the year plans were put out to tender for a Sixth Form house on St Cecilia's lawn and simultaneously an extension to the Science Block. Well-managed finances obviated the need for a further appeal.

The Sixth Form House (Joyce Walters)

In the summer of 1984 work was proceeding on the new boarding house. The hope was that it would provide an intimate and friendly environment which would nurture the spirit of the school. It was to stand in part of the staff garden, extending at the front into St Cecilia's garden, avoiding the much-loved copper beech tree. The development was to have three sections: common rooms for study and recreation; 40 study bedrooms and a flat for the housemistress; and a bungalow for the deputy head. An 18th-century temple, once gracing St Cecilia's garden and more latterly a potting shed, would now stand in a courtyard.

Additions to the Science Block provided a new laboratory and a classroom for the Sixth Form, which in the future could be adapted for science.

Above: *Joyce Walters House*

Left: *Alison Mayhew and Priscilla Bain in a Plumer Wing study bedroom in the 1980s*

Right: *A trip on the Kennet and Avon canal after O Levels*

The house was furnished with the help of Mrs Rachel Benson, one of the governors (and Old Girl); the curtains were made by the housekeeping staff under the guidance of Mrs Robinson; the garden was redesigned using shrubs given by the leavers of 1984 and the pond refurbished. The whole project was ready for use by September 1985, but Mrs Walters' years at St Mary's had by then drawn to a close.

Mrs Walters Moves On

Joyce Walters had set out as headmistress with clear ideas as to how St Mary's could develop in order to help her girls rise to greater academic challenges and embrace a wider range of activities, while at the same time improving the well-being of the staff and pupils. She single-mindedly pursued her goals and saw her determination bear fruit. After nearly 13 years she had the opportunity of returning to her own city, Bristol, to take up the headship of Clifton High School.

Mrs Walters' path at St Mary's had not always been easy, but she gained much admiration for the leadership she had displayed, the enthusiasm she engendered and the respect she gave the girls. She had personality and style, as well as a shrewd understanding of the individual pupils who shared their time with her at St Mary's. Her commitment to the school, to reaching out to the wider community of parents and Old Girls and to developing ideals and standards in the girls that would serve them well in their future lives, is now part of the fabric of St Mary's history. The school took a large step forward during those years thanks to her vision and guidance; as Kay Stedmond said, she was a 'special' headmistress. Looking back in her retirement she in turn wrote, 'St Mary's was, and is, a very special place.

Sport

In the ebb and flow of school life sport had always held its place, sometimes with great enthusiasm and success. The changing seasons brought a different set of activities both inside and out and gave a pace and familiarity, as one term slid into the next. Occasionally a new sport was added which brought a surge of redirected enthusiasm for new experiences. Or perhaps it was a more niche sport at which some pupils already had some expertise. In these years, both horse-riding and a skiing holiday were on offer.

Towards the end of the 1970s there was concern that team games were not popular. Two senior girls were given positions as head and deputy head of games in order to encourage and support the teams. Soon participation picked up and results improved, so that by the end of Mrs Walters' time there was a thriving department which, as well as the main games, offered a raft of individual sports and clubs, including a hockey club which was so successful that it produced its own team. Award schemes were followed in gymnastics, life-saving, athletics and trampoline, and girls took part in county tournaments.

Above: *Mrs Bailey presenting prizes at the St Margaret's Sports Day 1975*

Left: *The St Mary's gym in the 1970s*

I remember the School and the girls who were there with me, with great affection'.

She was delighted with the appointment of Delscey Burns, the next headmistress, commenting later, 'We thought alike and I was confident the School would flourish under her leadership, as indeed it did'. In characteristic generosity of spirit, Joyce introduced Delscey to the staff at a number of small dinners. She herself was given a good send-off by the parents, staff and girls at a series of parties at the end of the spring term.

Mr Colin Carter – Acting Headmaster

St Mary's now had an interregnum of one term before the new headmistress was to take up her post. Colin Carter had become a loyal and highly effective deputy to Mrs Walters and it was to him that the task fell of carrying the school though this period. Paying tribute to him when he left St Mary's in 1986, Mrs Colette Culligan remarked on him steering the school 'with an absolutely characteristic vigour which earned him the increased respect of colleagues, pupils and parents alike'.

Top right: Pupils in the orchard by Gibbins House in the 1970s

Bottom right: A letter to Arabella Fitzmaurice from her father on their arrangements for attending a Rolling Stones concert

BOWOOD HOUSE
CALNE
WILTSHIRE
SN11 OLZ
TEL. CALNE 813343 (HOUSE)
TEL. CALNE 812102 (OFFICE)

23rd June, 1982

Darling Arabella.

Mrs. Walters has kindly given permission for you to go to the Rolling Stones on Friday night, and I will collect you and Imogen after our Estate Meeting.

The time of the concert is 7.30, and perhaps we might want to change and have a bath before we go to it, so we should leave here just before 5 o'clock.

All love
Daddy.

Lady Arabella Fitzmaurice,
St. Mary's School,
Calne

107

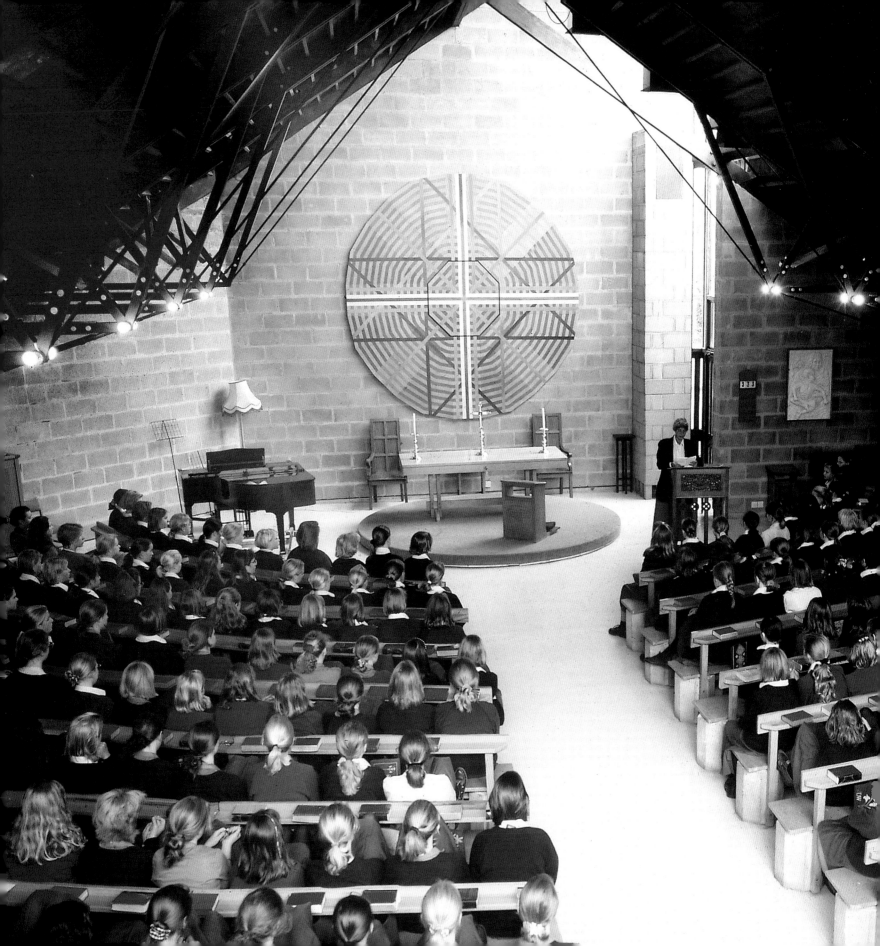

CHAPTER FIVE

Delscey Burns
1985–96

'**O**ne of St Mary's greatest strengths is the sense of continuity which underpins the everyday life of the School.' These words were written by Miss Delscey Burns at the end of her first year. Among her early duties as headmistress had been to host the opening of the new boarding house in the presence of two of her predecessors, Mrs Walters and Miss Gibbins. It was a happy occasion which brought together many visitors, including pupils past and present, in celebration of another milestone in the history of St Mary's School. Then in May of 1986 Miss Burns and the school community said goodbye to Kay Stedmond who, from 1947, had served with three headmistresses and taught both mothers and their daughters.

Above: *Miss Delscey Burns*

Left: *The school Chapel*

'Imagine a school of 120 girls. After a morning's work and lunch, a time for rest and quiet reading is scheduled though not easily enforced. The whole school then goes out to games or for a walk. The single PE teacher expects the help of senior girls to supervise the games. After two more lessons and tea, two hours of prep runs up to 7.00pm supper. The LIV Form leave prep at 6.20pm and armed with Bibles, they visit the headmistress to read and talk about a Bible passage and anything else that crops up.

'There is a careful procedure for granting freedoms. Starting as a "Nothing", when any step out of school has to be accompanied by an adult or Sixth Formers, a girl eventually becomes a "Half" when she may go out with those more privileged. Finally the status of "Whole" is reached which permits those now deemed to be really sensible to go for a walk or shop in a foursome'.

– Kay Stedmond looks back to the St Mary's she knew when she arrived nearly 40 years before

With Delscey Burns' arrival, St Mary's entered a time of youthful enthusiasm, of joy and of sadness. Her headship was to challenge her in ways she had not imagined, but her personality shaped the lives of many of those who were with her at St Mary's during those years.

Miss Burns was writing up her doctorate in educational management at Oxford when she was approached by Margaret Ellis, one of the governors of St Mary's and later chairman. The Governing Body was searching for a new headmistress with little success until Delscey Burns was suggested. She perhaps did not fulfil the criteria they had in mind as she was young and had not held a deputy headship. However she was well prepared for her interview and, most impressively, she had energy. She clearly made a strong impression and the governors, in a leap of faith, appointed her.

Miss Burns describes being flattered by the appointment but unrealistic as to what the role involved. Her experience in teaching was as head of the English Department at St George's School in Ascot, but she had never chaired a meeting and was to be faced with staff meetings of over 70 people. Having done no public speaking prior to arriving at St Mary's, she would practise every public utterance beforehand.

Despite these drawbacks, Delscey Burns was familiar with the place of management within education and she had the gift of being able to communicate and empathise with those she met. Whatever anxieties she felt, she presented a confident face to the outside world.

Left: *Pupils at the opening of Joyce Walters House*

Right: *The Governing Body*

Back l–r, Mr Henly, the Revd Reynolds, Mr Southwell, Lord Farnham, the Earl of Shelburne, Mr Morgan,

Front l–r Mrs Ellis, Miss Burns, Dr Cameron, Mrs Rotherham, Mrs Benson

Top right: *A school magazine cover designed by Honor Peters and Charlotte Patrick*

The Governors

Dr Bremner Cameron, Chairman of the Governors, oversaw the appointment of Miss Burns. He is remembered as a kindly man with a sensible approach to life: a steady pair of hands. Towards the end of Dr Cameron's time as chairman, and with a number of retirements on the horizon, the governors reviewed how they functioned as a body and what particular skills and interests should be represented as they looked to their future composition.

In 1987 they amended the Articles of the Association on the suggestion of Canon Reynolds, Vicar of Calne and a member of the Governing Body. He looked back at the principles on which Canon Duncan had founded St Mary's and posed that, in the current more ecumenical age, they should consider that Christians of denominations other than the Church of England might be eligible as governors, subject to the majority being communicants of the Church of England. This change was soon ratified by the Bishop.

In 1988 the governors were joined by Miss Pat Lancaster. She seems to have been one of those people who stand out in memories. In her obituary in the 2004 News Sheet, Delscey Burns described her passion for education and English literature and her concern that her pupils should develop an 'inner resilience and resourcefulness'. She had been a member of staff at St Mary's in Miss Gibbins' time, and later Delscey Burns' own headmistress. When she joined the governors she was headmistress of Wycombe Abbey School. Miss Lancaster is remembered by Mr Richard Southwell QC, who later became Chairman of the Governors, as a wonderfully warm person with huge experience within education. She was a great support to Miss Burns.

On her second day, Delscey Burns was confronted with addressing the whole school in Chapel. Unsure what to say, she asked for advice. With nothing specific forthcoming she put her own mark on the occasion by speaking of the school rules and saying how she wanted the girls to be able to talk about any problems rather than stepping out of line. This helped set the ground rules for when discipline problems inevitably arose, and epitomised Miss Burns' preference for discussion over confrontation.

The 1980s were a period of change in the world of education. The introduction of GCSE to replace O Level would have a significant impact on all secondary schools including St Mary's. Staff needed training, resources acquiring and timetables adapting. Soon after, the National Curriculum was introduced, prompting the publication of league tables, and the Children's Act coloured the approach to boarding. Life at St Mary's would be busy.

Looking Forward

After his term's tenure, Colin Carter had reported that the school was well organised with a high level of competence and enthusiasm among the staff. An impressive school magazine produced at the end of Miss Burns' first year presents a well-focused, busy, happy face to the outside world. Many aspects of school life are shown, with contributions from staff and girls. It conveys a great sense of optimism and community at St Mary's. Miss Burns certainly felt that the 'warmth, friendliness and trust' she found in those around her helped her to settle in quickly. In return, her youth and energy made it easy for the girls to relate to her.

St Mary's had been experiencing an increasing demand for places and this was now intensified by press coverage of the new headmistress. However the governors had to be realistic about the future, and at the end of her first

the options available and encourage them to be receptive to the opportunities, particularly the shift of emphasis in girls' education towards science and engineering. Group activities would pool their talents and open their eyes to the power of co-operation. They would need to be competent computer users and aware of the technology of design and its impact on the environment.

Delscey Burns recognised that good teaching helped the pupils develop a framework that allowed them to make well-informed, intelligent decisions on ethical and topical issues and to present their opinions effectively in private or public. Greater access to newspapers and journals and opportunities for debate would further develop these abilities, while closer involvement with local causes would encourage a wider altruistic outlook.

In recent years St Mary's had seen a great improvement in the facilities for some areas of the creative arts. Miss Burns' belief that the girls should have experience of a broad range of leisure activities chimed with the recognised need for improvement in other areas. She wanted to promote all aspects of athletic, creative, aesthetic and cultural activities, including the Duke of Edinburgh's Award Scheme, which had started at St Mary's the previous autumn.

She also felt that the school should look at how different facets of health education, including health-related fitness, could be made relevant to the pupils' physical and emotional development and incorporated both within and outside the curriculum.

year Miss Burns presented a paper on how St Mary's might develop. Well aware of changes in society at large, she looked at their possible impact on the pupils' education.

Careers were no longer for life and the girls would need to be flexible in fitting family life into a changing labour market. Good careers advice could make them aware of

Left: *In the school laboratories*

Below: *From the school magazine*

Above: Delscey Burns with pupils in Coulter Library

Other Matters

Miss Burns, however, had more immediate issues to manage. The heavy demand for boarding places at St Mary's required astute decisions on when to close the waiting list, but at the same time there was a need to encourage good candidates for Sixth Form entry. The number of pupils in the school was a careful balance of the boarding places available and the desirable number of girls for economic purposes. A steady entry of day girls was important for the school and with more day places to fill, a publicity drive, which included local advertising and open days, was begun.

The staff were investing time and effort in managing the challenges of implementing the new GCSE courses, and Miss Burns recognised that the school had a responsibility to them beyond their statutory rights. She wanted to ensure that they had opportunity within the school to gain maximum experience, so placing them in a good position when applying for promotion. She described them as 'efficient, loyal and dedicated', and the records show clearly the thought she put into the welfare of the staff. She awarded incentive allowances to those who were particularly hard working, who had contributed greatly to the school, or who had taught an unusually demanding range of classes.

Calne and St Mary's School

St Mary's School was born of Calne and has its roots within the local Church and community. As years have passed, it has looked further afield in order to sustain itself, but it is situated in the town and feels a commitment to it. At the time of Miss Burns' arrival the school employed 73 Calne residents and used local traders, bringing nearly £300,000 annually into the area's economy.

In 1981 Harris' bacon-processing factory, which had dominated the centre of the town, was forced to close, with the loss of 20 per cent of local jobs, and in 1984 the buildings were demolished. The Calne Civic Society looked to regenerate the town centre, work which St Mary's actively supported. The following year the school lent its backing to the community in opposing the plans for a theme park, Frontier City, described as the 'Cowboy Capital of the West', on the outskirts of Calne.

Community service in the town became part of the Duke of Edinburgh's Award, and the girls frequently had combined musical and sporting events and lectures with the John Bentley School. The Calne Music and Arts Festival was strongly supported by the girls and staff, two of whom were on the committee, while others performed for the event.

Local groups used the school facilities, as they still do, and when St Mary's theatre was opened in 1990, the school was able to offer a wonderful venue in which the West Wiltshire Youth Orchestra could perform.

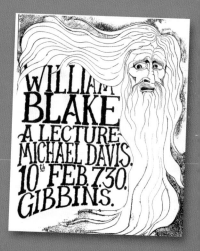

A 1987 poster

On the pastoral side Miss Burns was keen to provide accommodation for a third residential couple. With the movement of personnel there had been a change of emphasis again within the boarding houses. There were no longer many residential academic staff but Delscey Burns was content with this, as she wanted to promote the sense of the girls returning to a 'home' after their school day. The housemistresses at this time reported to the headmistress via the deputy head. Communication systems were not always strong and so she enrolled a senior housemistress who could support the house staff and provide a link with the academic side of the school. Looking back at this time, academic staff remember that the only duties they had in the houses were 'knicker checking' at the beginning of term, when they made sure that all clothing was named.

Another area Delscey Burns was very keen to establish was the employment of a chaplain, but despite much outside help it proved very difficult to find a suitable person. Eventually, in 1991, a parish team lead by the Vicar of Calne, the Revd Alan Woods, who as tradition had it was a governor of St Mary's, was engaged to prepare girls for Confirmation, help with services within the school and to act as counsellor. This appointment released some time for Miss Burns.

Plans for Development

On Delscey Burns' arrival, St Mary's had 315 girls in the school, 78 of whom were in the Sixth Form. The governors knew that some departments felt keenly the need for more space. High on the list were better facilities for music, but close behind was the hope of a larger assembly hall which would provide improved space for drama. The PE Department were lamenting the poor state of the grass tennis courts in front of the Dining Room and the lack of an all-weather surface for winter games. All hoped that the swimming pool could be covered, enabling it to be used throughout the year.

Many alternatives were contemplated for the positioning of new buildings, change of room use, opening up of attic spaces and conversion of cellars. During Delscey Burns' first term some minor work was done to provide rooms for the Companies which could also accommodate visitors, and to enlarge the kitchen. The domestic staff mess room was moved to the floor above, so releasing space within the kitchen. At Miss Burns' request, plans were laid to open up the cellar of School House as a games room for the youngest pupils. This cellar is approached from Red Hall down steps, at the top of which is an area that for many years was used to store large bottles of ink for the girls' pens.

In June 1987 the governors were presented with possible sites for a Music School, including the sunken garden near Plumer Wing and in the Top Hall above the Dining Room. In the event, the place chosen was between Plumer Wing and the Matthews Building, its position at the centre of the school mirroring the place music has always held at St Mary's. The Jubilee Building, which had stood nearby since St Mary's 50th birthday in 1923, would have to be demolished and its facilities relocated, some within a new extension to the Art School. Its weather-vane, with an image of a pig in recognition of Calne's main industry, was moved onto the roof of the pottery section of the Art School, where it can be seen to this day.

Developments in the near future were to be financed by a bank loan and an appeal, taking advantage of favourable tax laws on charitable giving. While St Mary's was advancing with its building programme the junior school, St Margaret's, was also beginning a major phase

Left: *The weather-vane was moved from the roof of Jubilee Building to the Art School*

Music

In Miss Burns' first couple of years, before the luxury of the new Music School facilities were available, music-making continued in its many forms, as was the tradition. A highlight of 1986 was a service presented by the choirs and orchestra of St Mary's in Calne parish church in aid of the Salisbury Spire Appeal. Focused round the theme of 'praise', the school raised £600 and received a letter of thanks from the Prince of Wales, President of the Salisbury Spire Project.

In 1987, despite the promise of a new building for music on the horizon, the school set up a music laboratory with ten keyboards, and an adjoining eight-track recording studio with synthesisers, and as the Music School was rising from its foundations, St Mary's resounded to the practice sounds of 14 enthusiastic players of a new drum kit.

In the autumn of 1990 the music at St Mary's had the huge benefit of the arrival of Keith Abrams as music director. The following summer he took the Chamber Choir, with Mr Field who had coached them, to Wales for a week taking in an international Eistedfodd, where the girls came fifth to the likes of choirs from Lithuania and Spain. They also performed in a concert with a male voice choir. Exceptionally well looked after by their hosts, between various engagements they had a chance to explore the Welsh countryside.

St Cecilia, the patron saint of church music, is a name strongly associated with St Mary's, reflecting the importance of the musical life of the school. During Joyce Walters' time the tradition had arisen of an annual St Cecilia's Day concert within the school, and this continued under Miss Burns. The format varied from year to year with outside performers, the school music staff or pupils taking part.

Each year St Mary's girls participated in the Mid-Somerset Festival with considerable success. Visiting professionals gave recitals and master-classes, informal music-making groups formed, events were celebrated and the school's musicians presented a highly acclaimed *Last Night of the Proms*.

Many people remember this period of St Mary's for the exceptionally high standard of the music, overseen by Keith Abrams, Geoff Field and Colin Howard. Past members of staff describe it as 'fantastic' and as 'taking a leap forward'. It helped to reinforce the strong place that Chapel services held in the daily lives of the girls. As always in a shifting population, old friends moved on, new young talent emerged and the musical years turned full circle.

Top left: *Busking for Charaday 1994*

Left: *Keith Abrams*

115

of development, and even as the Music School was going through a detailed planning stage, thoughts were moving ahead to funding a hall for drama. The careful juggling of the budget was now about to fall to a new bursar as Commander Harwood, who had been at St Mary's for 11 years, was due to retire.

The Music School

St Mary's were lucky at this period to have Sir David Willcocks on the Board of Governors. He had joined in 1985, around the time of his retirement as Director of the Royal College of Music, and was already known to St Mary's as he had been the school's own visiting director of music in the late 1940s. He was able to give professional advice on the requirements of the Music School. Because of the site, it was to be a four-storey building with teaching rooms, practice rooms, a recording studio, a classroom and an orchestral room large enough for small recitals on the top floor. This room, as well as having excellent acoustics, has a wonderful outlook over the school grounds and to the White Horse and the Monument on the distant downs.

Looking ahead to the new Music School, a pupil wrote in the school magazine, 'No more queues for practice rooms, no more struggling to hear your piano teacher's words of wisdom because of the saxophone next door and no more practising in the cupboards'.

By the autumn term of 1989 the Music School was ready for use; a greatly improved environment for continuing the musical tradition that had beat through the heart of St Mary's for so long. The link with the past was clear as the orchestral room became known as Nesbitt after Barbara Nesbitt, who for so many years had fostered the School's music.

It was of some concern when it was discovered that owing to the dimensions of the two grand pianos, a crane had to be used to lift them into place through the windows. However this was achieved and, thanks to its timing with bonfire night, the new building's opening by Dr Cameron was followed by an evening of fireworks and celebration.

Above: *The Music School*

Left: *Keith Abrams with the orchestra*

Right: *Staff members Liz Thompson, Philippa Hobson and Jane Dickson*

The Curriculum

Both the introduction of the GCSE courses and the demands of the National Curriculum were to influence the school's approach to planning its academic programme through these years.

Establishing the foundations for the new courses required thought and time but they were soon underway, despite some inevitable teething problems. The first girls to take the examinations in 1988 achieved excellent results, which was encouraging but, as following years showed, not necessarily a good indicator of potential at A Level.

St Mary's, along with other independent schools, was not bound by the stipulations of the newly introduced National Curriculum. It seemed wise, nonetheless, to consider its requirements in order that pupils were not put at a disadvantage in the long term. Miss Burns and the governors were keen to preserve the school's strong academic bias and wide choice of GCSEs, including minority subjects such as Latin and Greek, but alterations were made to its science course structure; a computer and IT course was added, including keyboard skills; and the staff looked at the area of creative arts, which had until then fallen under the extra-curricular programme.

Room changes gave more space for practical science work, an improved computer centre and a bias towards design and technology in existing classes. A compulsory creative arts course was added for the LV pupils.

The Staff

There is no doubt that during the introduction of the GCSE courses the staff were required to put in a great deal of extra time. The weaknesses that they found in the curricula and the adaptations that the examination boards were forced to make over the first few years must have caused frustration. However, Delscey Burns found the staff receptive to her leadership and she had the confidence to delegate to them, recognising them as 'bright and hard-working'. Together they steered the school through the difficulties, with the girls gaining some excellent results in the process.

Delscey Burns had her own ideas on the sort of school that she wanted to promote. In later years she described how she felt that organisations should ideally be light-

> *'Their unstinting support and generally humorous approach, combined with the same attitude within the senior staff, made my experience of being a head a lot less lonely and a lot more fun than it would have otherwise been.'*
>
> – Miss Delscey Burns remembering her office staff

hearted and purposeful, with members showing kindness and respect to each other. Staff remember this as a time of informality, of packed meetings in the staffroom when many decisions were made. Miss Burns was assiduous in discussing each girl with all members of staff before a parents' meeting. They felt well supported by her and recognised her total commitment to the welfare of the girls. She describes how she would try to find the innate nature of each girl, and that she wanted the staff to believe the best of a pupil. The school felt comfortable and, as one member of staff remembers, 'cocooned'. Another described these as 'golden years'.

By all accounts Delscey Burns drew around her staff who had vision, who with her support could observe, listen and be critically supportive of the pupils. Her senior team made a great contribution over the years. Colette

Culligan, who taught English, became deputy head and was an immense support to Delscey Burns, helping to drive through many policy changes. She arrived at St Mary's while Joyce Walters was headmistress and remembers knowing that the school was special when at her first staff meeting, along with academic matters, there was a long discussion as to why one of the girls was having trouble sleeping.

Margaret Beater is remembered by a governor as 'an old-style teacher who was firm but kind and to whom the girls could respond'. She arrived to teach Classics in 1976, becoming senior mistress in 1987 after Mavis Hunter. She replaced Kay Stedmond in the staffroom, taking over her desk by the door and monitoring the comings and goings, always supportive of the staff. She and Mrs Culligan worked together to ensure the daily running of the school, both leaving St Mary's in 1998.

Rather than the many administrative staff that St Mary's has today, Miss Burns had one secretary when she arrived, Anna Blundell, who combined the roles of both the headmistress and the school's secretary. Together they worked long hours, and when Anna left her job was split into two, with Jane Bull as PA and Jill MacLaine as school secretary. Miss Burns describes how they all did an extraordinary job in presenting the ethos of the school to the outside world and conveying to her the concerns of staff, parents and pupils, taking some of the pressure off her. They remembered her as great fun, appreciative and supportive of them, but challenging to work for, as she thought and acted so quickly.

The Fabric of the School

The grounds and maintenance staff had a continual programme of work to see to, including any unexpected problems that arose. In 1988 St Cecilia's was being used as a roost by a flock of pigeons that had been displaced by the demolition of the Harris' factory. 1990 blew in with a storm that damaged some of the school's roofs and uprooted 40 trees, leading to the closure of the school for a few days. Later the bursar announced that death-watch beetle had been found in the floor joists of St Cecilia's and a colony of bank voles had taken up residence by the hockey pitch. Among those overseeing the many problems was a young

Vince Pennock, who had joined the ground staff in 1985, later becoming head of the department and continuing at St Mary's to the present day.

Miss Burns' desire to make the boarding houses and common rooms more comfortable and welcoming as places to return to during breaks in the school day led to an upgrading of the boarding houses. Better use of rooms and new curtains, carpets and furniture helped deal with overcrowding and a 'tatty' appearance. Carpeting the dormitories in School House was a luxury of which girls of previous generations could not have imagined. Along with these changes the accommodation for the house staff was greatly improved.

Through its history, St Mary's had from time to time to deal with planning matters within Calne that affected the school. In 1989 the school were once again faced with a scheme that proposed to manage congestion in Curzon Street by running an inner relief road through St Cecilia's garden. After a strong petition to the County Council by the bursar, and supported by town councillors and the local MP, the plan was overturned.

The entrance hall in the Theatre

Left: West Side Story
*(1995) with Kate Dierckx
as Riff and the Jets*

Below: *The Delscey
Burns Theatre*

The Delscey Burns Theatre

The governors at this time did not let the grass grow under
their feet. Having seen what was needed to give St Mary's
the facilities of an up-to-date school as highlighted by Miss
Burns, they pushed on with planning and funding a new
hall for drama. At first a site had been considered at the
corner of the lower pitch at the east end of the Matthews
Building, but later an area was chosen by the path leading
up to St Margaret's, which offered space for parking.

The Theatre was designed to be flexible: able to be a
theatre-in-the-round, an apron-and-thrust stage theatre
or a proscenium theatre. It could also be used for Mark
Reading, lectures, films and recreational sport. After a
visit to the newly converted Marlborough College theatre,
refinements were made to maximise efficiency. Cost
restrictions meant some additions, including the scenery
dock and green rooms, were added in later phases, with
the help of a grant from the Wolfson Foundation. Initially,
the green room accommodation was deployed as a fitness
space for PE, but this was changed when St Mary's Sports
Centre, with its spacious fitness suite, was built.

A blizzard just before Christmas in 1990 did not deter
the parents who came to watch the first production, *The
Importance of Being Earnest*. Delscey Burns remarked that

the 'quality of the acoustics and flexibility of the seating
and acting space make it a joy to work in'.

The Delscey Burns Theatre was a tribute to the
headmistress and her love of the performing arts. On
Founders' Day 1996, in a ceremony presided over by
Rachel Benson, Chairman of the Governors, the Theatre
was named after Miss Burns. Some years after she left
St Mary's, a portrait of Miss Burns by Bradford-on-Avon
artist David Cobley was hung in the Theatre.

Drama in the Delscey Burns Years

There are some things that linger in the memories of our school days and high among them must be the theatrical performances that we took part in or watched. Whether produced by forms, dormitories, companies or as the main school play of the year, the performances bring together groups of pupils in ways that challenge, broaden horizons and give fun. Within St Mary's drama holds such a position.

When Miss Burns arrived at St Mary's the main school hall, now known as Top Hall, was the setting for many of the plays. It had served its purpose for 50 years and had seen some exceptional productions. Despite the limitations, the staff and girls often put on works that drew admiration from those who witnessed them. In 1987 a parent wrote that 'There are school plays … and there are school plays, and occasionally, just occasionally, one experiences a major dramatic presentation. Such was the case with *The Crucible*'.

With the completion of the Theatre, St Mary's was able to move into a whole new arena: to discover the magical technical opportunities now open to the directors and to explore the possibilities of an adaptable space. It was a challenge that they grasped enthusiastically, producing a show that traced the history of the British stage musical in a collaboration of drama, music and the PE Department. This was followed later by an exciting lower school production of *Bugsy Malone*. These however were a toe-dip in the water for what was to come. The arrival in 1992 of Lilian Leadbetter in the English Department as head of drama brought a professionalism which would in time match much on the public stage. Before long Lilian had formed

Georgina Briscoe as Titania in A Midsummer Night's Dream *(1993)*

a separate department for drama and the enthusiasm among the girls was immense. *Jesus Christ Superstar,* in 1992, drew together 96 girls from throughout the years in a production of which Miss Burns commented, 'I have seldom felt so proud of the school'. She praised the 'maturity, depth and power of those playing the leading parts'. It set the standard very high for the future. It also marked the beginning of a wonderful working relationship with Sir Tim Rice, whose daughter, Eva, played Mary Magdalene.

Following years saw LVI Form productions including *Murder in the Cathedral,* and in 1994, a whole school staging of *Amadeus*, described as 'an enthralling and disturbing experience for cast and audience alike', in which the audience sat 'riveted'. A visitor from Marlborough College said that it was the best production he had ever seen in a school. In the autumn of 1995, Delscey Burns' last year, the Drama Department returned to a musical, *West Side Story*, which required complex staging and musical arrangements, with 'resounding success'.

Boundaries were being pushed and drama was moving higher up the agenda. The enthusiasm and talent now being shown prompted the school to incorporate drama more fully into the curriculum. It soon became a GCSE option, and a year's A Level course in theatre studies was begun, with immediate success. This was enriched by a series of workshops lead by RSC actors, including David Troughton, in which the pupils learnt, through physical, vocal and improvisation exercises, the rhythms and movement of Shakespearean verse.

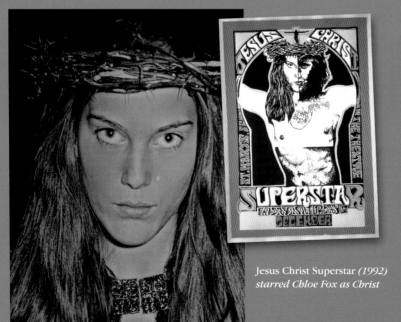

Jesus Christ Superstar *(1992)*
starred Chloe Fox as Christ

Other Projects

With the completion of the Music School and Theatre, the PE Department staff were keen to promote their needs. They produced a comprehensive report which highlighted the inadequacy of many of their facilities: the warped wall bars, the undulating pitches and the fact that in order to use the tumble-drier in the swimming hut, the heating had to be turned off. These were only a few of their concerns. The low height of the ceiling in the gym meant that St Mary's own form of badminton had to be played, and even then not during the summer term, when the gym was used for examinations. And always, simmering in the background, was the issue of a very cold and antiquated swimming pool. In response, the governors agreed that a sports hall should be included as a priority of future projects.

Along with the eye-catching building developments, St Mary's had more utilitarian matters to deal with, ones that involved a large financial commitment. In order to comply with the Food Safety Act of 1990, new equipment for the safe storage and preparation of food was required which needed additional space. The existing kitchen had been built in the 1930s when the school was much smaller.

Mrs Tilley retired in 1986 after 19 years at St Mary's

In 1991 the kitchen staff were providing several hundred meals each lunchtime, including those for St Margaret's children. Plans were made to extend the kitchen onto the platform area outside, redesign the internal space and re-equip it. After some unforeseen setbacks the cost came to around £450,000, but the kitchen was ready for use by September 1992. Gone now was the pig-swill bucket collected by the pig-man and remembered by Rita Hulme in Housekeeping, who is still working at St Mary's. When she arrived in 1976 milk churns stood by the cold-room door from which jugs were filled and carried to the San. Although for 25 years she was an assistant housekeeper, at busy times she would help in the kitchen.

In the PE Department

Among the earliest work after Miss Burns' arrival was the replacement of the four grass tennis courts with an all-weather surface primarily for tennis but also for hockey practice and six-a-side matches. It was expected that the work would be complete by the summer term of 1986 but a series of problems with the quality of the workmanship meant that only two courts were of an adequate standard for a demonstration match by Frew McMillan and three others from the All England Lawn Tennis Club. However the match did go ahead and was umpired by the school's first team captain, Camilla Benson, with the U15 team as ball boys. Each player then played mixed doubles with members of the school teams. The sorry state of affairs with the courts continued and the whole surface had to be re-laid, until finally in September of 1987 the courts were all ready for use.

Despite the far-from-ideal sports facilities, the school at this time had some excellent sports teachers, including lacrosse players with national and international experience. Among them was Sharon Cole, an England player, and Liz Thompson (then Miss Smith), who played for Wales and has continued to teach at St Mary's up to the present day. She also ran the Duke of Edinburgh's Award expedition work which was becoming increasingly part of the school's activities.

Liz remembers the sport at St Mary's when she arrived in the late 1980s as being taken less seriously than later, with limited skills practice sessions. There was enthusiasm,

MADHOUSE

St. Mary's is one of those schools,
In which all of the pupils are fools,
They are raucous and mad
And hopelessly bad
And they like to break all of the rules.

Miss Burns, the unfortunate head,
Was heard, I believe, to have said
"This school is so wild
I can't find <u>one</u> good child,
Very soon I shall end up near dead!"

From the teachers, the point is agreed
"The school is a madhouse indeed –
A night on the tiles
Is preferred to their files
And 'O' Levels are things they don't need!"

But us pupils don't see why we should
Be angelic, even if we could –
You have to agree
How boring we'd be
If we were so delightfully good!

NICOLA WAINMAN

And the Rest of School Life

A pupil writing in 1996 pondered the fact that though she knew that so many St Mary's girls had walked the path of discovery before her, she felt as if the experiences were unique to her. Miss Burns had talked of how St Mary's 'fostered the individuality of the girls within the framework of a lively community in which high standards are achieved in a wide variety of spheres'. Through the range of activities available to the girls outside the curriculum they could wend their own distinctive way.

Reading the school magazines of this period one gets a strong sense of issues of wider interest being of concern to the girls. They explored the arguments around the depletion of the ozone layer, nuclear power, the destruction of the rain forests, Britain's place in Europe and animal testing. They looked at the work of Amnesty International and Greenpeace and at racism, particularly

Above: *A school trip to the downs*

Left: *From the 1986 school magazine*

Right: *Lucinda Browne 1988*

however, and girls joined in early morning runs, lunch-time clubs and evening fitness groups.

As the school moved into the 1990s they had success in many areas of sport. The year 1991 saw a great improvement in athletics, with 12 track and 18 field event school records being broken, and the following year 11 girls represented North Wiltshire in the county trials. By 1993 St Mary's girls made up half of the county lacrosse team. They also had representation on county cross-country, netball, athletics and tennis squads.

In among the tournaments, rallies and trials there was time for some more light-hearted friendly matches, including hockey against a series of Eton teams in which St Mary's more than held their own.

'I feel that these worlds are entirely my own domain, that I was first to have my eyes forced open by Orwell, or to be inspired by Elizabeth I, but I feel sure that in reality I am going along a well-trodden path. I am insignificant, but in the same way special, for I am a part of an exclusive band of kindred spirits, searching together for some unknown ultimate aim.'

– WRITTEN BY RACHAEL SAUNDERS, AN UV FORM PUPIL IN 1996

in South Africa, and when world-changing events such as the fall of the Berlin Wall and the first Gulf War were in the news, they investigated the surrounding issues.

There was also an interest in feminism, and one of the many lecturers was Mrs Lamplugh, who spoke on women's self-awareness on behalf of the Suzy Lamplugh Trust. Another lecture was given by Irina Ratushinskaya, a dissident poet who had been held in a Soviet labour camp.

The pupils were making trips abroad as part of their curriculum studies, foreign exchanges were taking place and some girls were undertaking adventure holidays. A highlight of 1988 was a visit to the Soviet Union. Delscey Burns' keen

interest in things equestrian was matched by some of the pupils. Regular riding lessons were taken, one-day-events, for which St Mary's had several teams, were on the calendar and some girls learnt carriage driving as part of their DofE Award. On the science side, a group of LVI Form girls, wanting to construct a robot, attended a micro-electronics club at Chippenham FE College.

In 1993 the Young Enterprise business scheme was introduced to the school. Members of the LVI Form set up a stationery company, Scribo, which produced calendars and writing paper that incorporated some of the school's art work. With the help of outside advisors, they developed many skills and made nearly £1,000 in profit that first year.

Events in the Early 1990s

Despite the recession of this time, pupil numbers at St Mary's remained buoyant. Managing the intake at the different stages of the school was a constant juggling act, with flexibility the secret. Against the national trend, the demand for boarding places was high, as was the desire of the girls at Sixth Form level to stay on. This was welcomed as the sign of a successful school but demanded careful management. Miss Burns had said that she wanted to be free of having to use bunk beds for any of the girls. It became a bit of a running joke that no sooner had she achieved this in one place, then they had to be added somewhere else. Greater numbers in the Sixth Form had led to some girls not having single rooms. The cottage had been renovated to provide beds for four of the girls and in 1993 the extension added to Joyce Walters House gave eight new study bedrooms. Sited in the house car park,

Art

As the Music School went up, and the Jubilee Building came down, some of the Art Department was displaced. A new studio for fine art was added to the existing art rooms, a large kiln was installed and a three-dimensional-design studio was created. The changes enabled the school to more easily meet the challenges of the GCSE course and a new A Level syllabus, both with an emphasis on coursework.

St Mary's girls now had the possibility of hands-on experience in many areas of the creative arts, both as part of the curriculum and in the after-school activities. History of Art courses flourished, and throughout the years, national and international art trips took place, exhibitions were visited and workshops attended.

The year 1993 saw the first exhibition of the work of the Art Department staff in London, opened by the Romanian Ambassador and raising over £800 for Romanian orphans.

The Romanian Ambassador with pupils

three-metre piles had to be driven into the ground for the foundations.

By now the classrooms needed up-grading. The desks that had been intended for exercise books were not coping with the increasing use of ring-binders, the rooms did not have uniformity and the provision of electronic teaching aids was patchy. Improvements to the common rooms helped discourage the use of the classrooms as social spaces.

The staffroom had by now begun to bulge at the seams, with some staff having to share desks. There was no social area separate from the work area, and those preparing audio tapes were aware of their intrusion. Delscey Burns described it as 'anarchic'. Plans were made for a two-level extension to be built in the summer holidays of 1996.

Pastoral Care

Delscey Burns saw St Mary's as holding a special position in that it managed to combine being a happy, reasonably small boarding school with achieving very good academic results – something that she felt was an unusual combination. Under her leadership the school gained a reputation as being person-centred. It offered a safe environment to girls with particular problems who in other places might have been taken out of school, and gave them the chance to obtain good A Level results.

The implementation in 1991 of the Working with Children Act was taken very seriously by St Mary's. Although the school broadly conformed to its requirements they knew that, being a boarding school, the inspectors would look particularly at the quality of their parenting role. The position of the housemistresses was now fully reviewed and a detailed job description issued to them all.

The inspection highlighted that along with the house staff, all adults dealing with the children on a regular basis held the same obligations. This meant that tutoring was given a greater role in providing an opportunity for the pupils to talk to someone privately and regularly. The school day was changed in order to allow specific slots for tutors and tutees to meet and there was recognition of the need for relationships to be based on mutual respect and trust, with the staff having the right counselling skills. A further outcome of the inspection was that telephones for the girls were moved to places with more privacy.

After considering the review, Miss Burns decided on a restructuring of the school. Staff had been heads of Companies for many years and now she wanted them to have a greater leadership role in training both the academic and pastoral staff in their Company and to take on more evening and weekend commitments. Other members of staff would carry the positions of heads of the Fourth, Fifth and Sixth Forms. This installation of a middle management led to a network of channels by which the girls could find support and advice when needed.

Among those members of staff who were gradually taking on different roles, was Sara-Jane Socha. Mrs Socha arrived at St Mary's at the same time as Delscey Burns, to join the History Department, where she became head for

Above: *Founders' Day 1995*

Right: *Mary Hibberd (Combes)*

Day Girls

St Mary's had begun as a day school and continues to welcome day girls, but life for them now is now far more inclusive than in the past. In the early years the day girls often did not feel fully part of school life but despite this, one, Mary Hibberd (Combes), a pupil in the 1930s, remembered her school days with affection. The daughter of a farmer in Bishop's Cannings, her father would drive Mary and her three sisters in either their pony and trap or open-top Morris over the downs to St Mary's.

In her old age Mary recalled how she loved all sports and school work, particularly Classics, and was disappointed that continuing with Latin meant she had to give up geography. She was part of the team that represented the school at the All England Girls' Schools spelling competition. Spelling was a skill that stayed with her, and which she put down to her good grounding in Latin. In the drive home at the end of each day Mary would begin her two hours of homework, which often included learning one of the Collects.

Things changed for day girls over the years, but when Delscey Burns came to St Mary's 50 years later she needed to work at maintaining their numbers and providing a better environment for them. The increase in boarder numbers over the previous years had meant pressure on work space for day girls to study in school. Both girls and their parents began to insist on better facilities, particularly at Sixth Form level. This led in 1992 to some of the old music rooms at the back of the hall being adapted to create a day girls centre, called the Harwood Room after the bursar who took a particular interest in their well-being. An extension added to Joyce Walters boarding house released space, giving the Sixth Form girls private study areas in some of the double bedsits and allowing them to be more fully integrated with the boarders.

'It was as if she took a run up; you could hear her coming, in what I thought were hugely high heels, all the way along Curved Passage, up towards the Chapel, down the aisle and then two quick short steps up the steps and then she swept round to face us. She had the most amazingly commanding presence and more fool you if you weren't listening to every word she said, usually a brilliantly thought out message brought home to us through the world of A.A. Milne's Winnie the Pooh. Her presence resonated far beyond the walls of the Chapel and during her time at St Mary's she always created an element of excitement and awe and huge respect'.

– Sitting in Chapel waiting for Miss Burns to arrive, as remembered by Georgie Bell-Nugent

a time on the death of Mavis Hunter in 1994. In her role as head of the Fifth Form, she oversaw the academic side of the girls' schooling, liaised with the house staff and was responsible for induction into the year. She later became head of the Sixth Form, and under future headmistresses her position changed further. She is remembered affectionately by one pupil from this period, who commented on the 'amazing A Level lessons with inspiring teachers such as Mrs Socha and Mrs Footman. We learned so much from their depth of interest and understanding of their respective subjects'.

Earlier difficulties in finding the right house staff had been exacerbated by their concern at the increasing security problems within the grounds. In 1989 St Mary's employed its own security guard to replace those of an outside company. Sergeant Geoffrey Hunt, previously of the Royal Air Force police, joined the school's residential team (as did his dog), and later his wife worked as a housemistress.

Miss Burns's own personality was a factor in how she approached the care of the pupils. She was aware that she

Above: *Unpacking trunks in St Cecilia's garden 1992*

Bottom Left: *From the school magazine*

Right: *From the school magazine*

had a tendency to side with children against authority, and if she felt that a child was vulnerable she had to do what was right for them. However it was paramount that she did this while still holding in mind the overall interests of the school and the other pupils. She remembers that this led her to some unusual decisions which were helped by having the ability not to lose her nerve.

These were years when St Mary's girls achieved highly within an easy-going relaxed environment. One said, 'I remember laughing, so much laughing with my friends. Friends who are friends for life'.

The House System

It is unusual for a school the size of St Mary's to arrange for pupils to live in houses with their own year group rather than in a vertical age structure. It gives St Mary's a feel of a smaller school and allows the girls to have their friends around them outside the work day. Contact with others in the school is achieved through the Company system, which provides inter-year events, and in the Dining Room where the girls eat together each day.

Delscey Burns tells of how early on a governor, Pat Lancaster, in reassurance of particularly high-spirited behaviour, explained to her that St Mary's had a definite character and energy of its own which came partly from the house system, which allowed the younger years to have a

certain amount of freedom without the weight of too much authority bearing down on them.

Miss Burns supported her introduction of exclusively non-academic house staff by providing them with good working conditions and securing better liaison with the academic staff. In 1992 she looked at increasing their profile within the school. She changed the working pattern of the housemistresses so that, with the help of the relief staff, the houses could be staffed throughout the day, and there was time for the staff to attend staff meetings and help in other houses if needed. The changes paid dividends, and in time Miss Burns was reporting that the staff involved were 'very flexible and generous with their time'.

Melanie, Elinor and Katie

By 1993 Miss Burns was presiding over a highly successful, happy school community, riding the vagaries of the curriculum changes and watching the girls taking their skills into the wider world. But St Mary's now met with a series of events that caused it to draw deeply on the spirituality, resoluteness and compassion that were fundamental to the beliefs on which it was founded.

In the summer holidays of 1994, Melanie Richardson, who had left St Mary's the previous year, died of cancer. Delscey Burns remembered her as 'a bright, bubbly, gregarious 17-year-old' who, faced with the extreme challenges of her condition, grew into a person of 'extraordinary bravery, maturity and depth'. Melanie received treatment at the John Radcliffe Hospital in Oxford, sometimes on an adult ward and at other times with children.

While Melanie was going through her treatment a second St Mary's girl, Elinor Green, had also been taken ill. Elinor was a great-niece of Old Girl Gladys Beale, herself a great-niece of the renowned women's educationalist, Dorothea Beale. Elinor, a scholar in the LVI Form, had a wonderful gift for words which round the time of her own illness she used to express her thoughts on her life and her impending death. She was described by a friend as having 'humour, energy and a remarkable selflessness'.

Comparing the specialist adolescent unit at the Middlesex Hospital in London where Elinor was receiving her treatment with the lack of facilities for teenagers in Oxford, Melanie and Elinor were inspired to initiate an appeal for a similar unit at the John Radcliffe. This led to a massive fundraising programme which was spear-headed by Melanie's family, and in which St Mary's was to play a very considerable part. Still a pupil within the school, Elinor was able to help other girls confront the reality of what she was experiencing and inspire them to raise money in many ways. In a little over two years an adolescent unit was opened in Oxford, though sadly Melanie and Elinor did not live to see that day.

Even as the project was coming to completion, St Mary's was to suffer another tragic loss. Katie Plunkett, a Sixth Form pupil, lost her fight for life in February 1996. Katie's tutor, Mrs Socha, wrote about her in the school magazine: her enthusiasm and energy; her quick mind and her perception; her open-heartedness and her enormous potential. Katie shared Delscey Burns love of horses and was a valued member of the school's one-day-eventing team. It was a sad period through which Delscey Burns gently guided the school.

The house system provided the younger pupils with some cushion against events in the upper part of the school, but Miss Burns later recalled spending a great deal of time talking to different year groups. The girls experienced many emotions, and by discussing what they were feeling much of the energy was dissipated. The fundraising provided a focus for the girls, but those days were not always straightforward. For her own part Delscey Burns says she believed in her ability to find the resources to do what needed to be done. It was not an easy time for either her or her staff.

Above: *Charity fashion show 1993*

Left: *St Mary's School 1989*

Charity Support

There were some hugely successful fundraising undertakings during Miss Burns' time in support of both wider appeals, such as the Ethiopian famine relief and the Romanian orphans, and of local charities. Within Calne the girls helped clear Doctor's Pond on the river Marsden, where Joseph Priestley is reputed to have discovered oxygen, and with the OGA raised money for the repair of one of the windows in the clerestory of the parish church. In a series of plain leaded windows two have small flower motifs: a lily for the St Mary's School window and a violet on a window funded by a local family, the Downhams. Both images were designed by Hilary Downham, a young stained glass designer.

In a glance back to those years when the school's pupils spent many of their afternoons on rambles in the lanes and meadows around Calne, sponsored walks featured large in Miss Burns' years, including a Bath to Wells walk which raised money for Save the Children Fund.

Nothing, however, was on the scale of the work put into the MRJR Appeal for an adolescent unit at the John Radcliffe Hospital in Oxford, an effort supported wholeheartedly by the wider St Mary's community. A group of Sixth Form girls masterminded the major school fundraising events with great success, and by Founders' Day of 1995 they had made £123,000. They received many generous donations from parents and friends and arranged a wide variety of activities within the school. Girls in all year groups contributed in different ways: the Fourth Formers took to the downs on a sponsored walk; a fashion show was staged; and a St Cecilia's restaurant and an UV Form soda bar brought in more funds. There were also individual efforts, including Shara Dorman's scaling of the Matterhorn.

129

The Duke of Edinburgh's Award

These were the years that the Duke of Edinburgh's Award became established at St Mary's. With an initial 29 pupils, after a couple of years 110 girls were in the scheme, and the governors recognised that it was a development that chimed with the spirit of the 'Way Ahead' paper that Miss Burns had written at the end of her first year. There were considerable costs involved that they decided, as with other subjects, should mostly come from the fees, with the staff receiving incentive bonuses. By 1989 St Mary's was hosting the scheme's award ceremony for the North Wiltshire area.

In 1991 Jane Dickson arrived to teach some geography and act as extra-curricular activities co-ordinator. She remembers that also under her remit fell the maintenance of bicycles. She helped to raise the profile of the Duke of Edinburgh's Award further into the prominent position that it holds today. The upbeat encouragement of Jane Dickson and Liz Smith (now Liz Thompson) spurred on the girls in these years in treks across Somerset, over the Brecon Beacons and up the Welsh Mountains. Meanwhile some of the Fourth Form had a taste of adventure during their annual week in Bude.

Delscey Burns Leaves St Mary's

In 1993 the governors congratulated the teaching staff on the 'wonderful' examination results achieved by the girls, including the 'spectacular' GCSE results. St Mary's held a high place in the league tables, and the leavers of 1994 gained 13 Oxbridge places. Miss Burns was running a very successful school where strong pastoral care was considered of high importance. The pressures of the past few years had taken a toll, however, and Delscey Burns decided that for the sake of her own health she needed a change. In fact she had exceeded the ten years she had originally envisaged and so at Easter of 1996 she handed over the reins of the school to Colette Culligan for an interregnum of one term. Miss Burns had the summer term as a sabbatical, returning for Founders' Day to say goodbye to St Mary's and to unveil a plaque in her name above the Theatre entrance.

Paying tribute to Delscey Burns' achievements around the time of her departure, Richard Southwell commented on the high standard Miss Burns set for herself and how this was to be seen in her excellent choice of staff, her care for the pupils and the way both she and Mrs Cordon had turned around the fortunes of the junior school, St Margaret's.

Delscey Burns was a much-loved headmistress with a 'light-hearted certainty'. One governor said that Miss Burns was unusual in that she had a strong empathy with everyone, and everyone had affection and respect for her. She also had an 'innate vision'. Another remembers her as a 'wonderful' headmistress. Jane Dickson, who was one of those appointed by Miss Burns, remembers her as a great support to the staff and totally committed to the welfare of the girls in her care. A parent remembers her as someone who helped each girl to find her 'self-start button' so they did well for themselves. Past pupils remember her as a

Left: *Duke of Edinburgh's Award expedition*

Below: *Mr Richard Southwell*

Above: *A portrait of Delscey Burns by David Cobley*

Right: *Collette Culligan*

Mrs Colette Culligan

With a term to go before the new headmistress was to join St Mary's, Mrs Culligan, the deputy headmistress, oversaw the running of the school during the summer of 1996. The busy nature of the term and the many achievements of the girls emphasised how St Mary's was flourishing. In DofE Jane Dickson now had 94 girls working for their bronze award, 60 for their silver and 23 for their gold; the School's U16 and U14 tennis pairs represented Wiltshire in a regional tournament; and the Music Department brought the whole school together in a celebration of British folk music. This was an undertaking called 'Distant Voices', in which all the pupils explored unison singing for the term, culminating in a concert of contemporary folk music with solo and ensemble numbers, followed by music and dancing at a party in the Dining Room.

Through the term St Mary's made preparation for the new headmistress, Mrs Carolyn Shaw, and her family. The old matron's house at St Margaret's was extended and modernised, allowing for the first time for the headmistress to live away from the immediate school buildings. Mrs Shaw made several visits during that term to attend the new girls' day, open days for prospective parents and the first sports afternoon which the school had held. As the new millennium approached St Mary's looked towards the arrival of its 12th headmistress.

person whom they respected: 'She was formal but stylish, vigorous and fun.'

Delscey Burns career after she left St Mary's took her into different fields, including coaching in personal development. Although her time at St Mary's threw up enormous challenges, she now feels that it was the making of her. She was pleased with what she achieved while at the school but senses that she was also very lucky: lucky to be appointed; lucky that admission numbers were never a problem; lucky in her staff; and lucky in the support she received. From all accounts St Mary's was very lucky to have had Delscey Burns as their headmistress for those years.

CHAPTER SIX

Carolyn Shaw

Carolyn Shaw
1996–2003

When Mrs Shaw joined St Mary's in the autumn of 1996 it was to lead a school of nearly 300 girls. Coming from Cheltenham Ladies' College, where she had taught English and chaired the staff common room, she was used to a far larger school. However, the 'legendary friendliness and relaxed atmosphere' of St Mary's and the commitment of the staff which she had witnessed when she had visited in the summer, clearly impressed her.

Above: *A portrait of Mrs Carolyn Shaw by Keith Breeden*

Left: *The Carolyn Shaw Swimming Pool*

In her letter in the school magazine at the end of her first year Carolyn Shaw recalled her nervousness on her first morning, and on entering Chapel being met with an 'ocean of unfamiliar faces'. But as she, her husband and children settled in to their newly renovated house Mrs Shaw began to get to know all her staff and pupils, sitting in on lessons and visiting boarding houses.

Mrs Shaw was seen by many as someone to steady and consolidate the school. She was described as a positive person, with the right attributes to provide a more conventional stability that some felt the school now needed. The staff recall how she was approachable, kind and thoughtful, sometimes joining them for supper in the staffroom and listening to their comments on the daily workings of the school.

Mrs Shaw's First Year

As the new academic year began, the staff had the luxury of a greatly improved staffroom. The existing one had been extended out to one side towards the edge of what, more than 100 years previously, had been the quarry. Before work could begin on building the new section, the original staffroom had to be underpinned. The remaining

rock could then be taken down to the level of the roadway below. This gave two floors to the extension, linking it to the main staffroom and providing space for many more desks. The staff, along with the girls, were also enjoying the use of the new fitness centre in the Theatre.

In the October of Carolyn Shaw's first term, St Mary's underwent a Social Services Department inspection which was positive about the pastoral care that the girls were receiving and the systems that were in place to act as a safety net. It did however highlight outdated living conditions in Gibbins House, in which some of the LVI Form girls and the UV Form lived.

Later in the term Mrs Shaw and the governors discussed the need to encourage more of the UV form to continue into the Sixth Form in the face of increasing competition from outside. This prompted a detailed study, carried out by Sara-Jane Socha, head of Sixth Form, into how the Sixth Form could develop, of its strengths on which the school could build and the problems which had to be addressed. The report included both short- and long-term actions that showed the need for improved study and accommodation facilities, particularly for the LVI Form.

Following these findings it was decided to look at the LVI Form boarding accommodation, along with the redevelopment of Gibbins House. The bursar, Mr Paul Norton, worked with the architect in planning an extension of the Mews House to link it with Gibbins. This would provide extra study bedrooms, so improving the accommodation for the LVI Form and allowing them to all live in one house. Eleven rooms in Gibbins House would be freed for redevelopment.

Mrs Shaw's Approach

The character of St Mary's, which the headmistresses had recognised as so significant, to some degree gives the school its own momentum. Values are transferred down the year groups and carried into life beyond school. However each headmistress brings her own ideas and leaves her own imprint.

Carolyn Shaw's management of the direction of the school brought a shift in approach that reflected her personality. She felt there was now a need to put some more structure into the lives of the girls, to give a greater

Above: *The junior library 2000*

Left: *Mrs Carolyn Shaw with pupils*

Right: *A trip to the Dorset coast 1998*

discipline to areas that might have become over-relaxed. Two tactics directed her approach: one, which she called 'Straight and Wide', allowed for tolerance within firm boundaries, and the second, 'Kaleidoscope', was a way of nudging girls into new patterns of behaviour through small changes. The transition was not always smooth but gradually things settled down, and Mrs Shaw felt she gained the respect of the staff and girls.

As time went by Carolyn Shaw drew a senior team around her with whom she was able to effect changes, and within the staffroom she set up a consultation group: a forum for dialogue and discussion that involved the staff in decision making. Staff acknowledged how she encouraged an open-door ethos between the teaching staff and the management team which made for good working relationships.

The Academic Side of the School

Over the previous years St Mary's girls had achieved some outstanding results in their examinations. In 1997 another set of pupils were highly successful and an academic meeting in November recognised the hard work of all those concerned with helping the girls. In a report Miss Lancaster wrote, 'In short, after splendid results the staff

remain serene, though like swans they are no doubt paddling furiously underneath'.

In the term that Mrs Shaw arrived new GCSE syllabuses were being introduced, and the staff were looking ahead to the publication of the Dearing Report on education for 16 to 19 year olds, expecting some reorganisation of the A Level curriculum. Inevitably this was to be a further educational development that within the school required careful planning on the part of the staff.

One early change in the curriculum throughout St Mary's was the introduction of personal and social education, a cross-curricular syllabus. In the autumn of 2000, and against the backdrop of some exceptionally good examination results in the summer, the new AS courses began, among them the additional ones of sports science, and government and political studies. The increasing popularity of science and mathematics led to more sets for these subjects.

Prep in the dining room 1997

School magazines of this time describe some of the activities the departments undertook. In 1998 the geography staff took the MIV Form to the Dorset coast, the UIV surveyed the River Kennett and the A Level students had a trip to Arran. Other years featured visits to a nuclear power station and down a coal mine. There were tours abroad for different year groups and for the language and art students. On several occasions the St Mary's History of Art students won the Duke of Marlborough's Annual Heritage Educational Prize.

The Science Department entered St Mary's students into national competitions such as 'Paperclip Physics', run by the Institute of Physics, and 'Top of the Bench', a competition run by the Royal Society of Chemistry and the Science Museum. Cross-curricular cooperation was fostered by the Science Centrestage project run by the Wellcome Trust, in which scientific issues were explored through drama in workshops run by scientists and drama specialists. In mathematics all sections of the school entered national mathematics challenges.

Throughout the time that Mrs Shaw was headmistress St Mary's remained high on the league table of results and the flow of girls to Oxbridge and other universities continued.

Other Concerns

With changes afoot, the governors brought in a planning consultant to look at the whole school area and to report on the best use of land resources for future developments. Outcomes arising from this were the need to provide more office accommodation, to improve the entrance to the school and to upgrade the boarding accommodation in some houses. He also recommended a tree survey to be conducted by a specialist to assess the condition of the trees in the school grounds, maintain their population and supplement them where possible in order to distribute the age groups evenly. The report listed over 100 trees, commenting on their age and condition, including the copper beech in St Cecilia's garden which was considered to have reached over two thirds of its natural life.

While the building plans were going ahead, news was coming in of a proposed housing development on the allotments west of St Margaret's. This was a time of expansion for Calne, with development of a northern ring road and nearby housing. The governors saw this as an opportunity to buy some additional staff housing, taking over three houses that bordered the lane by St Margaret's Preparatory School.

With an eye to the school's anniversary in 1998, Carolyn Shaw suggested to the governors that the occasion might be marked by launching an appeal for a sports hall and a new swimming pool.

This was a major appeal and a huge undertaking. An appeal chairman, Mr Mark Jackson Stops, and an appeal director were appointed; a steering committee was created and initial contacts made. By the spring of 1998 the first plans for the new building were drawn up with recommendations from Liz Thompson, head of the PE Department. After presentations by competing architects, it was found that the initial sum envisaged for the appeal was unlikely to meet the costs, and that the project would have to be split into different phases. The swimming pool would be first, as many felt that there was a greater need for this.

As the school's anniversary approached, other plans were made for a number of events during that academic year. Just before Christmas St Mary's came together with St Margaret's for a joint production of Benjamin Britten's *Noyes Fludde* in the parish church. Over 100 singers, dancers and instrumentalists performed, and St Margaret's children provided a chorus of animals. Mrs Shaw wrote that 'We were entertained by Mrs Noye and her gossips, inspired by Noye's gentle humility and moved by the fresh enthusiasm that the cast brought to the ancient story of God's covenant to mankind'.

St Mary's School has always marked the great milestones in its history by joining as a community for a service of thanksgiving, whether in chapel, church or cathedral. At the 125th anniversary, Salisbury Cathedral was the setting for a wonderful celebration, attended by around 1,200 people, among them many Old Girls. A programme of readings and music had been arranged by Lilian Leadbetter and by Keith Abrams and his staff. The readings, drawn from old school records, formed a thread that wound back down the years to Canon Duncan's Speech Day address of 1896.

On Founders' Day of 1998, an art exhibition showed work by both pupils and Old Girls, including some beautiful pencil sketches of St Bridget's boarding house drawn by Peggy Wilson when she was a pupil in the 1930s. The Old Girls' Association had always been mindful of the help they could give towards the education of daughters of Old Girls. They marked the year for St Mary's by raising funds for an Anniversary Bursary Appeal.

Above: *A sketch of St Bridget's from the slicket drawn by pupil Peggy Wilson in the 1930s*

Left: *The school magazine*

ST. MARY'S SCHOOL

Celebrating 125 Years

1997-1998

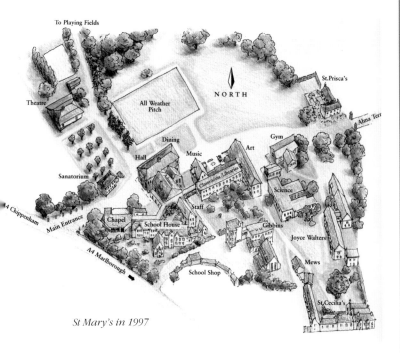

St Mary's in 1997

The Swimming Pool Project

The decision to proceed with the swimming pool was
to herald the start of a long and complicated process of
funding demands that required a great deal of time and
imaginative thought on the part of many people. It was a
costly scheme that needed some substantial donations and
for a time the future of the project was in the balance. In
2000, sensing the value of a reappraisal, Richard Southwell
approached Michael Pipes, whom he knew through their
positions on the Governing Body at Warminster School.

Michael Pipes had a strong background in education
having taught at Oundle, been both head teacher at
Portsmouth Grammar School and a Schools' Inspector. He
acted first as a consultant and later joined St Mary's as a
governor. His business plan for the swimming pool looked
at bringing in more income. By including a fitness centre
in one of the areas of the design and having it open to the
public along with the swimming pool, the project became a
more attractive proposition for seeking a loan.

Through its history St Mary's School had had to take
great care with the management of its finances. The school
has no major endowments but, thanks to the generosity
of some of its early benefactors, it owns its own freehold.
Partly in light of this, the loan was secured. Another major

The Governors

Some families have been linked with St Mary's down several generations.
Margaret Maclean (Randolph) was head girl in 1919 and later became
a governor of the school. She was the first member of the only family
to have had four generations of girls at St Mary's. The Chairman of the
Governors when Carolyn Shaw was appointed, Rachel Benson (Woods),
was a pupil in Miss Gibbins's time along with her two sisters and was then
followed by her daughters and nieces. Rachel's father, Robin Woods, the
Dean of Windsor and later the Bishop of Worcester, was a great friend of
Miss Gibbins and gave the address on Founders' Day in 1972, the year
of her retirement. Mrs Benson was asked to be a governor a week after
visiting St Mary's as a prospective parent and continued in her post until
her retirement in 1997, having followed Margaret Ellis as chairman.
Anne Ferguson (Smellie), an Old Girl and governor, said of Rachel that
she 'led the school with a light but firm hand and an ever-present sense
of humour'.

Richard Southwell became acquainted with St Mary's through his
wife, Belinda, who had been a pupil at the school. Their daughter was
also a pupil. He had joined the Governing Body in 1983 towards the end
of Joyce Walters' headship. On the retirement of Rachel Benson, Richard
Southwell became chairman and remained until 2005, when he moved
to the role of Patron. He saw St Mary's through some interesting and
challenging times and his wise counsel was of immense value.

factor in the successful funding of the project was the great generosity of the Sackler family whose contribution is recognised by a plaque within the entrance hall to the building. A trading company, St Mary's School (Calne) Services Ltd, was set up to manage the swimming pool, with pupils among the first members.

The swimming pool is situated on part of the old workhouse site with the original boundary wall, now listed, running behind. By the autumn of 2001 the governors declared the building was looking 'magnificent', being particularly pleased with the roof line on the north side. A room that had at first been intended to be a classroom was now equipped as a fitness suite.

The fine 25m swimming pool with six marked lanes, the fitness room and the series of changing rooms, all provided ideal facilities for use by St Mary's and St Margaret's pupils as well as for members of the community, being available for swimming lessons, for individual members, and for general leisure use. A manager, Lee Chalk, was soon appointed and got the whole enterprise up and running. Before long the centre became financially sound. A further development of the facilities converted a roof space to a dance studio, which is now also used for many other activities.

The last event in the old open-air swimming pool was a gala in the summer of 2002, rounding off what was the

end of a memorable place for so many St Mary's girls. From the large windows which make up the end wall of the new pool, one can look towards the wind-swept site of the old swimming pool, now filled in and grassed over. For many past pupils this would be with perhaps a qualified nostalgia.

Concurrent Projects in the Boarding Houses

Around the turn of the century a flurry of activity within St Mary's saw considerable changes to a number of areas. The planning and overseeing of the swimming pool building was the major focus of this time but alongside this there were many other projects that improved the fabric of the school.

When Jane Dickson became responsible for the pastoral care of the girls, she carried out a study of how the boarding side of the school should be developed. At the top of her list of areas that needed looking at was School House. This was the original nucleus of St Mary's, with a warren of rooms whose use had changed and changed again. It is where the girls lived for the first two years of their time at St Mary's, and by 1999 it was clear that it was sleeping too many girls for the staff to be able to give enough time to individuals. Jane recommended that the two year groups should be allocated different areas with separate house staff.

Above: *Plumer Wing and the Music School*

Left: *Jane Dickson at Bude*

By the autumn term of 2000 the changes had been made. The LIV Form house, known as Gabriel, now occupied the first floor of the Bodinnar Wing and the house that had for many years been used by the headmistresses. The MIV Form, in Wordsworth House, took over the first and second floors of the other half of School House, where some of the dormitories were rearranged. The old Wordsworth dormitory became part common room and part bedroom. Two new dormitories took the names Benson and Dyas, after Rachel Benson, the previous Chairman of Governors, and Miss Dyas, an early headmistress.

When the UV form arrived back for the new school year in 1999 they found a completely renovated Gibbins House: study bedrooms had been enlarged; new electrical, water and central heating systems had been installed; there were new carpets, furniture and decoration.

Following on from improvements to The Mews, School House and Gibbins, was building work at St Prisca's. Additional staff accommodation was needed, as were extra dormitories for the girls. The house has a small area of ground at the back which for some years had held a portacabin used as a common room. Plans were now produced to extend St Prisca's on to this site, giving the extra rooms needed. Planning permission was not granted, however, owing to the impact it would have on nearby residents. A new plan extended the house to the west. Reorganisation within gave the girls a new common room and kitchen area looking out over the playing fields towards the main school. Three four-bed dormitories and a staff flat were also part of the development. A planting scheme on one side completed the changes. The UIV Form were now more comfortably housed.

The LV Form house, St Cecilia's, was in need of improvement, but now budget constraints restricted immediate work. However the front of the house facing on to Curzon Street was considered by North Wiltshire District Council to be in need of preservation for which they, with English Heritage, gave the school a grant. Work included repairing stone work, clearing pigeons and netting areas to prevent their return. The council took the occasion to run a pilot scheme on traffic-calming in the street.

Art During Carolyn Shaw's Time

Through the generations St Mary's has opened opportunities for the girls to experiment with different media and produce artwork either as part of an examination syllabus or as an extra-curricular activity. Some pupils have taken up careers as artists or within the art world, exposing their talents to a wider audience. The Art Department lies at the centre of the school and work is displayed prominently. During these years the girls were exhibiting their examination work, attending workshops and enjoying gallery visits, including a trip to Venice. In a cross-curricular event the Art Department was part of an inter-Company arts festival in which each Company created a mime, a poem and an instrumental piece along with a programme and poster to advertise their work. This period produced a number of commissioned artists, some of whom displayed work later at an exhibition by St Mary's in Cork Street in 2012.

Above: *A school magazine cover with a painting by Emma Dodson entitled* Wiltshire Landscape

Left: *The Cork Street Exhibition brochure*

Developments in Other Parts of the School

Parts of the school other than the boarding houses were also benefiting from changes. Prime among these was an assembly hall at St Margaret's. This was a most welcome addition to the flourishing junior school and was named after Richard Southwell, Chairman of the Governors, who played a significant role in steering it through.

The classrooms in Plumer Wing in need of refurbishment were decorated, and received new tables and chairs, lockers and shelves with the understanding that the girls would be encouraged to keep them in good order. Once completed Carolyn Shaw reported that the girls were now 'taking ownership of the rooms'.

Bodington Library, in one wing of the main classroom block, was the next room for improvement. All the books were boxed up for the summer while internal walls and shelving were removed and replaced with moveable shelves and desks, making a flexible and attractive working environment for the girls.

Since the 1930s the main entrance to St Mary's had been through the large doors of the Matthews Building. This was not well placed for the administrative offices, and following a report commissioned on ideas for marketing, Mr Southwell was keen to create an entrance that would be stylish, welcoming and convenient. Through the summer holidays of 2000 the Curved Passage, linking School House with other areas, was transformed by the insertion of a copper-roofed rotunda. It provided a light space suitable for displays of art, with seating where visitors could be welcomed. It was also convenient for the offices.

The entrance to the school

Mrs Shaw and Her Staff

In the summer of 1998 two of the senior members of staff left St Mary's. Margaret Beater retired after 22 years at the school, and Colette Culligan took up the post of headmistress at Clifton High School.

After losing two such senior people, continuity within the school was provided by the appointment of Jane Dickson as deputy head on the pastoral side of the senior team. Mrs Shaw then proposed advertising for the equivalent on the academic side.

The successful candidate, Mrs Sue Tomlin, had been head of English and drama at a Church comprehensive school in Harrogate. In addition to her teaching timetable, Mrs Tomlin filled in gaps where needed. She managed staff development, introduced some early GCSEs and tidied up the curriculum so that class sizes made the best use of the staff. She was of great support to Carolyn Shaw, who said of her, 'She was a wise and thoughtful leader, respected alike by staff and girls and noted for her vivid way with words'.

Mrs Shaw later ranked among her achievements at St Mary's the quality of the staff appointments that she made. A year later she brought in a new bursar, Alison Martin, who proved to be 'outstanding'. She is remembered as an empathetic person who engendered respect among her colleagues. Among her many duties she was instrumental in driving through the swimming pool project. In the autumn of 2001 St Mary's welcomed their first Newly Qualified Teacher (NQT) under a new government scheme.

The previous year, a change in the senior management team had occurred, prompted by Jane Dickson relinquishing her role as deputy head while continuing as head of extra-curricular activities and in the Geography Department. Most of her pastoral duties were passed to a new head of boarding, Mrs Di Riley, and her other

responsibilities went to Sue Tomlin, with Judith Milburn as her assistant. Two years later Judith took over as head of history and Sara-Jane Socha focused on her role as head of Sixths.

In 2002 Mrs Shaw asked Caroline Adler to take on one of the deputy headships. Caroline had been a science teacher at St Mary's since 1982, later becoming head of science and the senior resident teacher. In 2007 she left St Mary's for a few years before returning in 2011 to teach science and serve as a deputy housemistress.

Carolyn Shaw had the advantage of having her home away from the main hub of the school – a place to which she could return at the end of the day. She had great support from her husband, and their generosity and warmth is remembered well. On occasions they would invite staff from each Company to supper. Carolyn was seen as a calm, family person, 'with her feet on the ground'.

Above: *The staff v pupil lacrosse match 2001*

Right: *Pupils' stained glass hanging in the Chapel window*

Far right: *The shield given by the leaving girls of 1927 hangs in the Chapel*

Religious Life in the School

When the Revd Canon Alan Woods left Calne in 1996, St Mary's, for the first time since its foundation, did not have a clergyman on the Board of Governors, as the new Vicar, the Revd Bob Kenway, had a daughter within the school. A shortage of clergy in the parish had also left the school with virtually no chaplaincy, but the Revd Kenway was able to give some help, along with a number of his assistants.

The governors and headmistress had for some years hoped to appoint a chaplain to the school staff. In March 2000 the Revd Peter Giles, a local solicitor, was licensed by Archdeacon Hopkinson representing the Diocese of Salisbury at a service in St Mary's Chapel, and was presented with a special stole which members of the Fourth Form had helped to make. Alongside the Revd Giles was his wife, Elizabeth, who worked as his assistant. They had been associated with St Mary's since 1987, when their daughter Rachel became a pupil. With the arrival of the Revd Giles, the parish church relinquished responsibility for conducting services in the school and for preparation of Confirmation candidates.

As had always been the case, the girls of St Mary's continued to attend the church, and occasions such as Confirmation, the school carol service and the Founders' Day service took place there as it offered more space for parents and guests. Within the school daily services and Sunday worship remained.

In light of the competitive climate for enrolment towards the end of the century, St Mary's considered it appropriate to open the school to pupils of other faiths in addition to those belonging to the Anglican church.

Marketing and Enrolment

For some years the governors at St Mary's had hoped to raise the number of pupils in the school to well above the 300 mark. Marketing became an important tool and Mrs Shaw now had the help of Mrs Forbes-Welch, a St Margaret's parent with a marketing background. Advertising and contact with prep schools' head teachers were an on-going process, and taster days for children became a regular feature, but numbers were volatile and stubbornly remained in the 280s. It was not an easy period for boarding schools, as prep schools began to provide for more children until 13, an arrangement which appealed to the parents as it was less costly. With fewer pupils registering for 11+ and 12+, Mrs Shaw began to develop 13+ entry. A greater interest in an English education from Russians, Hong Kong Chinese and later mainland Chinese required some difficult decision-making. The school was able to take some but felt it had to keep a cap on the number of foreign students in the school. In 2001 St Mary's enrolled in the Dresden Scholars' Scheme, a charity which offered up to a year's schooling in Britain for a pupil from Dresden.

The school felt strongly the value of the UV form girls remaining at St Mary's for their final two years. Sara-Jane Socha's report on the Sixth Form followed one she had done earlier in the year with Judith Milburn into how best to present the attractions of staying on for A Levels. This led to the production of a brochure called 'Sixth Sense'.

The emblem of a lily in a shield had been the signature of St Mary's since the early days. The image has been interpreted in different forms over the years, whether on badges, clothing, book plates or in stained glass. In the Dining Room during Miss Matthews's time, 'neat little round pats of butter' all bore the St Mary's lilies. When Mrs Shaw was headmistress, in line with the times, St Mary's began to realise the value of promoting a corporate image. New and better signage for the school was one of the outcomes.

Music During Mrs Shaw's Time

During the previous two decades, St Mary's' Chamber Choir had performed in great cathedrals, minsters and festivals around this country. Now came the opportunity to venture further afield. At the school's 125th anniversary in the spring of 1997 the choir went to Italy, giving an impromptu concert in the amphitheatre in Verona and singing Mass at St Mark's Cathedral in Venice to a congregation of around 1,000 people. This was followed in 2000 by a tour to Sweden.

The Schola Cantorum, under the leadership of Mr Field, also began to reach a wider audience through radio and television broadcasts. A regional television *Sing Out* competition took the girls to third place after being interviewed, recorded and filmed in St Mary's Church. The following year the choir became the BBC Church Minstrels of the Year, giving St Mary's the springboard for two further BBC broadcasts and the opportunity for the whole school to record *Sunday Half Hour* and *Sunday Worship*. In the summer of 2000 St Mary's received the news that the choir had reached the semi-finals of the Sainsbury's Choir of the Year and would be singing in the Albert Hall.

The girls were also performing the great oratorios along with other school choirs, works such as Fauré's *Requiem* and *Carmina Burana*, the latter of these featuring Keith Abrams and Colin Howard as soloists.

In 2001 Geoffrey Field took over the running of the Music Department from Keith Abrams, who was unwell. The standard of orchestral music had slipped and was becoming of some concern, but the choir was flourishing and that year recorded a CD, took part in a live BBC broadcast, and sang in an eight-part choir on the occasion of a visit by the Queen to Malmsbury Abbey.

Along with all the high-profile events throughout these years music examinations continued; in-house concerts, musical evenings and competitions took place; and recitals, concerts, master-classes and workshops were attended. A newly formed jazz band was among those performing in the spring concert in 2003.

Above: *The Chamber Choir*

Left: *Choir practice in the Music School*

The junior pupils at the end of the day

In the Boarding Houses

The school's policy of having a separation between the boarding house staff and the academic staff had continued through this period, although there were some who felt a greater integration might be valuable. It was not always easy to recruit staff in the houses and there was considerable movement to fill spaces that arose. In 2002, to help give some consistency, Caroline Adler became the new deputy head with pastoral duties and Jenny Lacey took on the role of pastoral tutor.

Information Technology

St Mary's had gradually embraced the advent of the IT revolution but it was during Carolyn Shaw's time that a greater leap was made to bring the school up to the minute. In the past computers had been bought on an ad hoc basis without an overall strategy, and there now became a need for a policy covering computer use and the training of staff. The Computer Department, under the direction of Mrs Clark, had given both girls and staff good tuition, but it was in urgent need of more staff and greater technical support. It was now recognised that the school should appoint a technician.

By the end of 1999 a new network was installed giving internet access throughout the main school, later extending to the boarding houses. All girls and staff had an email address and a code of conduct was put in place. St Mary's also had a new website, a new digital camera was available for departmental use and 'Computing' now became known as 'IT'. Two years later, with further advances in the technology, the bursar decided that a wireless network was the way forward, leading to the Plumer Wing classroom block and the Music School being fitted with access points. Advice was also given to the girls and their parents as to suitable laptops. The introduction of broadband to Calne in 2003 led to further improvement in the network.

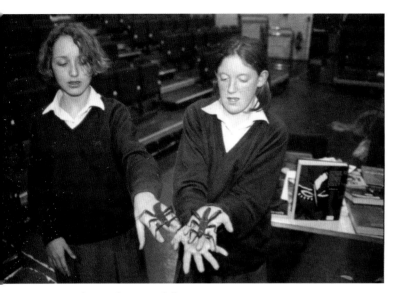

The Rainforest Road Show

Through the School Year

How often it is the events that break the normal routine of school life stand out in our memories. A junior pupil wrote of 'The Rainforest Road Show': 'This was one of the best things I remember about LIV Form'. She wrote of the bugs and the butterflies, of spears and blowpipes, of tribes and village life. The years around the turn of the millennium offered many such occasions: the visits to theatres, concerts, galleries and museums; the field trips and foreign tours; the visiting speakers, the inter-Company activities and the charity events. Each termly calendar shows the school offering a range of opportunities and experiences for pupils of all ages, leading to a rich and lively community.

The Duke of Edinburgh's Award scheme features large in the lives of the girls, giving adventure, social work, a variety of challenges and fun. In 2001, despite the restrictions of the foot-and-mouth epidemic, 168 girls took part in the award, including the entire UIV who started their Bronze Medal.

There was a lot of lighter entertainment in these years, be it Sixth Form bops, fashion shows (in partnership with Eton boys), visits to Marlborough Mop Fair or celebration of the Queen's Golden Jubilee.

The many charitable endeavours of the girls reached the far corners of the world as well as closer to home, with support for the Mayor of Calne's chosen charity. Charaday

The Millennium

Jennifer Fisher as Ophelia

As the world slipped into the new millennium St Mary's School made its own tribute to mark the passage of time, by the creation of an interactive sundial. It was placed near the Delscey Burns Theatre, where once the old rose garden had stood, and pupils of Miss Matthews' time had passed afternoons learning the names of flowers.

The project was initiated by Christina Smith, head of physics, and involved all departments and the pupils of St Mary's and St Margaret's in gathering ideas and drawing up the design. It included the signatures of all the staff and pupils etched in brass; the school's shield and lily emblem; the town crest of Calne; and the footsteps of Mrs Shaw and of Leonora de Ferranti, the girl with the smallest feet. Historical events from each century of the last millennium were depicted in granite and marble plaques. Near the sundial is buried a time capsule with photographs of the school, a copy of a timetable, a video of a school play and examples of pupils' work. The hope is that it will be dug up in 2073, the year of the School's 200th anniversary. The sundial was officially opened with a piece written especially for the choir by pupil Alexandra Coghlan, 'Sol Gloria Mundi'. Each pupil received a commemorative coin to mark the millennium.

In the first half of the 20th century, when the time pressures of the curriculum were less demanding, Miss Matthews would occasionally abandon the timetable and take the school on an outing. In such a spirit, St Mary's had a day off in February of 2000 and all went to the Millennium Dome in Greenwich to see the exhibitions and shows. The occasion was conceived and arranged by Caroline Adler, head of science, and despite some initial scepticism was seen as a great success.

The symbolism of celestial time passing in the nature of an eclipse formed the central tenet of the Drama Department's production of *In Love with Shakespeare*. Set in the Forest of Arden, 50 of the bard's best-loved women gather to hold a symposium on love. It was clearly a wonderfully evocative occasion, which Carolyn Shaw remarked had been 'brilliantly conceived and beautifully directed' by Lilian Leadbetter.

As the world rung in the new millennium, St Mary's ceased to ring its loud electric bell that had signalled the lesson changes. It was now the responsibility of the girls to manage their own time.

St Mary's School has kept its past alive to the current generation through naming rooms and buildings after many of those who held significant places in its history. As well as working for the success of the school, many have shown a further generosity through donations.

During Mrs Shaw's time a number of legacies were received: Elizabeth Gibbins, headmistress, remembered St Mary's in her will; Miss Thouless, a deputy headmistress, left money which was used to improve the Coulter Library; and the school was among the beneficiaries of the trust fund of Sir John Bodinnar, a school governor during Miss Matthews' headship. This led to the establishment of the Bodinnar Scholarship for an all-round pupil, the first being awarded to Sophie Russell in 2002.

was always a high point in the school calendar. One year money was raised by a themed restaurant at St Cecilia's, a beauty parlour in St Prisca's and tea-time in the Gibbins Café.

At this time the head girl of St Mary's had a team of up to seven members, spearheading initiatives within the school and attending the Head Girls' Conference. Among their many achievements the team of 2002 managed to obtain a water fountain for the girls, and were instrumental in establishing a school council, the foundations having been laid by previous years. Responsibility was also filtered down the school, with the LVI Form taking the lead in organising the junior dormitory plays.

For many decades the pupils had used trunks to move their belongings to and from school. In the early days they had arrived in advance by railway. In 2002 St Mary's decided to replace them with soft bags, so reducing man-power and storage space.

Above: *A Duke of Edinburgh's Award expedition 2000*

Right: *A poster from 2002*

Drama and Theatre Studies

A new pupil arriving at St Mary's described how surprised and delighted she was to find that drama was a subject that could be part of the curriculum. The success of the Theatre, and the exciting productions that were staged, ensured that theatre studies and drama activities in general became very popular. Involvement was seen in plays other than the main productions. Dormitory plays put on by School House pupils, the occasional Form Shakespeare and the Junior Drama Club productions all gave the younger girls the opportunity to perform, and the enthusiastic take up of LAMDA sessions developed their skills further.

In 1999 Elinor Cook became the first Sixth Form drama scholar at St Mary's. The following year a LVI Form student-led production of *Trace of Arc* was directed by Clare Diacono, that year's scholar. During that summer the UVI Form took their much-acclaimed A Level theatre studies' production of *Shall I Compare Thee* to the Edinburgh Fringe. Gaining three stars from a review in *The Scotsman*, it was a forerunner of many such occasions.

The director of drama, Lilian Leadbetter, often chose texts that explored female-centred issues or stretched the conventions of theatre. In 2002 she combined *Steel Magnolias* and *Machinal* to create a production which was a tribute to America and its heritage. The girls were having their eyes opened to the possibilities of theatre as a medium for exploring subjects in new and interesting ways.

Left: *Lilian Leadbetter*

Far left: *Victoria Parker as Lady Politic Would-be in* Volpone *(1998).*

2002 – a year in St Mary's

A glance at the school's records of one year – the minutes, the magazines, the calendars and the photographs – opens a window into a moment in time. We catch a glimpse of life in the classroom, in the dormitories, in the staffroom and on the playing fields. We sense the big decisions being taken by the governors and the planning by the staff; we see cameos of serious study and faces of laughter; we feel the pulse of the school. And 2002 was that sort of year. Daily events flowed on to create a community that worked and achieved, that was stimulating and fun, where lasting friendships took root and preparations were made for the future. It was also the last full year at St Mary's for Mrs Shaw.

Mrs Shaw Moves On

The threads of tradition and spirit that traced back to the days of St Mary's on The Green, were secure. Carolyn Shaw had overseen a great improvement in the living and working conditions of the girls in her care and academic results had remained strong. Mrs Shaw's successor, Dr Helen Wright, commented that 'The whirlwind of activity at the educational heart of the School – education in its broadest and fullest interpretation – makes it easy to see what lies at the core of St Mary's: a determination to succeed, an impression that there is something out there worth striving for and a strong sense of humour and fun'.

Mrs Shaw had been the guardian of these values and she was now ready to move on. She left St Mary's School at Easter in 2003 to take up the headship of Roedean School, where she remained until her retirement, after which she took up an active role in her community.

Sport

The slogans 'Sport for All' and 'Sport for Life' which St Mary's adopted at this time summed up the ethos of the PE Department. The wide range of sporting activities available offered something for all the girls, either competitively or for leisure. The highlight of these years was the opening of the new swimming pool (later named the Carolyn Shaw Swimming Pool) and St Mary's Sports Centre. At long last St Mary's had the opportunity to compete equally with those schools that had been able to practise swimming throughout the year, and the girls had wonderful facilities for fitness training and relaxation. In the summer of 2002 the first two swimming galas were held against other schools, with St Mary's winning both.

These years were notable for the great success that the St Mary's girls achieved, representing county teams in lacrosse, hockey, netball, tennis, cross-country running and athletics. Lucinda Ball qualified for a national fencing championship and Kate Fyfe was selected to play for the Scottish U18 lacrosse team. The school's equestrian team did exceptionally well in the annual inter-schools' one-day-event championship at Stonar School. In 1999 Laura Bechtolsheimer reported on taking part in the European Pony Championships in Sweden as part of the British Pony Dressage team. It was an event in which she placed ninth, commenting 'I have never felt so honoured'. In 2012 Laura was part of the British Equestrian dressage team at the London Olympics which took the gold medal, the first British medal since the sport was introduced in 1912, and she also gained an individual bronze medal.

Within the school there were inter-Company competitions, tennis ladders, father-daughter tennis matches and an annual Calne-Eton lacrosse match. In 2000 the lacrosse team went on tour to Toronto, taking in sights such as the Niagara Falls. Each year the LIV Form had the opportunity to try many activities on their trip to Bude, and Sixth Form activities included sailing, wind-surfing and jet-skiing. In 2002 St Mary's sent two ski teams to the Alps.

In 1996 Mrs Shaw introduced the first Sports Day, with a programme of inter-Company sport and field events. In 2001 it was moved to the day before Founders' Day. Girls were then able to go out with their parents in the evening which helped reduce the over-excitement which had tended to build up towards the end of the summer term.

Top left: *Laura Bechtolsheimer Olympic medal winner London 2012*

Left: *The winners of the father-daughter tennis tournament 1998*

Below: *U12 lacrosse team 1996–7*

CHAPTER SEVEN

Helen Wright

Helen Wright
2003–12

Possibly the most vital decision for the governors of a school is the appointment of the head teacher. They have to judge character, see potential, assess the needs of the school at a particular time and, if necessary, be patient. They may also require good fortune. All these factors came happily into play when they were looking for the next headmistress of St Mary's School. In 2002 Mr Richard Southwell QC was Chairman of the Governors. Alongside him were those with backgrounds in education, business and finance, a parent governor and past pupils of St Mary's. The governors followed the usual channels for appointments but, feeling they had not found a suitable candidate, waited. And then at the last moment Mrs Helen Wright contacted the school.

Above: *Dr Helen Wright*

Left: *The Helen Wright House*

Helen Wright with pupils

Like many of St Mary's headmistresses before her, Helen Wright was young when she took up the post, being still in her early 30s. After her childhood and schooling in Scotland she had studied Modern Languages at Lincoln College, Oxford, where she met her husband. She joined St Mary's from Heathfield School, having arrived there as deputy head before being promoted to the headship after one term, a position she held for two years. When she came to Calne, Mrs Wright was working on her thesis, *Understanding Moral Leadership in Schools*, and gained her doctorate from Exeter University in 2004.

Dr Wright was offered the post by the governors but the appointment could have been complicated by the fact that she was expecting her first baby in the summer term. To the governors this was not an obstacle; they felt they had found the right person to lead St Mary's into the future and they had the bonus of having chosen someone who would be a strong role model for the pupils. Helen Wright's position as a mother was to play an important part in the life of the school.

Helen Wright had felt drawn to St Mary's Calne, sensing that the core values of the school tallied with her own, and that it could aspire to be the best. She later said that the school felt good, that she was determined and she

wanted the challenge of leading such a school. She had seen the flexibility of the governors and knew them to have ambitious but realistic expectations of her.

Dr Wright's First Term

Dr Helen Wright's 'incisiveness and vigour', recognised at her interview, were soon seen in practice. One member of staff recalls how early on Helen Wright asked the senior staff to go round the school as if they were prospective parents and look with fresh eyes. It was the start of her move to build up a strong team with common goals.

During her first term Dr Wright established herself in her new role and sought to gain the confidence of all members of the school community, beginning with the departmental heads and the UVI Form girls. She took time to observe and listen.

She then identified two main areas for immediate development which she wanted to pursue. One was to improve communications both internally and with the parents, and the other was the integration of academic and pastoral matters in the school, building on ideas contributed by the staff. The role of year heads would be developed as the centre of contact for all issues concerning the girls in their care, and the school office

Sixth Form lessons

would be centralised so all correspondence could pass through it. Every Sixth Form student was to have her own director of studies who would tutor and monitor her academic progress. In line with the wishes of many of the governors, a mix of teaching and non-teaching housemistresses would be introduced. Improved accommodation to attract more married teachers with families was key to this move.

Dr Wright and Alison Martin, the bursar, recognised that careful budgeting, financial accountability of departments and good marketing were essential for the progress of the school. In time this would lead to some departmental changes and the formation of a working group to lift the profile of St Mary's. Above all, there was a pressing need to increase the number of pupils.

There is perhaps a temptation for a new head teacher to rush into ambitious plans for the more distant future. Helen Wright took a more considered approach because she wanted to involve the staff in her strategic planning and have them contribute to the future direction of the school.

Dr Wright's choice of staff had reflected her belief that they must be right for the school, and the school

right for them, by providing opportunities for their career development and by recognising their particular needs. Personal experience had shown her how school commitments sometimes have to take second place to family matters.

The Heads of Year Roles

With the closer relationship between the academic and pastoral areas of school life, the learning and progress of the pupils could be put at the heart of St Mary's. The school aimed to provide the girls with an outstanding education that motivated, challenged, encouraged and inspired them, and through which they developed confidence and a respect for all people. The head of the Fourth Form became responsible for the induction of the new girls into the school, helping them to balance their time between academic studies and extra-curricular activities, and to make their GCSE selections.

The head of the Fifth Form, Judith Milburn, aimed to help the girls manage their workload, extend themselves into a variety of other activities and give them academic and pastoral support.

In the Sixth Form this support was overseen by the director of studies. The head of the Sixth Form, Sara-Jane Socha, helped the girls both with their university applications and to develop their responsibilities within the school. The role of heads of year gradually evolved as ideas emerged in the following years, until eventually the positions disappeared following a redefinition of responsibilities.

Marketing and Admissions

It is clear from records that a strong focus was now put onto reaching more prospective families. This new approach, ably led by Mrs Cari Depla as director of admissions and marketing, ensured that potential pupils enjoyed an interesting programme of activities when they visited St Mary's, and that there was good follow up. Very soon the school hosted a sports science preparatory school day, with great success. Later open days featured science demonstrations and art activities. The staff were seen as ambassadors for the school and became part of the enrolment process. The potential of admitting overseas pupils had been recognised in recent years and a strategy was developed to manage the process including an electronic prospectus.

Dr Wright held a strong conviction that there should be wide access to the high-quality education at St Mary's. Over the years the school had steadily expanded its scholarship scheme, and in 2005 a Foundation Award was launched for academic pupils who would otherwise not have the opportunity to attend as full fee-paying pupils. In 2007 it was possible to take in more students at different ages after the Adelman Foundation had been established with generous funding (courtesy of Mrs Georgina Illing and her family), and in 2008 a Sixth Form Foundation Award was introduced. The school's scholarships, grants and bursaries are extensive and support many families at St Mary's, recognising potential or need and helping to extend its education.

In 2004 the first issue of *The Lily*, the school newsletter, was produced. A lively termly booklet with information about recent school activities, it allowed the school magazine to become a formal record of the school year, increasingly in colour. In 2007 the magazine was named *Oxygen*, capturing the energy and ethos of the School and inspired by Joseph Priestley, who discovered oxygen in Calne in 1774. These publications, along with other communications, were well received by the parents of girls in the school, one of whom remarked that St Mary's was becoming 'increasingly professional'.

The rise in pupil numbers after Dr Wright joined St Mary's was at first a gradual process. Nationally there was less demand for girls' boarding school places, which led to the closure or merger of some schools. However the more attractive schools were taking the opportunity to grow that this offered. At St Mary's, the governors had responded early to the trend, by expanding St Margaret's School. By 2007 they were moving ahead with a new Sixth Form house as part of their programme to offer the very best. Despite some impact from the country's economic recession the school saw an increase in admissions which the governors attributed to the quality of education, leadership, staff and pastoral care. By 2009 numbers at St Mary's were well above 300 and the aim was to continue to expand.

Left: *Sara-Jane Socha*

Below: *The first edition of* The Lily *and* Oxygen

Lily Ball

The Calne Girls Association (CGA)

Generations of girls who had spent their school days at St Mary's had on leaving become members of the Old Girls' Association. Since 2002 Sue Ross had been chairman. With the retirement of a number of her committee members, a younger generation had begun to be represented, among them Cate Bell, daughter of a past Chairman of the Governors, Rachel Benson. Cate and others were keen that the magazine should have a new look, which led to a move to modernise further. In 2010 the OGA became the Calne Girls Association and past pupils became known as Calne Girls. The new-look magazine, *Calne Girls Connected,* was produced and a CGA website set up.

The CGA website

The Development Department

St Mary's school has attracted the support and goodwill of many people who have come to know it. It was clear that maintaining contacts and welcoming visitors into the school could give them a sense of ownership which would be invaluable in strengthening the school community and seeking support for future fundraising. In 2004, with a view to putting some structure into fundraising, Richard Southwell set up a committee of parents who were interested in helping. They provided leadership in the planning and operations of fundraising, and managed and developed alumnae relations in order to draw on the expertise and knowledge of Calne Girls. Known initially as the Fundraising Committee, it later evolved into the Foundation Committee, anticipating plans to set up a foundation trust to help secure the future of the school. At first the committee was chaired by Richard Southwell and later by Vicky Wilson (Richardson), a Calne Girl and governor. The Marchioness of Lansdowne became Patron of the Foundation Committee, carrying on a long connection between the Lansdowne family and St Mary's. The committee has initiated many new ventures and a number of their ideas, such as the annual Lily Ball for leavers, have become embedded into the school calendar.

In 2007 a Development Department encompassing Alumnae Relations was established to support the operations and bring ideas to fruition, headed by Lilian Leadbetter. The department soon became successful in raising funds (including those from the Adelman Foundation to support new Sixth Form students), while building contacts throughout the community and forging closer links with the OGA/CGA committee. Vicky Wilson, the development governor, was a key figure in

Far left: *Helen Wright and Simon Knight, Chairman of the Governors*

Top left: *The Armed Forces Fund brochure*

Left: *Jonny Wilkes swing night*

the latter process. As well as running the 135 Appeal which raised funds to support the building of a new Sixth Form house, the school's Development Department has arranged numerous events, such as weekend and year-group reunions, dinners, receptions, lectures and visits. Key events have included a celebration of the St Mary's Sports Centre's tenth anniversary and, more recently, two wonderful fundraising swing nights in the Delscey Burns Theatre, led by St Margaret's parent and West End star Jonny Wilkes. On both swing night occasions the whole community of both schools came together as one. Another significant fundraising event in the theatre was 'An Evening with Sir Tim Rice' in September 2012. The increasing number of events taking place in the school has led to great demands being placed on the housekeeping and catering departments. They have risen to the challenge magnificently and many visitors comment on the quality of the hospitality given by St Mary's.

The Calne Foundation Trust

With funds being received on a regular basis the time was right to create a charitable organisation to manage them and provide a transparent means of oversight. Through her position as chairman of the Foundation Committee, Vicky Wilson spearheaded work on setting up a foundation trust with advice from people outside the school. In 2011 St Mary's had joined Radley College and Downe House in establishing an Armed Forces Fund to provide bursaries for children of servicemen killed or wounded on operations. Their fundraising Silver Ball that autumn was hugely successful. Managing money such as this would be facilitated by having a more formal arrangement. On Founders' Day 2012 the creation of the Calne Foundation Trust was announced. It provides a structure to help the school raise funds for present and future generations, including important capital projects. It also gives a greater cohesion to raising funds for significant bursaries.

Developments in Room Use

As the expansion of marketing gathered pace, it became clear that the school needed an area for medium-scale formal entertaining and for conferences. The LIV Form classroom next to the Chapel was ideal but its change of use would have a roll-on effect in other areas. By moving the LV Form into St Cecilia's, which would become a study boarding house, the LIV Form classroom could move into the LV Form study area. This move conveniently supported the wish of the senior team to encourage more independent learning in the pupils. In the summer of 2005 an extensive development and refurbishment of St Cecilia's was carried out to provide the right facilities for the girls, including desks in the study dormitories for day girls.

The Academic Curriculum

A central strand of Dr Wright's approach to moving St Mary's to the next phase was to develop a curriculum for the whole child: one that was more responsive to the individual needs of the girls, encouraging intellectual curiosity and flexible thinking within the demands of the national assessment structure. While benefiting all, this approach allowed girls with particular educational needs to be stretched in some areas while spending longer on securing their foundation skills. Pupils of all ages up to LVI Form would now have lessons in critical thinking and it would be available at AS level for the UVI Form. The UIV Form would have the option of philosophy.

In the autumn of 2003 the governors reviewed the science provision within St Mary's, looking at the curriculum, staffing and the facilities. It led to a more detailed development plan being drawn up the following year by the Science Department and a report by one

of the school governors and Calne Girl, Professor Julia Buckingham. She wanted to extend scientific thinking to all areas of the school curriculum, encourage student-led activities and raise the profile of science throughout the school. Triple Award Science for GCSE became an option in September 2005. Professor Buckingham also commented on the inadequacies of some of the facilities in the labs, which led to a science working group being formed, chaired by Sir Brian Fall, one of the governors.

In 2007 further changes to the curriculum created a new and more demanding structure. A number of GCSE and AS examinations were now being taken early and the school had introduced various extension and elective courses, including Advanced Extension Awards. All the LIV Form now

studied Mandarin, and the Sixth Form had the choice of taking Italian and astronomy at GCSE.

Among those on the senior team was Mrs Nicola Botterill, who had joined St Mary's in 2007 as deputy head to Dr Wright. One of Mrs Botterill's first undertakings was to look at the pastoral side of the school, including all aspects of boarding, in preparation for an upcoming OFSTED inspection. She and Chris Strudwick, the director of studies, then worked together on responding to the curriculum changes.

By restructuring the school day, introducing new subjects and creating a range of examination pathways through the pupils' school years that accommodated the individual needs of the girls, the school was able to deepen and widen their learning. All these changes were made possible by the strong commitment of the staff at St Mary's: those who have seen the school through changes of leadership over many years and new members of the school community.

The New School Day

Changes in routine can be exciting but also unsettling – they can be seen to open up opportunities or as a threat to a familiar order. When Dr Wright and the departmental

Above: LIV Form history class

Top: Chris Strudwick with pupils

Left: Nicola Botterill

Above: *In the Dining Room 2008*

Right: *Pupils in the Chapel*

heads initiated a radical shift in the school timetable it was essential that all the staff were involved in the ensuing discussions.

It was proposed that the school day would begin earlier with two break times in the morning and a later lunch. After-tea sessions would be tailored to individual girls' needs for prep, activities, music practice and free time. All years would have plenty of opportunity for sport.

By having the Sixth Form supervising prep, teaching staff could put in two more teaching sessions each week. Their weekend duties were replaced by weekday evening duties.

The new timetable was in place in September 2004. The changes were not whole-heartedly welcomed by all the staff, and the senior management team recognised that it was important to develop a comprehensive programme of support and training. The girls when canvassed expressed particular delight with the new morning break, where they received an imaginative range of food as part of a 'second breakfast'.

The Religious Dimension of St Mary's during Dr Wright's Time

The manner and expression of worship, faith and spirituality within St Mary's reflects a changing world, but the Christian ethos remains paramount. The school's Christian foundation is never forgotten, and is honoured and acknowledged each Founders' Day. As with all previous generations of pupils, the morning service remains the focus of the start of each school day, bringing the community together in worship. On her arrival, Dr Wright changed the emphasis of services, giving more involvement to the girls through which they could engage consciously with the moral messages. They now all participate, along with many of the staff, in helping to lead the services, covering a wide variety of spiritual, educational and topical subjects, and with much use made of drama, poetry and music to enhance the liturgy. Sunday worship alternates between the Eucharist and morning services within the framework of the Anglican tradition.

Supporting the Revd Peter Giles, senior girls have responsibilities acting as head and deputy head of Chapel and as Chapel prefects. They also run a senior and junior Christian Union within the school. The chaplain prepares both Anglican and Roman Catholic girls for Confirmation.

By the door of the Chapel hangs the old brass plaque that remembers the founders of St Mary's School and nearby are those of some of the girls and staff who have

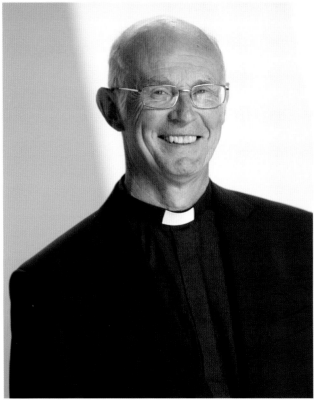

The Development of Responsibilities

As part of helping the girls to develop their potential and prepare for the future, Helen Wright was keen that they should begin to take on responsibilities through both independent learning and in leadership roles. In discussions with staff, the Sixth Form pupils all identified areas in school life in which they wanted to take a lead, with any pupil having only one role. These ideas were part of the ethos of being kind and caring across year groups, of leading by example and of self-responsibility. The emphasis of punishment was shifted to school-based community service tasks.

Building Developments

The arrival in 2005 of new chemistry and physics teachers and of a new head of science, Pam Maitland, allowed plans to be put together for improving the science laboratories. For some years a laboratory, Priestley, was situated with the classrooms. In 2005 this was given up to IT and in 2006 substantial improvements were made in the fabric of the science block, and new furniture and audio-visual equipment were installed.

The general expansion of Information Technology over the more recent years has necessitated a great deal of upgrading of facilities within the school and associated financial investment. The additional IT laboratory in Plumer Wing and its adjacent technicians' room, helped focus the IT resources. Later investment in IT throughout the school now means that St Mary's has among the very best facilities and well supported staff and pupils.

been part of the school community. Also among them is one remembering Martha Cole, who was a pupil in the LIV Form when she died in 2006. St Mary's held a memorial service for Martha in which her tutor and two friends read from a book of remembrances that had been created by the school.

Above: The Bishop of Ramsbury with Confirmation candidates 2012

Left: *Father Peter Giles*

Above: *A Sixth Form science lesson*

Top right: *LIV Form IT room*

Bottom right: *Angela Findlay with Sixth Form students after her lecture*

At the same time that the science area was being improved, a project was initiated to refurbish the Chapel and to equip it to become dual purpose. The primary use remained for worship and assemblies but the space can now also be used as a lecture theatre. The walls were plastered and painted, windows were renewed and cushioned chairs replaced the bench seats, some of them gifted by Calne Girls, staff and supporters and bearing their names on brass plates. Audio-visual equipment was added so that now the Chapel is used regularly by school and visiting lecturers.

In addition to staff accommodation within the school, St Mary's owns a number of houses round the perimeter of the school grounds, providing more living space for families, single staff and gap students. From time to time further houses have been bought.

Around 2006 the governors looked at improving access for parents to St Margaret's School through a gate at North End, and a new entrance was made to an area of land nearby for the Grounds Department of the school.

Extra-curricular Activities

As the academic curriculum was being developed, the role of those activities outside the curriculum was carefully considered. The governors and headmistresses of St Mary's had always recognised the place of sport, music, drama and art in the education of the girls. Many of the activities of these departments fall within the curriculum leading to examinations and awards, but outside the timetabled programme there are sports fixtures, concerts,

Clockwise from top left: *Challenge and Adventure; Challenge and Adventure sailing; Bushcraft; Young Enterprise*

drama productions and clubs. These, with charity work, adventure training, community contacts and the wealth of other events for which the school is now known, weave themselves into the lives of the girls.

In 2010 the school magazine reported on the reintroduction of the Young Enterprise Company Programme which had been in place for a few years under Delscey Burns' headship. The scheme is open to LVI Form girls and gives them the opportunity to develop negotiation, innovation and problem-solving skills. They learn to devise a business plan leading to the design, production and marketing of products and culminating in a company report presented at an Annual General Meeting. In 2011 two companies were set up: 'Made in Calne', which produced a celebrity recipe book, and 'U', which produced personalised clothing and accessories. At the Wiltshire County Final the girls won four awards and 'Made in Calne' went on to the regional final.

The opportunities now on offer made a reality of Dr Wright's desire to provide an education tailored to the needs of each individual girl.

Clockwise from right:
Isabella Hay; Consider
the Lilies *exhibition
in Cork Street; Sylvia
Syms opens the Plumer
Galleries 2006*

Art

The Art Department at St Mary's is essentially one of
fine art. The scope has widened extensively in the last
ten years and the work that the girls study is now more
contemporary, with the staff keeping an eye on what is
happening on the art scene in London and bringing ideas
back to St Mary's. The whole scale of the department is
more ambitious. While continuing to endorse the tradition
of teaching drawing, painting, sculpture and print-making,
a greater number of girls are taught, some of the projects
are physically large and the media used are more diverse.
Exposure to visiting artists within workshops brings in fresh
ideas and experience.

The girls regularly enter competitions such as the
Oexmann Art Award Competition at the Wiltshire Heritage
Museum, where in 2010 Isabella Hay won first prize for
her paintings of domestic animals and received many
commissions. Also that year, Daisy Sims-Hilditch's work was
exhibited as one of the 20 shortlisted entrants in the annual
Sunday Telegraph Art Prize for Schools at the Saatchi
Gallery, and Jessica Wheeler exhibited at the Morton
Metropolis Gallery in London.

For the artists in the school, the opening of the Plumer
Galleries by Sylvia Syms in 2006 provided a significant space
in which to display their work. The corridors of Plumer
Wing were fitted out to allow a changing body of work to
be hung professionally. An exhibition *Exits and Entrances*
by the UV and UVI Forms of painting, printmaking and
sculpture, launched the project. Further work by pupils is
displayed around the school.

The arrival of the first artist in residence a couple of
years later was a new direction for St Mary's. James Jones,
a sculptor, gave the girls the chance to work outside the
curriculum and with the local community, learning about
new materials and processes and gaining an understanding
of the role of the artist.

In 2012 St Mary's brought together artists from the
School, past and present, for *Consider the Lilies*, an
outstanding exhibition at Gallery 27 Cork Street in London.
It was a remarkable event which presented the work of many
artists in addition to the superb work of current pupils. ➤ *165*

The school magazine of 2003 commented that 'swing fever' had hit St Mary's with the establishment of the jazz band earlier in the year, under the baton of Mr Harries. In the next years this band would grow in size and ambition, becoming a regular mainstay at Founders' Day and the leavers' Lily Ball in school, and by invitation for garden parties and festivals outside, often joined by singers from the school. A new venture in November 2010 was a Jazz Soirée in the specially decorated Top Hall in which parents enjoyed wine and food with the musical entertainment, an event which has continued and replaced the St Cecilia's Day concerts of previous years.

Keith Abrams, who had so ably headed the Music Department, continued to teach until his retirement in 2005. He is very fondly remembered by those who knew him, and one parent, who with his wife met Mr Abrams in passing when they visited the school, credits him with their decision to enrol their daughters at St Mary's, describing him as 'exceptional'. Mr Field, who had stepped in as director of music, left in 2006 and was followed by Mr Edward Whiting.

In 2007 Edward Whiting wrote that 'Music at a school such as St Mary's must never stand still, particularly when there is such enthusiasm and talent, nor is it likely to when initiative is so readily found amongst both the girls and their teachers.' Mr Whiting's arrival saw the birth of an opera group, a flute choir, two string quartets and a string ensemble. He reflected how, as significantly musical pupils come and go, groups coalesce and disperse, changing the direction and focus of the Music Department. A link was also established with the Royal Welsh College of Music, giving the school's most talented musicians an opportunity to compose, listen and study theory with others.

The centrepiece of the musical year at St Mary's is the annual spring concert, when pupils are able to present their work in front of a hugely appreciative audience of parents and visitors. This is an occasion when the major musical groups perform and the music scholars leaving that year give solo performances.

Until 2010 the St Cecilia's Day concert was held in the autumn term, in 2004 raising money for the church organ in a concert in which over 100 girls took part in different musical groups around the church. Wider recognition later led to many requests for the girls to stage fundraising concerts in towns and villages around Calne.

The enthusiasm and fun of music at St Mary's is clearly seen in the new form of an annual Company musical festival which was premièred in 2007. In an afternoon and evening of competition, each Company

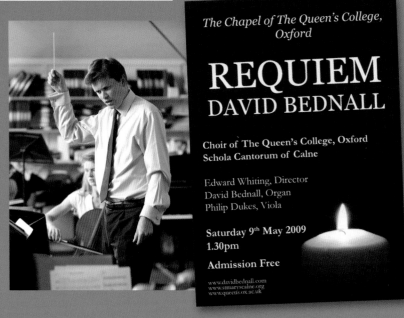

Edward Whiting and advertising flier 2009

presents vocal and instrumental ensembles and musical solos in brass, wind, piano and voice, with the winner from each solo section going on to perform for the Cecilia James trophy. In the evening the whole school comes together for Company songs taken from a theme such as The Beatles or Michael Jackson. These songs, known as the 'Company Shout', have been described as 'an explosion of noise and colour' involving music, costume and dance moves. Keith Abrams is among those who have been asked to adjudicate for the day.

The flowering of further music groups has provided a platform for girls of all ages to develop their musical skills and to perform in front of many people. In addition to the larger events, the pupils put on small concerts for occasions such as open days and new girls' days. An annual Fourth Form music competition, a junior choir and instrumental ensembles give encouragement to the younger pupils to extend themselves.

It is hard to describe the heights to which the music at St Mary's has climbed in recent years: the quality of the achievements; the diversity of the musical calendar; the scope of musical experience; and the commitment of the staff and the girls. Enrichment weeks have introduced the girls to lesser-known musical styles such as gamelan workshops, and they have been entertained by visiting musicians, including a group from Yale University.

135th anniversary celebration (top) and the spring concert (above)

The Golden Lily Awards

The Chamber Choir, made up of pupils from throughout the school, does much to keep alive St Mary's Anglican legacy through their large repertoire of spiritual music. The increasingly high standard that this choir has achieved has led to them being invited to perform in many wonderful settings, such as St George's Chapel, Windsor, St Paul's Cathedral and Christ Church Cathedral in Oxford. In 2008 the choir visited Paris, where in Notre Dame they premièred the first four movements of a Requiem composed for them by David Bednall. Later in the year they recorded the complete work, receiving widespread praise and excellent reviews. The first full performance took place in the church of St James, Spanish Place, in London, and the Requiem became the cornerstone of a wonderful tour the following year to America where they sang in churches in Maryland, Washington and New York, including the singing of 'Lux Aeterna' at Ground Zero.

Edward Whiting has taken the girls out into the world and given St Mary's a recognised place on the national stage. His time at St Mary's ended in the summer of 2012.

Four evening receptions drew many visitors including the artists and their friends and families, art dealers, collectors, journalists, school staff and passers-by. Many pieces were sold and offers were made on current pupils' work. Calne Girl Endellion Lycett Green, who opened the exhibition and helped to curate it, wrote, 'It has been an honour to work with an Art Department that keeps pushing boundaries, inspiring enquiring minds and encouraging students to dig deep and find their own voice.' The opening night saw the unveiling of Dr Helen Wright's portrait, commissioned from Daisy Sims-Hilditch by the school to hang with those of other St Mary's headmistresses.

St Mary's values highly the place of the arts within the school and provides scholarships to recognise excellence. Annually the music, drama and art scholars, with the pupil heads of the departments, arrange a Golden Lily Award evening: a celebration of achievements in each of these areas. This has developed into a red-carpet Oscar-like evening for the older girls where awards are presented over dinner by a special guest. It is a glittering event which puts the arts right at the centre of life at St Mary's Calne.

Drama and Theatre Studies

Each year, as the summer term draws to a close, the school looks towards the staging of the autumn drama production. These require a huge commitment from both girls and staff, but the magic that they sprinkle over the lives of those that experience them is a lasting reward.

All pupils at St Mary's have access to drama or the Theatre throughout their school career. Both classroom and exam drama can lead to opportunities to either perform in ambitious productions or to learn about and practise the technical side of theatre. An annual production by the Junior Drama Society gives all LIV Form and MIV Form the chance to take to the stage.

Over recent years the juniors have presented their own interpretations of *Animal Farm, Peter Pan* and *Robin Hood*, and have worked stories into stage plays in *Madiba Magic* and *Arabian Nights*. In 2009 the girls had the chance to explore the ideas, language and characters of Shakespeare through a staging of *The Tempest* and, as in many of St Mary's plays, the script was adapted by editing parts of it, creating new characters, and by having nine Ariels ensuring that he was 'everywhere'.

2011's ambitious production was a double bill of *The Pilgrimage and The Circle*, partly an adaptation of *The Caucasian Chalk Circle*. The girls excelled themselves in 'assured and compelling performances' in a challenge that saw actors in multiple roles and non-naturalistic sets and props.

While the younger girls follow their individual pathways of LAMDA, classroom drama and plays, they have the great inspiration and example of the work being undertaken further up the school. The build-up to the main autumn production permeates the corridors, creating a sense of excitement and, based on past experience, the knowledge that a treat is in store. This play, established and directed by Lilian Leadbetter, is led by the older girls but often includes some of the more junior and is always a stunning evening for the audience. The emotions evoked, the complexity of the productions, the standard of acting, singing and staging and the sheer spectacle are extraordinary.

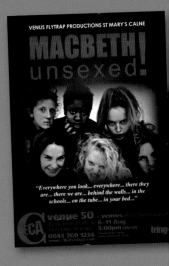

Victoria Price (top left), Nyasha Mugavazi (top centre), Matilda Ellis (top right), Charlotte Bell (front left), Olivia Gosling (front centre) and Nicola Randall (front right) as the Lady-killers

The production of *Cabaret* in 2003 combined elements of the stage musical and the film version and was described as a 'tour de force'. The following year St Mary's staging of *Chess,* a challenging choice, was greatly helped by advice from Sir Tim Rice and his daughter Eva, a past pupil of the school. In 2005 the psychological drama of *The Crucible* made terrific demands on the girls which they tackled with a sensibility that was mature and moving.

In 2006 we read of how in *All the World's a Stage,* 'across time and space, through juxtaposed genre and disciplines, the value of contemporary art, the nature of the universe, human rights, heavenly justice, musical genius and artistic and scientific endeavour were explored'.

Under the directorship of Lilian Leadbetter some exciting reworkings of established plays challenge the audience to view the familiar from a new perspective. In *The Taming of the Shrew and The Tamer Tamed*, she combined Shakespeare with Fletcher to produce the ultimate battle of the sexes. The action shifted between the two texts and from side to side of the stage, a process in which the audience became intimately engaged.

In *The Royal Hunt of the Sun*, an all-female cast tackled an all-male epic play in what proved to be a new departure for St Mary's, as Lilian Leadbetter took the play to London, where they performed in the Vanburgh Theatre at the Royal Academy of Dramatic Arts to capacity

Emma Pearce (Sixth Form Drama Scholar 2005–7) as John Proctor in The Crucible *(2005)*

Alexandra Webb (Sixth Form Drama Scholar 2007–9, left) as Petruchio and Elizabeth Dykstra-McCarthy (Sixth Form Drama Scholar 2008–10, right) as Kate in The Taming of the Shrew *(2007)*

Rebecca Rothwell (foreground centre) as Sandy and Davina Pearce (foreground left) as Danny in Grease *(2009)*

audiences. Those watching were described as being 'horrified and moved in equal measure by the portrayal of the conquest of the Incas'. This was the start of a close association with RADA.

In 2009 the Drama and Music Departments combined to put on *Grease*, 'a high-impact production'. It was visually stunning, with high-speed lighting effects, film montage and artwork by the LVI Form artists. *To Kill a Mockingbird* the following year was presented in a new adaptation by Lilian and the cast, a production that wove live gospel, blues and jazz music of the 1930s into the dramatic action. The autumn 2011 production of *Les Misérables* was described by Lilian Leadbetter as probably her most successful, but 'like going into creative battle with a theatrical juggernaut'. This huge production attracted record audiences who were entranced and entertained by the powerful presentation of acting and music.

Curriculum Drama at Sixth Form level has produced another strand of high-quality work both at AS and A2 level. The girls have for a number of years had the excitement and fun of taking plays to the Edinburgh Fringe, where they have received some excellent reviews. This has put St Mary's on a wider stage, as has the Shakespeare Schools Festival, an annual event in which thousands of secondary pupils perform half-hour plays in theatres across the country. A new venture, 'Acting Up', which is part of the National Theatre's Connection programme, takes acting into the community. Drama at St Mary's is now multi-faceted, and in the autumn of 2012, the Drama Department was privileged to have Sir Tim Rice as its official patron.

So many cast and crew members have been involved in St Mary's productions over the years. To be remembered among them is Mrs Debs Price, who worked tirelessly in the Theatre as wardrobe mistress and production manager from 2007 to 2012.

One of the highlights of Dr Wright's final year at St Mary's was the school's staging of *Hamlet*. Drawing on the tensions of 'To be or not to be', the play was an ingenious double ensemble, one in period costume followed by a second in contemporary dress. The large cast allowed many girls to be part of a production greatly praised for its acting, sets, music and costumes. The audience were drawn into the powerful portrayal of extreme psychological states which the actors presented with an impressive maturity.

LAMDA and RADA: Dramatic New Ventures

Almost 20 years after being the first to take a LAMDA examination at St Mary's in 1993, Kate Dierckx wrote to say that she was amazed to read that there were now over 100 LAMDA pupils. In fact 115 girls from throughout the school were being taught by a staff of five LAMDA teachers. Examination results for acting and the speaking of verse and prose up to Grade 8 Gold Medal have become increasingly impressive, with distinctions and merits being the norm.

In 2006 a unique venture evolved which saw the collaboration of the Royal Academy of Dramatic Art (RADA) and the St Mary's Drama Department. This resulted in the establishment of an advanced communications course for the UVI Form. This is the only course of its kind in a UK school, or indeed anywhere. The 'RADA Speak Out!' course includes weekend master-classes by RADA tutors and 12 weekly sessions delivered by St Mary's RADA-trained drama teachers. It ends with final student presentations at RADA in London.

To the delight of St Mary's, one of those RADA pupils, Olivia Gosling, later gained a place on a foundation course at RADA starting in September 2013.

In the Physical Education Department

Traditionally it was thought that the greatest strengths of St Mary's lay in areas other than sport. As the school moved into the early years of the 21st century, this was no longer the case; sport now takes an important place in the life of all the girls and with it comes increasing success. The indoor swimming pool, the fitness suite and the wide range of extra-curricular sport give a variety of opportunities to suit all the pupils. Among the biggest changes during Helen Wright's time were the introduction of sports' scholarships at 11+, 13+ and in the Sixth Form, and the extension of the timetable into full afternoons of sport both on weekdays and Saturdays.

On arriving at St Mary's at the youngest end of the school, the pupils are all timetabled to play the main sports of hockey, lacrosse, netball, swimming, tennis, athletics, gym and dance, and in the evenings they can then pursue the many extra-curricular sports. As the girls move up the school they opt for particular sports, become part of teams and plan their own programmes of fitness.

Netball, one of the first games that St Mary's girls played when the school came to its current site, continues to be popular. In 2005 the teams played 84 friendly matches and took part in 11 tournaments, scoring a total of 1,559 goals in the season. The U14 squad went on to represent Wiltshire in the South West regional tournament. In 2008

three girls were talent scouted and took part in additional training at one of Wiltshire's new satellite academies.

Lacrosse has developed through these years as well, with some of the girls attending lacrosse camps in the summer, and in 2007 a Welsh international player and her team ran a lacrosse clinic for the girls. An outreach programme has brought other schools to St Mary's, with an American coach teaching pop lacrosse. A ten-hour lacrosse festival one weekend in 2005 involved the whole school in a series of competitions between Companies, year groups and teams, raising money for charity in the process.

The lacrosse season at St Mary's in 2011 was described as a 'breakthrough season', when teams gained victories at the National Schools' Tournament and at the Marlborough College Invitation Tournament. Annabel Wright took a place on the U17 Wales Lacrosse Team following Grace Haworth who a few years before had been part of a Welsh national team.

During the summer term, trials in the week leading up to the inter-Company sports day give many of the younger girls the chance to compete in athletics, some of whom also take part in the many county competitions. Hannah

Above: *Netball team practice*

Left: *Amy Williams – the guest speaker at Founders' Day 2012*

Thompson, one of the school's many talented athletes, qualified for the National Pentathlon competition as part of the South West team in 2005 and in later years Hannah went on to participate in further national championships. Also in 2005 a new race, the cannon relay, was introduced at sports day, in which successive girls ran increasing distances.

The sports successes of 2007 were recognised at the annual sports presentation dinner that year with girls represented at county level in lacrosse and tennis, nationally in athletics and internationally in horse riding by Olivia Kuropatwa. By 2009 the girls were achieving so much in riding, both regionally and nationally, that riding colours were awarded for the first time. Success continued with Jessica Mendoza, Lucy Rogers and Franziska Goess-Saurau each representing England on equestrian teams in 2012.

In 2010 a group of LV form took part in an award in sports leadership, and they were later involved in running a prep schools' netball tournament, and led games sessions throughout the year in school.

Help from professionals can be stimulating and inspiring and perhaps all the more so when that person is a past pupil. In 2010 Emily Knight returned to St Mary's to run a lacrosse training session. Emily had gone on to play for Scotland's Senior Women's Lacrosse Team and

had had experience playing in a World Cup. The following year three Olympic athletes visited the school, including the skeleton racer Amy Williams, who was a speaker at Founders' Day in 2012.

To celebrate the tenth anniversary of the laying of the foundation stone of the swimming pool, the girls put on a display for invited guests, which included a synchronised swimming routine by Henrietta Page and her sister Verity from St Margaret's.

'Swifter, Higher, Stronger' were perhaps apt words to describe the place of sport at St Mary's in 2012, the year of the London Olympics which saw medals for a past St Mary's pupil, Laura Bechtolsheimer.

Above: *Annabel Wright playing for Wales*

Top right: *Jessica Mendoza*

Bottom right: *Emily Knight with pupils*

known as The Oratory, leaving the old Coulter Library
free to become an ICT suite. The junior library was moved
from above the seminar room to a room near the new
Oratory library.

The senior and junior non-fiction was now combined in
the Bodington Library, an area in which any girl may study,
and the younger girls learn to use the room for research in
support of curriculum work.

The libraries had always been overseen by a staff
member, with senior girls in charge of the day to day
running. In 1999 a librarian was first appointed, later
helped by an assistant, with girls still taking responsibilities.
With developments in technology, audio books are no
longer stocked, but the vast resources available online can
be downloaded straight to the girls' devices.

An active programme within the libraries brings visiting
authors and illustrators in to speak and to lead workshops,
run creative writing days and to arrange events for World
Book Day. In recent years the school has put more
emphasis on the libraries being used for personal research
and teaching.

Above: *The Oratory Library*

Top left: *Santa Montefiore talked to the girls in 2010*

Bottom left: *World Book Day*

The Libraries

The early records that St Mary's holds show how gradually
the library shelves were filled through the generosity of staff
and friends of the school. Each book given is recorded in
the diaries of Miss Matthews' time, with St Mary's bookplates
recognising the donor. As the collection expanded, rooms
changed to house them. With the reorganisation of School
House in 2009, what had once been the Chapel and later
a classroom was converted into the school's fiction library,

Off Timetable Time

As part of Helen Wright's wider look at the curriculum, she and her senior team viewed the timetable in terms of weeks, terms and years. This was a more fluid, cross-disciplinary approach that led to the introduction of Enrichment Weeks and Flexible Fridays.

The start of Enrichment Weeks in 2008 moved St Mary's into an exciting area that perhaps had its first stirrings in the themed weeks of Miss Matthews' time. Now every term the Fourth Form have time to focus on project work, problem-solving and out of school visits which nurture independent work and creative thinking. Departments are able to bid for blocks of time and also combine for activities. In its first year the events of Enrichment Week included bush craft, a Roman day, a tango workshop, a philosophy workshop, a Fairtrade day, several outings and a look at the challenges posed by the development of the Amazon rainforest.

The introduction of Flexible Fridays for the Fourth Form in 2010 gave much greater opportunity for longer sessions in subjects where this would be of benefit. The programme was devised by Mrs Botterill and Mrs Strudwick, who put together scenarios of how the time would be allocated in subjects such as art, music, personal development, critical thinking, swimming and Challenge and Adventure.

A Fifth Form programme of weekend workshops for critical and creative thinking has extended the academic life of these girls into wider areas. Those not following a geography course which takes the students on field trips to Iceland or Poland have immersed themselves in research projects. Each year after GCSEs are completed the UV form spend a week gaining work experience.

In the summer of 2009 the school introduced the Extended Project Qualification at Sixth Form level to develop skills such as research, evaluation and autonomous learning. The EPQs are now taken up by individual girls who want to look at a subject in greater depth and have covered areas such as the Spanish Civil War and the Higgs

Pastoral Care

A change of culture meant that there was now an understanding among the senior staff that the school and the boarding houses were intimately linked in how they worked with the girls. As the years have gone by, the support for the pupils has evolved. When the housemistresses, who are now all academic staff, became increasingly pivotal in the daily lives of the pupils, the role of the heads of year was no longer needed. The girls and the tutors are now matched from across the whole school rather than through the Company system, giving each girl the individual support best suited to her. The tutors and housemistresses see each other on a daily basis and are backed by staff on the senior team. Every member of the teaching staff is employed also as a house tutor with evening boarding duties.

Day girls are integrated totally into school life, with all the opportunities that are on offer to the boarders available for them. They have work and leisure areas among those of others in their year, and they can opt into any of the activities that are on offer.

boson. They are a hugely valuable way of extending their learning.

From early on in her time at St Mary's, Helen Wright promoted the weekly Sixth Form lecture programme. It is a very significant part of school life for these girls, bringing in a wide range of speakers from many areas of interest. In more recent years visiting Calne Girls have brought their knowledge and expertise back to St Mary's Calne in their own series of lectures.

In 2006 St Mary's began what is now an annual Women in Corporate Culture Conference at the school for the LVI Form. Each year a group of successful women from many career backgrounds speak about their professional lives, offering advice, sharing their views and giving more specific direction.

This opening up of ideas and pushing the boundaries of education was described by Dr Wright. She said, 'I believe that it is our mission to enable each individual girl to grow fully into the person she can be and is meant to be, releasing from within her that deep creativity and spirit which makes her truly who she is – an individual with a perceptive and inquiring mind, a generous heart, a grounded and creative sense of self, a great sense of humour and the ability to retain that childlike fascination that we all possess, and to be a joyful human being as a result.'

Left: *Natalie Baldwin with a tutee*

Below: *Mathematics Challenge in Top Hall*

Above: *The opening of Helen Wright House*

Right: *The Marchioness of Lansdowne*

With the girls grouped in their boarding houses by age, the Company system has always been an important way to mix the year groups. Charity fundraising, Company dinners and competitions in maths, drama and music, as well as in the many different sports, provide a way of creating a network of relationships among the age groups.

Helen Wright House

At some points in the history of St Mary's, projects have been undertaken which have had a major impact on life within school and the perception of those viewing it from outside. With the building of the Sixth Form Centre in 2008, the physical orientation of the school shifted. Looking from the main school towards the so-familiar lime kiln, there was now something to draw the eye beyond to what had once been a quarry boundary. Named after Helen Wright in 2012, the house is a striking timber-clad building partly sited on an area which had been the quarry pond. This boarding house for girls in their final year is phase one of a building which will eventually house all of the Sixth Form and encompass a courtyard garden.

The vision behind the plan was to give the older girls greater independence in their living and studying. It sets the Sixth Form slightly apart from the rest of the school and provides an environment which is more akin to a university residence. However the girls, while valuing the privileges of their living space, display a strong loyalty to their responsibilities within the school. They speak of their contacts with the younger girls through activities within the Companies, through drama, music and sports events, and with the help they give through clubs, St Mary's retains its sense of a caring community.

The Helen Wright House also gives the school wider opportunities to open up the premises to others. In its first years it was quickly seen as an ideal place to hold weekend reunions for Calne Girls and even hosted a hen weekend.

Looking ahead to the opening of the new building, Helen Wright chose 24 October in 2008 after realising that through a neat coincidence of timing this date would be exactly 100 years to the day after St Mary's relocated to Lansdowne Villa from The Green in Calne. The Marchioness of Lansdowne presided over the ceremony,

Above: *School House*

Left: *In the classroom*

as had a previous Marchioness all those years before. Rather than solely afternoon tea as then, the opening was celebrated with a champagne reception, lunch and a charity fashion show by Moberly Company.

Subsequent Building Developments

With the UVI Form moving into the new boarding house, space within the rest of the school could be reorganised for the other girls. When planning the new building Helen Wright and the governors wanted the accommodation for the middle school to also be improved. In the spring of 2008 work began to adapt Mews, Gibbins and St Cecilia's, creating spaces for 46 boarders and ten day girls in each of the houses.

An extension to St Cecilia's was now added beside the main house on a site which had once held three Curzon Street houses. When the only remaining wall fronting onto the road was stripped of rendering, the original window and door apertures were uncovered. Planners required that the new building had to use material of certain heritage standards. The extension provided 17 additional dormitory places and a staff flat. St Cecilia's now housed the UIV Form, Gibbins the LV form and Mews the UV Form. The changes were ready in September 2008 and the LVI Form were now able to take their place in Joyce Walters House. Plans were made for an extension to Joyce Walters to provide ten additional rooms in 2009. There was also need for new accommodation for the housemistress of Gibbins House.

The LIV Form were huge beneficiaries of the changes, as their domain in School House was soon completely reworked, with classrooms and areas for craft, textiles, model engineering and creative thinking and learning. The old Chapel now became the fiction library and named the Oratory and the small rooms opposite were mostly opened up to accommodate a textile area and a junior library. The first-year students at St Mary's now have all their living and classrooms in School House. Red Hall, which had seen many transformations over its life, is now furnished with comfortable seating and is used for displays of art work.

Careers

Records from the school archive show the ambition and success of many St Mary's girls down the decades from the earliest days. Far-sighted headmistresses opened up opportunities and tailored the curriculum to the demands of their times. Over the last ten years St Mary's has refined its personal development programme to give each girl support from their arrival to enable them to develop their talents and to make good choices for their futures. With the help of the dedicated staff at the school, the girls learn about work skills and risk taking and identify their strengths and their aspirations.

The Fifth Form girls receive career guidance from external advisors and the team within the school, and as they move into the Sixth Form the careers course is closely entwined with the university application process. The staff adapt the support they give the girls to the changes in this process, the ever-rising offer levels and the need for very thorough research and preparation. Sara-Jane Socha, whose career at St Mary's began under Delscey Burns and

Celebrating 135 years

Once again Salisbury Cathedral was the wonderful setting for the celebration of a landmark in St Mary's history. The Diocese of Salisbury has been there to support the school both spiritually and practically from its very earliest days. Many Bishops have confirmed pupils, acted as Visitor to the school and dedicated buildings. Historically the School Companies were named after people connected with the Diocese. The Cathedral is a fitting setting in which St Mary's can honour its past.

In 2008 a service led by the Dean, the Very Revd June Osborn and by St Mary's School chaplain, the Revd Peter Giles, celebrated the 135th anniversary of the school. The congregation were treated to the specially commissioned Requiem composed by David Bednall and sung by the Chamber Choir. Staff and parents joined the choir to sing anthems and the LIV Form and MIV Form choirs gave a performance.

At Founders' Day that year, the guest speaker at the commemoration service in the parish church was Mrs Anne Ferguson, someone who has given many years' service as a governor and who is also a Calne Girl. As a successful business woman, Mrs Ferguson has been in a strong position to give career advice and is a great role model for the girls. After the service, she joined the school for lunch and the annual formal prize giving, an event that Dr Wright had initiated early on at her time at St Mary's in order to celebrate publicly the successes of the pupils.

Celebrating 135 years in Salisbury Cathedral

*An Independent / State
Schools Partnership day*

which has evolved over the years, is now head of higher education and futures within the school. Her knowledge of universities and her experience and expertise are invaluable to the girls as she guides them through their UCAS applications, personal statements and references. Some of those now leaving are looking beyond the shores of Britain for their university education.

Contact with the Community

When Miss Matthews was headmistress of St Mary's she placed high importance on maintaining links within Calne. She herself took an active role in local organisations and encouraged the girls to be part of community projects. Like Miss Matthews before her, from early in her time at the school Helen Wright built up strong contacts within the town and felt it was important for the pupils to do effective work in the community. St Mary's School set up the North Wiltshire Independent/State Schools Partnerships Scheme through which it has established strong contacts with primary and secondary schools in Calne, as well as other organisations and churches. The schools have met for activity days, charity work and through events such as the lecture programme, the artist in residence exhibition and concerts.

An outreach programme, run by a member of the sports staff, takes pop lacrosse to local primary schools including St Margaret's and coaching is given to many other schools.

The Parents' Guild of St Mary's

The main concentration of girls in the school comes from Wiltshire or within an hour-and-a-half drive. Many families are able to visit St Mary's regularly and be involved in events that are taking place. Dr Wright's time saw the establishment of a Parents' Guild, the primary purpose of which was to provide an opportunity for social events in which parents within and across year groups could meet.

The Guild (PGSM) started life as the Friends of St Mary's in 2004, set up by Helen Wright and Lynn Copp, a parent of two girls in the school. They brought others together to form a committee with two representatives from each year group, the aim of which was to arrange at least one social gathering a year. The group now has a partnership with the Development Department, helping to raise money for charity and for the non-curricular needs of the girls. The largest event the Guild has established is a Christmas fair which draws together the whole school community before the carol service. There are now many social events both in and outside the school. The Guild runs a pimms and memorabilia stall at Founders' Day, and they have sponsored events such as a workshop run by the Royal Opera House, a tour of the casting studios at the V&A and a drugs education programme.

The establishment of the Foundation Trust in 2012 has given the Parents' Guild a secure future, but the PGSM maintains its independence and is run by the parents.

The Governors

Founders' Day of 2007 marked a significant occasion for St Mary's, as it was an opportunity for the school to thank Mr Richard Southwell QC on his retirement for all the years of service he had given, both as a governor and as Chairman of the Governors. Despite pursuing a very busy legal career in London he has given generously of his time to St Mary's and St Margaret's, overseeing key appointments, major developments in strategy and building, and by ensuring a robust constitution for both schools through his revision and review of the memorandum and Articles of Association.

Mr Southwell gave the address in church that Founders' Day and was, with the other guests, later entertained by a musical and dramatic tribute with an appropriate legal theme.

He was followed as chairman by Mr Simon Knight, who had had daughters in the school and who, with his background in land management, has brought his wide expertise to St Mary's. Since his arrival in 1997 Simon has been a member, and then chairman, of the governors' finance committee, where he has been able to take bold decisions about funding capital projects in the confidence that St Mary's future is well assured. Although living some distance away and having a demanding career, Mr Knight is a familiar face around the school.

The Governing Body

Back l–r Vicky Wilson, Anthea Griggs, Michael Pipes, Josephine Chesterton-Lam, Christine Lough, Alison Martin (Bursar)

Front l–r Simon Knight, Karen Cordon, Richard Southwell, Helen Wright, Peter Allen

Gladys Beale

Gladys Beale was a pupil at St Mary's from 1921 to 1926 when Miss Matthews was headmistress. Born in 1907 Gladys, the great-niece of Dorothea Beale, is at 105 years old the oldest Calne Girl. She was a member of the OGA committee and chairman when the Old Girls donated the cross and candlesticks to the school Chapel in memory of Miss Matthews.

Gladys took up teaching as a career and began her own boys' preparatory school in her home village of Minchinhampton. A colleague said of her, 'She had an affinity with pupils; she talked to them man to man.' In her old age, the local Vicar said, 'She is an extraordinary woman. She lives life to the full and makes the most of every day. Self-effacing and endlessly interested in others, she is quite simply an inspiration to us all.'

In Gladys Beale's 100th year, three Fourth Form girls, visited her and spent a happy morning talking to her about her time at St Mary's and her working life. She in turn was interested to hear of school life today and kept the girls well entertained with anecdotes and cake. The occasion was filmed for the school archives.

The Ellinor Gabriel Archive

St Mary's had never had a single dedicated place for its archives. Some had been kept in the headmistress's study, while others were scattered throughout the school in cellars or under eaves. With the establishment of the Development Department, the opportunity arose to create a room where all the archives could be catalogued, safely stored and displayed. Thanks to the generosity of the Old Girls' Association the room was fitted with shelves, cupboards and display cases and now provides an area where visitors can explore the history of St Mary's. During the 2010 reunion at the school, Sue Ross, Chairman of the Old Girls' Association, officially opened the archive room, naming it after Ellinor Gabriel, one of St Mary's founders. Miss Gabriel was a keen compiler of newspaper articles, two albums of which are in the archive.

One of the first undertakings related to the archives was to interview Gladys Beale, the oldest Calne Girl, who in 2008 was in her 100th year.

Above: *The Ellinor Gabriel Archive room*

Left: *The School Diaries*

Far left: *Sue Ross, Chairman of the OGA speaking at Founders' Day in 2011*

The Wider Educational World

Increasingly throughout her time at St Mary's Dr Wright made her name on the national stage. In 2011 as President of the Girls' Schools Association she was able to engage with the national debate on education and build relationships with other educators, confirming to her the dynamism and vision that is special to St Mary's. In her speech to the GSA conference with the theme of 'Making a World of Difference', Dr Wright looked at, among other things, the responsibility

of using the privilege of an outstanding education in making a difference to those with disadvantages in the wider world.

Helen Wright frequently espoused in public her enthusiasm for single-sex education for girls and her belief that it sets women on the track of becoming equal with their male counterparts. She also promoted her opinions on many issues related to young people and education and her concern about the early sexualisation of girls in the media, a further area which she highlighted in her role on the GSA.

A person of such forthright and vigorous views as seen by the outside world might appear to be intimidating to

those within the school. To the pupils, however, as well as being their headmistress she was a mother of three young children managing to balance her career and her family. Pupils were often invited into her home as baby-sitters and through their discussions with her they knew her to want the very best for each one of them. The girls were thrilled to meet Helen Wright when she returned to school within a few hours of giving birth to her third child, an event which made national headline news.

With greater globalisation, the opportunities for communication between schools across the world are enormous. In 2012 Dr Wright worked with colleagues internationally to set up a Global Girls' Schools Network to help establish contacts between schools. The staff at St Mary's Calne are also establishing worldwide links with charities in order to send girls out to work with them.

Charities

Every year St Mary's focuses its fundraising efforts on one main charity and nominated house charities but also supports many other causes, raising significant amounts of money in creative ways. When Dr Wright first arrived a charity day provided the main focus, with other events throughout the year. Soon the week preceding charity day was designated as charity week allowing for more research and preparation for the day. Sometimes representatives of the chosen charity visit the school, and lessons widen the girls' knowledge of particular issues such as spinal injury.

The charity of the year may be international, national or local, such as Calne First Response. Sometimes individual

Above: *Helen Wright with her daughter Jessica*

Top right: *Helen Wright (right) in Bangladesh for PlanUK*

Right: *Helen Wright and the Head Girls with the Tatler Award for the Best Head of a Public School*

girls or groups have a particular cause they are keen to support and for which they organise a fundraising event. In 2010 members of the UV form raised £3,550 for Help for Heroes through a party they organised as part of their Duke of Edinburgh's Award. Readathons and half-marathons, fêtes and cakes, film nights, discos and beauty parlours, these and many more events provide opportunities to raise funds and have fun.

In 2011, while President of the Girls' Schools Association, Dr Wright adopted two presidential charities to support and promote during her term in office. Both charities were also the beneficiaries of fundraising within St Mary's School. Funds for the Prince's Trust Enterprise Programme were channelled particularly into the needs of young women.

The GSA and St Mary's also supported the work of the international charity Plan UK, which highlights the plight worldwide of millions of girls without access to education. Their 'Because I am a Girl' campaign looked at fighting gender inequality, promoting girls' rights and lifting millions out of poverty. This was a charity in which Helen Wright took a great interest, travelling to Bangladesh to witness first-hand its work there. She hoped that one legacy of her time as President of the GSA was to have given the organisation a greater cutting edge in its approach to charity support.

Dr Wright described how the moral message that one must make a difference in the world became stronger for her over the years, seen in practice in the expansion of charities supported by the school.

The Adventures of School Life

Helen Wright once wrote about how the education the girls were receiving was a journey: 'They have learnt how to do and how to be, how to think and how to feel. I do believe that imagination lies at the core of this journey of life'. And as that journey takes the girls past the more familiar milestones that they expect on the way, sometimes the byways lead them into adventures and experiences that challenge and awaken them to new ideas. St Mary's Calne presents opportunities for the girls which they can explore as they wish.

There are none more so than the adventure trips to Bude for the Fourth Form, the school's own Challenge and Adventure programme and the Duke of Edinburgh's Award scheme. New skills are mastered, hidden talents discovered; they learn to care and share and cope; they develop self-awareness and tolerance. In one year of adventures, 'The girls survived the extremes of heat and cold, steep hills and unwelcoming terrain, unpredictable farm animals, disappearing paths, impenetrable jungle and their own cooking.'

Clockwise from top:
The Independent British Schoolgirls' Skiing Championships; A school trip to China; A school trip to Belize; The Duke of Edinburgh's Award; Bude 2012

In 2006 what was described as a 'cross-curricular adventure' took the LIV Form and the Year 6 pupils of St Margaret's to Cardiff for a day of mathematics, science and history. Here they learnt about binary arithmetic, the laws of physics and how to turn grain into flour.

Other visits took different year groups on field trips to rivers and seashores, for a Roman day at Westonbirt where they competed in their home-made chariots, and to see the old ships at Bristol dockyard. And always, every year, there are wonderful trips abroad either interdisciplinary or following a particular subject.

The LVI Form have joined other schools at the Winchester Symposium, where they have spent the day in pairs exploring English literature before presenting a paper for discussion. Among subjects covered have been ghostly literature, disease, villains and deceit in love. They have also, with the Fifth Form, been to workshops that have focused on developing their skills in learning styles, organisation, managing stress, responsibility, leadership and communication.

Then there are those special occasions that punctuate the school year: the carol service with its wonderful music; the staff entertainment; Burns' Night and its traditions that must have given Helen Wright a particular thrill; the mornings the girls awake to find the school grounds blanketed with snow, and the ensuing snowball fights with the staff. Memories are always being made and friendships are being forged.

Looking Ahead

St Mary's is a school that honours its past and values its traditions, but still has the confidence to look towards the demands and opportunities of the future.

In 2010 the senior master from Marlborough College, James Rothwell, was appointed by Helen Wright to review the curriculum and to develop academic initiatives. This led to a major on-going three-year study involving many of the staff, into how to develop and deliver a curriculum that would best suit the aspirational needs of young women today. Its preparedness to rise to challenges such as these has put St Mary's School in a strong position to continue to provide the highest standard of education and equips it well to surf the next wave of changes in the examination structure.

The high reputation of St Mary's has led to steadily increasing numbers. By 2012 St Mary's had 335 pupils on the register, the highest ever, with every sign that this would increase further. The balance of day girls and boarders and national and international students has been maintained. Greater pupil numbers and careful management have led to the robust financial health of the school, allowing for flexibility in planning. The governors had considered the optimum size of the school and had in place ideas for how the school buildings could be developed and improved. When the Helen Wright House was in the planning stage permission had also been acquired for a future extension to house the LVI Form. This

building programme began in the spring of 2013 and, with its completion, space will be released for development in the rest of the school. The governors were now also in lengthy discussion regarding the development of plans for the overall improvement of PE and sporting facilities for St Mary's and St Margaret's.

The increased numbers within the school had put pressure on the Dining Room, with the kitchen providing over 750 meals at lunchtime for St Margaret's and St Mary's pupils and staff. In 2012 plans were drawn up for a future extension to the building at ground-floor level, towards the tennis courts.

As electronic communications have become more diverse and widespread, St Mary's School has kept pace and made use of the new opportunities. A weekly e-Lily newsletter is sent to parents, and a termly one to prospective parents. The school's website is regularly updated. The school and the headmistress have a Twitter account; St Mary's Calne and Music at St Mary's Calne have Facebook pages; and school videos are uploaded onto YouTube. When the Chamber Choir made a tour to Florida a hugely successful blog was set up. The name St Mary's Calne is ever more widely recognised.

As the summer term of 2012 drew to a close, the school prepared to say goodbye to a number of members of staff. Among them were Nicola Botterill, deputy head of school, who was leaving to take up her own headship at Bruton School for Girls in Somerset, Edward Whiting, who had so

Above: *2012 geography trip to Iceland*

Left: *In Helen Wright House*

assuredly led the music in the school, and two members of staff who had been at St Mary's for many years: Mel Footman and Jane Dickson. Mel Footman appointed by Joyce Walters was an outstanding head of the English Department who maintained meticulously high academic standards. Jane Dickson had held such a significant place at St Mary's that on leaving, her roles were spread among 11 members of staff. She was one of those truly dedicated staff members that the school has been privileged to have known.

Dr Helen Wright's Time at St Mary's Draws to a Close

The raised profile of St Mary's is largely due to the huge amount of work that Dr Wright devoted to ensuring that St Mary's is firmly in the public eye. She became a regular contributor to educational matters on radio, television and in the major newspapers. The Director of the Wellington Sunday Times Festival of Education, Dr David James, wrote: 'She has transformed St Mary's Calne from being a good school in a rural part of England to being a high-profile market leader in single-sex education.'

By 2011 Helen Wright had developed St Mary's Calne into a school with an international reputation and now she received an opportunity to expand her own life beyond the shores of Britain. An approach by Ascham School in Sydney with the offer of the headship opened horizons for her, her husband and young family, and presented the natural next step in her career after leading St Mary's for nearly ten years. She felt the time was now right for both her and for

Top right: *Helen Wright with Calne Girls in Australia*

Below: *The 2012–13 Head Girl's team: Victoria Price, Isabella Warner, Georgina Terry (Head Girl) and Matilda Ellis*

St Mary's to move on. It was announced by the governors that Dr Wright would leave at Christmas 2012.

Helen Wright described how St Mary's held a very special place in her heart and will always do so. In the spirit of what is sure to be an on-going connection, she arranged that two St Mary's UV Form girls should spend three weeks in the summer of 2012 at Ascham School and a reciprocal visit was arranged for the autumn term.

Dr Wright's time at St Mary's was an extraordinary journey for both herself and for the school. It coincided with the birth and early lives of her three young children and she skilfully managed to nurture the well-being of her own family while overseeing that of all those other young people in her care. Helen felt that during her years at St Mary's she grew in wisdom to become more 'liberated and authentic'. She drew the admiration of many people and helped direct the lives of the generation of girls who were at St Mary's with her. When she left St Mary's Dr Helen Wright presented a prize in her name which recognises a girl who has demonstrated leadership through her strong integrity and values while at the school. This was awarded for the first time on Founders'

Day in 2012 to Georgia Perry, leaving head girl. She also set up the Helen Wright Bursary, as part of the Calne Foundation Bursary Fund, to support young women with leadership potential. During autumn 2012, Helen's last term, donations were made to this by parents who wished to recognise Dr Wright's enormous contribution to the school during her headship.

As the autumn term of 2012 drew to a close, the school gathered together to thank Helen Wright for her years of service to St Mary's and to wish her well for her future. Caroline Adler described how the governors, staff, pupils and parents had put their faith in her, saying, 'We believed that she could see the finished picture whilst we were still making the first tentative brushstrokes.' Lilian Leadbetter said, 'From the moment I met Helen I knew St Mary's was about to undergo a great period of change. As the school was once described, so was Dr Wright: "a pocket battleship". She was a truly inspirational and exciting leader and role model.' A parent, Lynn Copp, remembered the promise that Helen Wright had used which convinced her that St Mary's was the right school for her daughters: 'We teach your daughters how to learn', a promise on which she did not fail to deliver, the same promise that a previous headmistress, Miss Matthews, had made nearly 100 years before.

All those associated with the school can recognise the progress that has been achieved in the past ten years. Helen Wright hoped that she had 'reinvigorated the very essence of St Mary's'. Thanks to her vision, energy and total commitment, St Mary's School is now widely recognised as offering its pupils the very best education, and has stayed true to the ethos of its Christian foundation as a caring community, one of which all its members can be proud.

Canon John Duncan founded St Mary's School in Calne 140 years ago, praying that it would have a long and successful future. Arching down the years, a fellow Scot, Dr Helen Wright, left St Mary's in the sure knowledge that the school was true to its foundation, outstandingly successful and in a strong position to meet the challenges of the future with confidence.

Top left: Joyce Lynn (Walters), Delscey Burns, Carolyn Shaw, Helen Wright, Felicia Kirk

Dr Wright welcomed to St Mary's three of her predecessors and her successor during her final term in 2012

Left: Caroline Adler and Helen Wright at Helen's leaving reception in 2012

Dr Felicia Kirk, 2013–

As Dr Helen Wright was planning her move to Australia, the Governing Body of St Mary's was appointing a new headmistress, Dr Felicia Kirk, whose origins were in the United States. In January 2013 Dr Kirk took up the headship of St Mary's.

Felicia Kirk had lived in this country for some years with her British husband and was familiar with both day and boarding school life on this side of the Atlantic. She was brought up in Maryland and graduated with a BA in French and Latin from the University of Maryland. She later continued her studies at Brown University and in Paris. Dr Kirk's career began as an academic researcher in Cambridge before she took up teaching. She joined St Mary's Calne from Ipswich High School for Girls, where she was on the senior leadership team and head of the Sixth Form.

From her arrival Felicia Kirk focused on getting to know the girls as individuals. By asking the head girl, Georgina Terry, to introduce her to the assembled parents at her first open day, she put the pupils at the forefront of how St Mary's shows its face to the public. On that occasion Dr Kirk described the school as 'four walls around the future', a place where the aim is to foster 'confident, inquisitive and courageous young women' with the social and emotional intelligence to put their achievements to good use in their professional lives and to balance this with fulfilling relationships.

She believes that through their education the girls need to learn to be adaptable, to have the confidence to be risk-takers, to gain leadership skills and to have their voice heard. Felicia Kirk recognises the important part that her staff play in achieving this, how they work as a strong team to realise the expectations of a school such as St Mary's. Her passion for innovative teaching and learning and for high standards, in an environment where pastoral care is of the utmost importance, will see St Mary's School well on its way into the future.

Above: *Dr Felicia Kirk*

Left: *The 2013–14 Head Girl's Team: Jessica Fechner, Sophie Nye (Head Girl), Olivia Erwin, Emilia Flack*

Old Girls' Association/ Calne Girls Association

Records in the school archive show that Miss Dyas founded the St Mary's Guild in 1891 for the few early pupils who had been at the school while it was on The Green in the centre of Calne. In 1915 a later headmistress, Miss Donaldson, was urging Old Girls to join a re-launched Guild, and it was at this point that the organisation became better established. In 1916, soon after the arrival of Miss Matthews as headmistress, the Guild committee sent out their first copy of the News Sheet, a slender publication which they hoped would develop into a magazine with contributions from readers. A pupil list, school events, news of the Guild and individual Old Girls all featured. In the spirit of Miss Matthews' belief in service to others, each year Guild members were asked to send in particular garments they had made such as a pinafore, apron or a pair of knickers. These were then exhibited and sent on to a charity. Old Girls were also encouraged to subscribe to their branch of the United Girls' Schools' Mission.

Gill Everett, Mary Henly, Sue Rotherham and Rachel Benson with
Lilian Leadbetter at a reunion in 2010

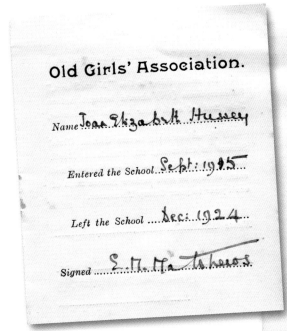

Old Girls' Association.

Name Joan Elizabeth Hussey

Entered the School Sept: 1915

Left the School Dec: 1924

Signed E. M. Matthews

Old Girls are asked to keep in touch with the School—

(i) By subscribing to the "News Sheet," Subscriptions (1/6) should be sent before July 2nd of each year to the Treasurer, The News Sheet, S. Mary's School, Calne.

(ii) By subscribing to the United Girls' School Settlement, 15, Peckham Road, S.E.5. Subscriptions (there is no fixed sum) should be sent before March 25th of each year to your Group Treasurer.

Name I. C. Martin

Address Hunsdon Mill House, Stanstead Abbotts Ware Herts

You are asked to remember the School especially on **March 25th and July 2nd.**

PRAYER FOR THE SCHOOL.

Vouchsafe, O heavenly Father, to direct and prosper all that is done for the welfare of Thy children in this our School; and grant that all members of this School may work together for the good of each other, and to Thy honour and glory. We commend to Thy loving care our parents, our relations and friends, the benefactors of the School, the Governors, and all who teach and all who learn in it; and because through the weakness of our mortal nature we can do no good thing without Thee, grant us the help of Thy grace that we may please Thee both in will and deed, through Jesus Christ our Lord. Amen.

Remember, O merciful God, the souls of Thy faithful departed servants by whose faith and works this School was begun and carried on. Grant to them, and to all who rest in Christ, refreshment, light and peace. And we beseech Thee O God, remember all those who have gone out from us into the world; pour out upon them Thy Holy Spirit to strengthen and to purify them, that giving themselves up to Thy service, they may reign with Thee in life everlasting, through Jesus Christ our Lord.

An early OGA membership booklet

From the early News Sheets we see that Miss Donaldson continued her association with St Mary's by holding the post of vice president of the Guild. There were three meetings each year: one, a 'Summer Festival' at St Mary's, was a reunion which included a Chapel or church service, tennis matches, dinner, speeches and entertainment by the girls and also by Miss Matthews, who read old favourites such as *The Highwayman* and *The Old Vicarage – Granchester*.

Miss Matthews was known to be a great letter-writer, and although the News Sheet appeared each year, it was largely through her efforts that the school maintained contact with all its Old Girls. By 1921 Miss Matthews was beginning to feel that the Guild did not supply the necessary link with the school, and she urged more Old Girls to subscribe to the News Sheet as a way of keeping contact and having notice of upcoming events. Later she wrote, 'As the years go on and new generations arise it is impossible for them to keep in touch with the older Old Girls; we can no longer all be known to each other in the same way.'

The need for more structure led to the inauguration of the St Mary's Association in 1928, later becoming known as the Old Girls' Association. Within a year, 102 Old Girls had paid their £1 1s life membership subscription and 35 had paid first instalments. Subscriptions for copies of the News Sheet were 2s annually. The hope was that in time there would be a 'complete chain' of those who had passed through the school. Miss Dyas was among those early subscribers.

The constitution stated that the membership should consist of a president and vice president, posts held at first by Miss Matthews and Miss Alexander; Associate members, who included Archdeacon Bodington and staff; and members, who were girls who had received their lily leaving badge at the end of their school careers. A committee was made up of the president, two representatives from each of the Old Girls' groups and the current head girl. A sub-committee was appointed to arrange the London reunions. Old Girls were divided into groups for the collection of subscriptions and news, each group headed by a secretary.

Katherine Barton, who had arrived at St Mary's in 1898, was the first secretary of Group 1. She represented all those who had left the school before 1915, but as she later wrote, despite writing to and visiting those she knew of,

As the years went by, the committee arranged both reunions and fundraising events. The money raised went towards projects within the school and also to the Bursary Fund, which provided support particularly for daughters of Old Girls. In 1975, after Mrs Bailey's arrival as headmistress, the school began producing its own magazine and the OGA News Sheet focused particularly on alumnae interests. For a time the finances were described as being on the 'breadline', but Old Girls rallied round and by 1993 mini-reunions were being arranged around the country, and indeed the world. This was the year that the OGA published *Portrait of Miss Gibbins* by Mary Warren-Smith, a collection of memories and the transcript of a conversation that Mary had held with Elizabeth Gibbins. It was not long before the OGA started a database of members.

Owing to a new method of paying subscriptions, by 1995 the OGA had an assured income and the committee decided to invest any surplus. Charitable status was sought and a new constitution was drafted.

Above: *Reunion of the 1981 leavers*

Right: *A letter to the OGA members*

she only had 14 members in her group. She was succeeded as group secretary by an even earlier pupil, Alice Frayling, who in turn was followed by Ruth Baker. Ruth had joined St Mary's in 1906 so was one of those who experienced the move from The Green to the new site. She was a regular attender at reunions and later, as treasurer, she husbanded and invested the small resources of the OGA.

Ivy Martin, the first secretary of the Association, wrote that they wanted reunions to be more than 'just a tea-party', and requested suggestions. Among those attending the reunions were members of the Sixth Form. The Old Girls were active in raising money for the Old Girls' Scholarship Fund through sales of work. Ivy Martin became chairman of the Association in 1936, a role she carried out for ten years.

In 1947, after Miss Matthews' death, the constitution of the OGA was changed to allow for the election of presidents for a term of six years, although in reality the current headmistress has always taken this role. London reunions had become a regular event, and there is a record of regional meetings when Gladys Beale became Chairman of the OGA after Ivy Martin.

S. MARY'S SCHOOL, CALNE.
Reunion July 27th—30th, 1945

Members of the O.G.A. are invited to a Reunion at the School from tea time on Friday, July 27th, until after breakfast on Monday July 30th. The new Headmistress, Miss J. I. Field, hopes to be present on Saturday.

Over 200 members have asked for further particulars of the Reunion so we are hoping for a large attendance. It may be difficult to find beds for all—our normal accommodation is for 150 all told—so members are asked to be very particular in filling up the form enclosed and to return it, without fail, **by the 5th July.** No changes should be made after that date except for exceptional reasons. Those attending should bring towels, soap, music, tennis racquets, and balls if possible. The charge will be 4/- for one night or 10/6 for the three nights.

No rations need be brought, but numbers expected **must** be given to the Food Office some considerable time ahead. (No evening dress expected.)

TRAINS:	Paddington	9.15	1.15	4.15	6.30
	Calne	12.10	4.45	6.55	8.50
	Calne	11.5	5.25	} Sunday	
	Paddington	3.50	8.45		
	Calne	7.40	9.0	} Monday	
	Paddington	10.30	12.45		

Please return to Miss Matthews before July 5th.

Those who have already said they hope to be present **must**, please, return this form.

I hope to be at the Reunion arriving on ....
at (approximately)................ ....p.m. and leaving on ....
at (approximately)..... .... a m. I should like, if possible, to sleep
in a room with ....

Signed ....
Address (which will find you
up to the last moment) ....

The Calneval Ball in 1970

Over time, the income from the Bursary Fund had diminished significantly, prompting the OGA committee, under the chairmanship of Sue Ross, to launch an appeal in order to reinvigorate it. Iona Wake-Walker (Maclean) wrote to every Old Girl and as a result of their generosity more than £22,000 was added to the Fund. A further fundraising project was the compilation of a booklet of prayers contributed by past pupils.

Calne Girls have always received a warm welcome when they visit St Mary's, and those lucky enough to be at the school for the reunion in 2006 witnessed a wonderful tribute to Miss Gibbins, celebrating the 60th anniversary of her arrival as headmistress. The girls of the lower school staged a play, *Where Angels Fear (to Tread),* written by the director of drama, Lilian Leadbetter, which represented the life of Miss Gibbins in small cameos of speech that illuminated aspects of her life as the narrative moved from girl to girl. It was a clever and evocative portrayal which charmed those who saw it and which would have touched Miss G.

Times were changing and in 2010, in order for the OGA to maintain its commitment to the alumnae, appeal to its future members and present a modern face to the outside world, the committee oversaw a transition to the Calne Girls Association. With this development came a modernised magazine and a greatly improved website.

Along with Sue Ross's retirement in 2010 were several other changes on the committee which, as Frippy Fyfe

Clockwise from top:
*2010 Calne reunion;
Fifth term reunion
in London; A Calne
weekend hen party 2012;
The cover of the first CGA
magazine 2011*

(Maitland), the new chairman, wrote, 'offers on one hand huge wisdom and experience and on the other hand a youthful enthusiasm and energy'. It was this committee which joined the school in setting up the Calne Foundation Trust that now oversees the Bursary Fund.

In 1946 Ivy Martin wrote, 'There is fun and interest and refreshment when St Mary's people meet – refreshment because we share a common heritage of thought and belief, and when we meet we find again values which in the hurly-burly of life have often become blurred or crowded out.' This sentiment remains as meaningful to Calne Girls today as it has been down the generations.

CHAPTER NINE

St Margaret's Preparatory School

There are some charming photographs from the early days of St Mary's of a few young faces, both girls and boys, among those of the older pupils of the school.

We do not know much about the younger children or what was the school's admission policy. What we do know is that when Miss Matthews arrived in 1915 as headmistress she employed Miss Abdy, a Froebel-trained teacher, to look after the juniors. She stayed until 1921, when the following tribute was paid to her: 'She has made the Kindergarten one of the happiest and best parts of the School; all the little ones who have been under her care owe to her far more than they will ever realise.'

The junior pupils in 1928

Far left: *Kindergarten pupils around 1918*

Left: *Kindergarten pupils in St Prisca's 1928*

When St Prisca's boarding house was bought by the school the following year, certainly more than one form of junior pupils moved in, and there is a photograph of some at work on the verandah. At the service on 11 November 1919 in the Chapel when, like the whole country, the pupils held a two-minute silence as ordered by the King, the Kindergarten and Form 1 were present, standing in the aisle. However, in 1925 the governors' minutes record that the Junior Department was having to close from lack of pupils. Two years later it reopened with ten girls and by 1929 there were three classes: Kindergarten and Forms 1 and 2.

In the 1936 News Sheet there is a description by St Mary's head girl, Suzanne Hobson, of how every morning the junior pupils had hymns and prayers, and of Miss Mosse teaching 15 children of different ages

If you were to look through the window one day you would see her sitting in the middle, perhaps listening to someone reading, while on all sides the work goes on, apparently by itself. Some are doing copy, others arithmetic or tables, while on the mantelpiece are the results of their handwork

– an illustration of a history story, a large picture of a Zulu village, calendars, bags and future Christmas presents. But no-one comes to school to learn lessons alone. You tie up your own shoe-laces, and see that your finger-nails are clean; if you wish to ask a question, you do not call out or run across the room, but put up your hand. Their games are as the sand of the sea-shore in number. They usually like to know all about the big school – what the badges stand for, why there are cages on the lacrosse pitch and who sleeps in each room. Life at St Prisca's is a goodly thing and lucky are those who begin their school life there.

The juniors were sometimes involved with events in the senior school. At Christmas in 1938 Miss Matthews held a musical 'At Home', at which staff played solos and senior girls sang carols to accompany a nativity tableau given by the Kindergarten. Every day they went to the main school for their lunch, and at break 'little blue-bereted figures rush round St Prisca's garden, or stand on the wall and wave to their friends playing lacrosse'.

For a time the Junior Department moved to the large room behind the dining room, as space was required in St Prisca's for boarding, and later again there was a spell in St Bridget's in the town. Then in 1940 the Juniors occupied the east wing of the old isolation hospital at the top of the school site. This was a temporary move though, as before long they had to make room for the evacuated Hammersmith School of Art and later for St Stephen's

School from Shepherd's Bush. Eventually, towards the end of the war, they were able to take up permanent residence, and have remained there since.

When St Mary's acquired the old hospital they named it St Margaret's, perhaps in recognition of Canon Duncan's Scottish roots. One of the rooms, which is now used as the staffroom, contains a small stone statue of St Margaret in a niche in the wall. The original building had a main central block of two rooms with two more running at right angles across the ends. These high-ceilinged rooms still exist, as do the wide doorways which allowed hospital beds to be moved around.

For many years St Margaret's functioned as a department of St Mary's, with Miss Joyce Gosney as mistress in charge from 1954 to 1977. Remembered by colleagues as a kind and gentle person, hers was a familiar face to the St Mary's girls as she led her pupils down to lunch in a room at the end of Long Passage. It was Miss Gosney who began a brownie pack at St Margaret's School.

In 1967 Miss Eason arrived from the Republic of Ireland to teach the youngest children, recalling in later years that at that time there were 39 pupils in the school, a few of them boys, who mostly came from the big farming families around Calne. On Joyce Gosney's retirement it fell to Joyce Eason to take on the running of St Margaret's, and when Kay Stedmond wrote her history in 1986 the school had become very popular, with 75 pupils and five full-time members of the teaching staff. Miss Eason was resident for some years in Gibbins House in the senior school, undertaking weekend duties such as supervising breakfasts and accompanying the girls to church.

Traditionally St Margaret's had been considered 'the school at the top of the path', but it gained the strong

support of two local governors of St Mary's, Mr Robert Henly and Lord Shelburne, both of whom had children in the junior school. Gradually the profile of St Margaret's rose and in 1988, the bursar announced that the governors considered the time had come for St Margaret's to become a separate school while continuing to make use of some of the St Mary's facilities. Numbers were to increase beyond the limit of 80; there would be a separate form and teacher for each year group, and a new building housing four classrooms had been commissioned. This came to be used for the infants while the juniors remained in the original building.

Over the years the demand for places had not always been as strong, and on several occasions the governors had had to consider whether to continue to support St Margaret's. A difficult period again arose when a further head followed Miss Eason in 1989 and numbers dropped. A governor's sub-committee was formed under the chairmanship of General Sir Maurice Johnston, who was

described as going to great lengths in giving support to the school. In time the governors asked Miss Burns, the headmistress of St Mary's, to take on the management of St Margaret's. She in turn asked Mrs Karen Cordon, who had joined the teaching staff in 1989, to act as deputy head and to oversee the day-to-day running of St Margaret's. She took up the role in January 1994 with such success that when Mrs Shaw was headmistress at St Mary's, Mrs Cordon was given autonomy by being appointed as the headmistress of St Margaret's, a post in which she remains

Above: *Year 1 sports practice*

Left: *Joyce Eason and St Margaret's pupils*

Right: *Karen Cordon*

the two schools have an exceptionally close relationship. Growing from a common foundation, St Margaret's, like St Mary's, has a Christian ethos running through all that the school does.

The late 1990s and early 2000s were years that had a profound effect on the future success of St Margaret's. Karen Cordon had been joined on the teaching staff in 1990 by Cath Jones and in 1991 by Sarah Giles. It was these three who drove the changes that have helped place the school in a strong position today. Cath Jones, at first a class teacher, later became deputy head. Sarah Giles was responsible for monitoring and assessment, a role that has helped push standards up. Mrs Cordon wanted the school to become a proper preparatory school, recognised by the IAPS. They began to create a full curriculum with primary specialists in ICT, music, languages and PE, as well as appointing some male teachers. The changes leading up to 1997 helped them to work towards their goal, and by early in the new millennium the school was full and they had a waiting list.

up to the present. Among her staff was Joyce Eason, who continued to give great service to St Margaret's until her retirement in 1999.

St Mary's Calne and St Margaret's Preparatory School are two schools run by the same Board of Governors, with their finances overseen by one bursar. Karen Cordon sees the schools working together as one community despite the fact that St Margaret's is broadly a non-selective co-educational day school while St Mary's is a selective girls' boarding school. Perhaps unusually this works well, and

The governors, under the chairmanship of Richard Southwell QC, now made the brave decision to double the size of the school to a two-form entry without increasing class sizes and with a particular desire to bring in more boys. This has always been a difficult issue for St Margaret's as, owing to the strength of St Mary's as a girls' school, perceptions were against seeing St Margaret's as being able to provide boys with a strong education that prepared them well for entry to secondary school. However things gradually changed, and from the ten per cent of boys when Mrs Cordon arrived, St Margaret's is now around 45 per cent boys.

As a governor, Richard Southwell had taken a particular interest in St Margaret's, confident that it could have a successful future and ensuring that funding for development was forthcoming. It was he, along with Karen Cordon, who formalised a Parents' Association which supports the school through its fundraising, social events and in its welcome to new families. The decision to expand led to a need for considerable investment in more facilities. In 2000 a multi-purpose assembly hall was built, more classrooms were added to the existing ones and spacious corridors linked the buildings. Fittingly the new assembly hall is called the Southwell Hall.

The Kindergarten and a reception class, the first of the parallel stream, were opened in 2003. For a while other rooms stood free but year by year were filled by new classes of pupils. In 2007/8 and 2010 further rooms were added, replacing various temporary buildings. The school then totalled over 200 pupils, with some of the children coming in through a community bursary scheme at KS2 level.

Along with the new rooms came an increase in staff numbers, with additional specialist teachers. Latin was added to the curriculum for Years 5 and 6 and Spanish has been taught since 2011. Specialist subjects, including swimming, are taken by the three-year-olds upwards. Learning support has grown from a part-time post in 1990s to two full-time teachers now working in two rooms, one a specially equipped speech and language room built in 2012.

As ICT has developed the school has moved from an initial typewriter, followed by six PCs to a fully equipped ICT suite, as well as computers and interactive whiteboards in every classroom. St Margaret's now has gap-year students helping in this area, as well as with sport and music. The high standard of music was recognised with a gold award as a Singing School, and St Margaret's now has an orchestra, as well as samba and rock bands.

Part of the 2007/8 build had included a room for St Margaret's after-school club, known as 'Maggots', embracing the name that the junior school had been fondly called by the St Mary's girls. A club had first been started in 1998 in a portacabin with eight children. There are now 50 to 60 in attendance most afternoons.

St Margaret's makes use of some of the senior school facilities: every day the children have their lunch in the Dining Room; the older children use the Science Laboratories each week; they make use of the playing fields; and all the children learn to swim in the St Mary's pool. St Mary's girls regularly help in the junior classes. The big occasions such as Harvest Festival and the Carol Service are held in St Mary's School Chapel and Revd Giles has been one of those visiting St Margaret's to take assembly.

Academic excellence is the driver of decisions, with an emphasis on the performing arts and sport. Expectations are high and every year girls who enter St Mary's from the prep school are often among the top scholars. Karen Cordon has forged strong links with other senior schools over the years and always recommends which school a child is most suited to.

Statue of St Margaret in the wall of the staffroom

Above: *Year 6 pupils walking up to St Margaret's 2011*

Right: *The Kindergarten children going swimming 2012*

St Margaret's sees itself as a school with traditional values but with an innovative and creative approach to education. OFSTED and ISI inspections have regularly recognised the school as outstanding in all areas. Parents are hugely appreciative of what Karen Cordon has done for the school. One commented that 'St Margaret's is a warm and friendly school with incredibly committed staff, particularly Mrs Cordon, who ensure all pupils, boys and girls, reach their fullest potential. Despite being non-selective, St Margaret's has a very strong academic focus and provides excellent preparation for senior school.'

The school is looking ahead to a new centre of learning with a library soon to be added to the technology area. This is a school which more than fulfils the aims that Miss Gabriel, Mrs Murray and, above all, Canon Duncan aspired to 140 years ago. It serves the community providing the very best education and even now, the present Vicar of St Mary's Parish church, the Revd Bob Kenway – like Canon Duncan – is a familiar presence in the school.

*At the centre of the grounds of St Mary's School stands
the lime kiln, a reminder of times past. From here
one can look over Calne towards the parish church
of St Mary and to the downs beyond, the landscape
that has been the backdrop to the school over the
decades. Nearer at hand are the familiar school
buildings representing developments under different
headmistresses. These were the women who with the
support of their governors and the dedication of their
staff did so much to shape the lives of those in their care.
Many were strong individuals who led from the front,
upheld the values of the school through their example
and carried it forward into the next generation. There
have been difficult times and glorious times, sadness
and joy, but above all has been the continuing spirit
of faith, determination and hope that the three founders
gave to us all so many years ago.*

*A drawing of the lime kiln from the
1995 prospectus (above) and St Mary's
School today (right)*

List of Subscribers

This book was supported by the generosity of the subscribers listed below.

Caroline Adler (Staff)	1982–2007	
	and 2011–	
Phoebe Aldridge	2010–	
Lucile Allender	2013–	
Rowena Annable	1983–89	
Samantha Axtell		
(née Benham)	1984–90	
Laura Barlee		
(née Attlee)	1936–40	
Julia Baron	1949–53	
Ella Bavinton	2012–	
Lara Bavinton	2012–	
Margaret Beckett		
Rachel Benson		
(née Woods)	1956–61	
Rosalind Birchall MBE		
(née Henderson)	1952–57	
Helena Boase	2009–	
Nicola Botterill (Staff)	2007–12	
Constance Bowkett-Pritchard		
	2005–12	
Emily Bradshaw	2009–	
Suzie Bradshaw	2009–	
Caroline Brenchley	2012–	
Julia Buckingham	1962–68	
Delscey Burns		
(Headmistress)	1985–96	
Virginia Butler	1975–81	
Claire Byrne		
(née Anderson)	1982–89	
Chiara Candido	2013–	
Anne Carter		
(née Garrad)	1938–42	
Emily Chaffer	2007–	

Lee Chalk (Staff)	2002–
Leonora Clark	2005–12
Emily Clarke	2007–
Celia Cotton	
(née Beale)	1955–59
Nicolette A. Cotton	1942–46
Kitty Crawford	
(née Hood)	1942–46
Kelly Crockett (Staff)	2007–
Daisy Crone	2010–
Jean Caroline Cross	1974–81
Colette Culligan (Staff)	1983–98
Ammy Davies-Potter (Staff)	2010–
Nick Davies-Potter	
Lesley Davis	
(née Lea-Wilson)	1941–45
Rodger Davis (Staff)	1964–2000
Elizabeth Dawson	
(née Copeman)	1947–50
Kate de Montjoye	
(née Mahaffy)	1970–76
Clare Denman	
(née Troutbeck)	1941–46
Isabella Depla	2011–
Lucy Depla	2006–12
Rosemary Devonald	
(née Herbert Smith)	1934–45
Jane Dickson (Staff)	1991–2012
Thea Dillon	2011–
Imogen Dobie	2008–
Laura Doel	2011–13
Joan Dorling in memory of	
Peggy Pepper	1969–84
Eleanor Dove	2007–
Flossie Dove	2006–13
Emily Dundas	2008–13
Joyce Eason (Staff)	1967–99
Jemima Ellis	2012–

Matilda Ellis	2006–13
Tabitha Ellis	2009–
Olivia Erwin	2007–
Lucy Evans	2010–
Vicky Eyre	
(née Huddy)	1976–83
Jessica Fechner	2007–
Zanya Fechner	2012–
Arminel Fennelly	
(née Sebesta)	1966–71
Annabel Fenton	2013–
Charlotte Fenton	2012–
Ella Fenton	2013–
Lara Fenton	2007–12
Victoria Fenton	2005–10
Alexandra Finch	1986–93
Isabel Finch	1989–96
Mary Ford	
(née Keevil)	1943–56
Sue Foreman (Staff)	1991–
Letitia Frome	2006–13
Frippy Fyfe	
(née Maitland)	1965–69
Deb German (Staff)	2001–
Tony German (Staff)	2010–13
Father Peter and Elizabeth Giles	
(Staff & Former Parents)	1991–2013
Marcia Gooderham	
(née Matthews)	1928–36
Olivia Gosling	2006–13
Polly Gould	
(née Horne)	1966–70
Sarah Gralla	2011–
Peggie Green	
(née Beale)	1929–33
Julia Hailes	1974–79
Marion Hamlin	
(née Jefferies) (Staff)	1965–67

Martin Harker	
Angelo Harrison (Staff)	2011–
Eleanor Harrison	2007–
Commander Henry Harwood	
(Bursar)	1977–88
Cynthia Haworth (née Aldrick)	
Josephine Herrlinger	
(née Guillaume)	1962–67
Jacqueline Hewitt	1972–78
Jocelyn Holland	1967–73
Athina Hostelet	2013–
Penny Howell	1960–66
Susie Hunter Smart	
(née Agnew)	1963–68
Sarah Ivatts	
(née Tolson)	1948–56
Isabella Iversen	2012–
Laura Cecilia James	
(née Livingstone)	1941–43
Rebecca Jump	2008–
Anne Kelly	1939–45
Anne I. Kerr	
(née Shaw)	1943–47
Dr Felicia Kirk	
(Headmistress)	2013–
Jennifer F. Lacey (Staff)	1974–2005
Joyce Lam	2012–
Louise Lancaster	
(née Arbuthnot)	1966–71
Eloise Le Fevre	2009–
Kate Le Fevre	2006–13
Lilian Leadbetter (Staff)	1992–2013
Anne Littlewood	1946–59
Susan Lloyd	
(née Woodroffe)	1944–48
Torla Mackarness	
(née Tidman)	1933–38
Sophie Mallinson	2012–

Joanna Martin		Angela Purdon	1970–75	Ros Senior		Shireen Uren	
(née Lamb)	1970–75	Camilla Purdon	1995–2001	(née Whinney)	1956–62	(née Moore)	1941–47
Annabelle Mastin-Lee	2009–	Eleanor Purdon	2002–09	Carolyn Shaw		Marina Vestbirk	2012–
Mary Mather		Alexis Purdy	2012–	(Headmistress)	1996–2003	Jasmine von der Esch	2009–13
(née Field)	1939–45	Juliet Purdy	2011–	Alexandra Slater		Janie Walker	
Jane Miller		Sarah Randall	2005–10	(née Reece)	1985–91	(née Marilyn Winther)	1957–62
(née Roberts)	1950–56	Nicola Randall	2008–13	Isobel Slater	2011–	Sophie Wallace	2001–08
Sophie Milne	2010–13	Rebecca Randall	2010–	Phyllida Smeeton		Chloe Waller	2009–
Sophie Montagu Douglas Scott		Victoria Rassmuss	2011–	(née Nicholson)	1952–59	Sally Walters (Former Staff)	
	1978–85	Henriette Reckhenrich	2012–13	Isobel Smith	2009–	Buffy Wareham	
Matilda Moore	2012–	Rosamund Reece		Sara-Jane Socha (Staff)	1985–	(née Barnett)	1968–73
Lali Naunton Morgan	1978–84	(née Roberts)	1960–64	Belinda and Richard Southwell		Alexandra Warner	1997–2004
Janet Morris	1939–45	Alta G. Ridgway (Staff)	2005–	(Chairman of Governors)	1997–2005	Eleanor Warner	2003–10
Georgina Mullins		Pamela Rifaat		Beth Spinks	2012–	Isabella Warner	2008–13
(née Gardiner)	1978–85	(née Pam Saxon)	1939–42	Susannah (Buzz) Stanton		Katherine Warner	1998–2005
Caroline Mytum		Jane 'Other' Ritchie	1962–67	(née Valli)	1965–71	Catherine Watson	2005–10
(née Reis)	1967–79	Seymour Rooke	1941–45	Paula Steensma		Jennifer Watson	2005–11
Evie Nicholson	2010–	Gill Ross		(née Herring)	1954–60	Eve Constance Webster	2010–
Georgina Nicholson		(née Johnson)	1945–49	Carina Stephens	2012–	Sarah J. C. Webster	1976–83
(née Stewart-Cox)	1948–53	Jane Ross		Sybil Stevens (née Barnes)		Iona Westwood	2010–
Hope Nicholson	2012–	(née Keevil)	1947–60	Sophy Stewart-Wilson	1979–84	Jessica Westwood	2011–
Louisa Nolte		Sue Rotherham		Hugh Sutton (Staff)	2012–	Diana Wheatley Price	
(née Legge)	1989–96	(née Hayter)	1931–37	Tessa Tarratt		(née Brocklebane)	1953–59
Olaoyin Okuboyejo	2010–12	Elizabeth Rothwell (Staff)	1985–	(née Dinnis)	1963–68	Alicia Whitaker	2012–
Oyindamola Okuboyejo	2004–06	Rebecca Rothwell	2003–10	Margaret Tatton-Brown	1962–66	Vicky Wilson	
Maeve Oram		Penelope Rowse	1973–79	Georgina Terry	2006–13	(née Richardson)	1962–68
(née O'Ferrall)	1949–53	Sophie Rushman	2007–	Angela Thomas (Staff)	1966–73	Susan Wood	1953–60
John F. Osborne		Sylvia Rutherford	2012–	Anna Tigerschiold		Catherine Woodman (Staff)	2011–
Henrietta Page	2008–	Amelia Saer	2010–	(née von Essen)	1978–79	Lucinda Woods	1996–2002
Verity Page	2010–	Jean Saxelby-Kemp		Aurore Tigerschiold	2010–11	Annabel Wright	2009–
Georgia Patterson	2012–	(née Turner)	1943–51	Hermine Tigerschiold	2006–7	Dr Helen Wright	
Dr Christie Peacock	1970–75	Fleur Scott	1998–2005	Tory Toler		(Headmistress)	2003–12
Claudia Pease	2003–10	Charlotte Scott-Barrett		(née Charrington)	1971–75	Nigel and Jane Wright	
Marina Pease	2007–12	(née Lindley)	1961–66	Mary Tredennick	1955–59	Elizabeth Yule	1950–54
Emily Peel	2012–	Clare Scott-Dempster	1980–87	Carolyn Trethowan			
Alice Pennington	2011–13	Millie Scott-Hopkins	2012–	(née Reynolds)	1948–53	St Mary's Calne Library	
Charlotte Pilcher	1976–81	Jill M. Seddon		Lady Arabella Unwin			
Megan Piper	2010–	(née Smeeton)	1939–46	(née Fitzmaurice)	1977–83		

Index

Page numbers in *italics* indicate captions for illustrations.

Acknowledgements

The contents of this book have been drawn from many sources both written and oral. The school archives have been invaluable in providing much of the material and in establishing an accurate timeline, as have Kay Stedmond's *St Mary's School Calne 1873–1986* and *Portrait of Miss Gibbins* by Mary Warren-Smith. A booklet written by Jean Hughes and Miss Thouless for the school's centenary has provided further material and I have also consulted Peter Treloar's *Calne's Heritage*.

I have been fortunate to have been able to speak to many of those who have been part of the school community both past and present: governors, headmistresses, members of staff, pupils and parents. I have also had help from residents of Calne. I am extremely grateful to them all, some of whom have given several hours of their time. Lilian Leadbetter has encouraged me throughout and I have had great support from the administrative staff at St Mary's, especially Kelly Crockett and Catherine Woodman. The team at Third Millennium Information have steered me through the production process, with the editor Pam Hartshorne being of particular help.

My thanks go to the following: Caroline Adler, Laura Barlee (Attlee), Cate Bell (Benson), Rachel Benson (Woods), Nicola Botterill, Ted Buckeridge, Jane Bull, Georgie Burnell-Nugent (Bell), Delscey Burns, Cinty Carr (Wake-Walker), Lee Chalk, Rebecca Clerke (Annable), Lynn Copp, Karen Cordon, Jenny Crossley (French), Colette Culligan, Cari Depla, Jane Dickson, Imi Dobie, Paula Doel, Flossie Dove, Joyce Eason, Margaret Ellis, Tildy Ellis, Anne Ferguson (Smellie), Kate Fielden , Angela Fish, Frippy Fyfe (Maitland), Sue Garrett-Cox (Guest), Deb German , Peter Giles, Angie Green, Juliette Green, Judy Hart (Elgood), Henry Harwood, Julia Henderson (Hissey), Mary Hibbert (Combes), Daphne Hort, Rita Hulme, Elizabeth Hunter (Ham), Lilian Leadbetter, Joyce Lynn (Walters), Lucy Key Stratton, Felicia Kirk, Simon Knight, John McCausland, Jill Maclaine, Janet McGarry, Jenny Moore, Rowena Overend (Annable), Vince Pennock, Michael Pipes, Celia Plunkett (Johnson), Angela Purdon (Topham), Penny Rawlins (Hann), Jane Ridgewell, Gill Ross (Johnson), Sue Ross, James Rothwell, Elizabeth Rothwell, Carolyn Shaw, Charlotte Smith, Sara-Jane Socha, Richard Southwell, Sybil Spence (Ford), Rebecca Spicer, Christiane Strudwick, Margaret Tatton-Brown, Sue Tomlin, Liz Thompson, Sue Tomson (Parry-Jones), Arabella Unwin (Fitzmaurice), Sue Rotherham (Heyter), Mary Warren-Smith (Rowley), Edward Whiting, Vicky Wilson (Richardson) and Helen Wright.

Photo Acknowledgements

Many of the photographs featured in the book are from the school's archive. The school and Third Millennium Publishing would like to express their gratitude to all contributors to the archive, to Bob Lunn for the use of a number of photographs included in the book, as well as to the following individuals and organisations: p18 (left) courtesy of Ted Buckeridge; p49 (right) the Bowood Estate; p107 (bottom) and back endpaper Arabella Unwin; p125 (right) family of Mary Hibberd; p151 (centre) Tempest Photography; p155 (left) Hallmark Photography, Calne; p181 (right) David Maitland; pp196/7 (centre), 198, 199 St Margaret's School.

Every effort has been made to trace copyright holders and to obtain their permission for the use of copyright material. Third Millennium Publishing apologises for any errors or omissions in the above list and would be grateful if notified of any corrections that should be incorporated in future editions of this book.

Front endpaper: A 1728 map of Calne showing strip fields on the area where St Mary's School now stands.

Back endpaper: St Mary's School in 2013.